The American History Series

SERIES EDITORS
John Hope Franklin, *Duke University*
Abraham S. Eisenstadt, *Brooklyn College*

Arthur S. Link
Princeton University
GENERAL EDITOR FOR HISTORY

Howard N. Rabinowitz
UNIVERSITY OF NEW MEXICO

The First
New South

1865–1920

HARLAN DAVIDSON, INC.
ARLINGTON HEIGHTS, ILLINOIS 60004

Library of Congress Cataloging-in-Publication Data

Rabinowitz, Howard N., 1942–
    The first new South, 1865–1920 / Howard N. Rabinowitz.
        p.   cm. — (The American history series)
    Includes bibliographical references and index.
    ISBN 0-88295-883-6
    1. Southern States—History—1865–1951. I. Title. II. Series :
American history series (Arlington Heights, Ill.)
    F215.R125   1991
    975.04—dc20
                                                    91-33997
                                                    CIP

Cover illustration: "Weighing and Sampling Cotton on Lee Street,"
from *Artwork of Montgomery* (1894), courtesy of the Alabama
Department of Archives and History.

Manufactured in the United States of America
96 95 94 93 92 1 2 3 4 5 EB

For My Two Favorite Southerners—
Diane Wood and John Hope Franklin

FOREWORD

Every generation writes its own history for the reason that it sees the past in the foreshortened perspective of its own experience. This has surely been true of the writing of American history. The practical aim of our historiography is to give us a more informed sense of where we are going by helping us understand the road we took in getting where we are. As the nature and dimensions of American life are changing, so too are the themes of our historical writing. Today's scholars are hard at work reconsidering every major aspect of the nation's past: its politics, diplomacy, economy, society, recreation, mores and values, as well as status, ethnic, race, sexual, and family relations. The lists of series titles that appear at the back of this book will show at once that our historians are ever broadening the range of their studies.

The aim of this series is to offer our readers a survey of what today's historians are saying about the central themes and aspects of the American past. To do this, we have invited to write for the series scholars who have made notable contributions to the respective fields in which they are working. Drawing on primary and secondary materials, each volume presents a factual and narrative account of its particular subject, one that affords readers a basis for perceiving its larger dimensions and importance. Conscious that readers respond to the closeness and immediacy of a subject, each of our authors seeks to restore the past as an actual present, to revive it as a living reality. The individuals and groups who figure in the pages of our books appear as real people who once were looking for survival and fulfillment. Aware that historical subjects are often matters of controversy, our authors present their own findings and conclusions. Each volume closes with an extensive critical essay on the writings of the major authorities on its particular theme.

The books in this series are designed for use in both basic and advanced courses in American history, on the undergraduate and graduate levels. Such a series has a particular value these days, when the format of American history courses is being altered to accommodate a greater diversity of reading materials. The series offers a number of distinct advantages. It extends the dimensions of regular course work. Going well beyond the confines of the textbook, it makes clear that the study of our past is, more than the student might otherwise understand, at once complex, profound, and absorbing. It presents that past as a subject of continuing interest and fresh investigation. The work of experts in their respective fields, the series, moreover, puts at the disposal of the reader the rich findings of historical inquiry. It invites the reader to join, in major fields of research, those who are pondering anew the central themes and aspects of our past. And it reminds the reader that in each successive generation of the ever-changing American adventure, men and women and children were attempting, as we are now, to live their lives and to make their way.

John Hope Franklin
A. S. Eisenstadt

CONTENTS

ACKNOWLEDGMENTS

I've had a contract to write this book for most of my professional career. Put another way, I've been working on the New South for so long it has begun to feel like the Old South. For that reason, I hope it is not unseemly to have such long acknowledgments for such a short book.

My major debt is to the series editors, John Hope Franklin and Abe Eisenstadt, who asked me in 1978 to do a book on the New South, then defined as the period between 1877 and 1913. I accepted somewhat reluctantly because I wasn't sure I could actually complete the task. As I was diverted by a variety of professional and personal matters in the years that followed, I'm sure that John Hope, Abe, and the staff at Harlan Davidson came to have similar, except perhaps stronger, doubts.

But the book did get written. And the primary reason for that was my year as a Fellow of the Center for Advanced Study in the Behavioral Sciences in Stanford, California. I am grateful for financial support provided by the Center, the National Endowment for the Humanities, and the Andrew W. Mellon Foundation. More than that, however, I am grateful for the Center's unrivaled intellectual environment. The Center staff wants you to have the most productive and enjoyable year of your life. They certainly succeeded in my case during 1989–90. Lynn Gale, Patrick Goebel, and Carol Baxter taught me

the computer skills that made it possible for a previous computer illiterate to prepare the initial drafts of the manuscript.
The Center's Librarian, Margaret Amara, and her staff quickly
met my seemingly insatiable requests for books and photo-
copied articles. And the rest of the class of 1990 set a good
example by combining hard work with an unstinting appreciation of the nonacademic aspects of life.

I also want to thank three administrators at the University
of New Mexico who understand what universities should be
about. Dean Hobson Wildenthal made it possible for me to
spend the year at the Center and still have a semester sabbatical
that gave me time to revise the manuscript; then Vice President for Research (now Provost) Paul Risser provided some
sorely needed additional financial support; and Jonathan Porter, the chair of the Department of History, strongly endorsed
my year-and-a-half leave and didn't do too many things I disagreed with in my absence.

Getting a manuscript done was one thing, but turning it
into something I wouldn't mind parading in public was another matter. Fortunately, I had the help of able and generally
tactful critics. Despite their very different styles, Abe and John
Hope both made clear what was good and what was not, and
offered suggestions to improve the manuscript. I especially
appreciated the amount of time they devoted to my work at
particularly busy times in their own lives. Don Doyle was too
kind, but at the same time subtly noted that extensive revisions
were in order.

Bill Chafe read an early version of the economics and the
politics chapters and provided the proper mix of criticism and
support to keep me going. Noel Pugach offered thoughtful comments about the preface and epilogue. Daniel Feller, Peter
Kolchin, and Arthur Mann read the entire manuscript at different stages of its development, and their trenchant comments
and questions proved indispensable.

Maureen Hewitt, vice-president and editor-in-chief of
Harlan Davidson, demonstrated great patience and tact over
the years. She also displayed her considerable editorial skills

in supplementing the work of my first-rate copyeditor, Anita Samen.

As usual, I want to thank my parents, Abe and Gertrude Rabinowitz, for their continued support, and my children, Lori and Debbie, for—well, being my children.

And then there's Diane. She was probably the only person who was convinced that I would write this book. That support meant more to me than she will ever know. She wasn't my wife when she became the first person to read and comment on the entire manuscript. It was in very rough form and she was not averse to calling my attention to things that didn't make sense or needed to be eliminated. She then waded through the revised drafts. And she agreed to marry me anyway.

Albuquerque, N.M.

Of New Souths, Past and Present

In the beginning, that is, before the Civil War, there was the Old South. Grounded in slavery, dependent on King Cotton, and neither industrialized nor urbanized when compared to the North, this was the South that lost the war. Although they nostalgically celebrated certain real or imagined virtues of the Old South, subsequent generations of white southerners sought to convince themselves and others, especially Yankees and southern blacks, that a new South had finally arrived. Most recently, former president Jimmy Carter, while governor of Georgia, claimed to be a representative of the New South of the 1960s and 1970s. Before that, in the immediate aftermath of World War II, other southerners had announced the presence of a New South. An even earlier generation of southern boosters had proclaimed its arrival in the 1920s.

Although there have been many "New Souths," the original, and most important for our purposes, was the one that contemporaries celebrated between the overthrow of Reconstruction in 1877 and the end of World War I in 1919, but whose roots lay in the immediate post–Civil War years. This South, what I am calling the First New South, allegedly contained the same basic elements that later generations would claim as their own achievement—impressive urbanization and industrialization, diversified agriculture, adequate public services, and enlightened racial policies. As one northerner who had enrolled in the New South promotional campaign put it in 1893, "the Southern States are now American States, moving along the highway of the new American life." Whether or not the South had become truly new by the 1960s and 1970s is still a matter of dispute. The fact that at least three separate New Souths have been declared since 1920, however, suggests that such claims were not warranted for the years between 1865 and 1920.

This book will therefore examine the myth and the reality of the First New South. I am especially interested in the claims of progress made by New South proponents and will assess their validity. By focusing on the degree of "newness," I will be able to address a number of academic disputes that have important public policy implications, including the transformation of slaves into free people, the origins of the region's economic backwardness, and the emergence of a one-party South. But newness is not simply a historian's arbitrary construct used to bring some order to a particular period of southern history. Late nineteenth- and early twentieth-century southerners themselves struggled with the issue of newness as they sought to hold on to what they considered worth saving from their past while confronting elements of change that might or might not improve their lives. Thus at the same time that advocates of a "New South" were trying to convince northern audiences that the region had broken completely with its past, they sought to reassure southerners who were attached to the old ways of life. Statements such as "the new South is simply the old South under new conditions," or, as one publicist put it in 1903, "The South of today ... is not a new South, but a revival of the old South," were meant to convey a sense of evolution, as opposed to the alternatives of stagnation and revolution, and to convince southerners (particularly whites) that they could experience change and still be true to their essential "southernness."

In describing the kind of South that took shape between 1865 and 1920, we will be dealing with the perennial question of the relative importance of continuity and change in southern history. To what extent was the South of that period similar to or different from the South of previous years in terms of its economy, politics, and society? Although it is now fashionable among historians to challenge the value of this approach, in one way or another everyone working in this field comes back to it. There is a second dimension to this issue, and, like the first, it was initially noted at the time. To what extent had the South become more like the North than it had been before? Put another way, this is the issue of southern distinctiveness. According to contemporaries as well as most historians, in order to be truly new, the South had not only to be different from what it had been, but it also had to resemble the North, the model for New South advocates. At times I will use this yardstick because it was the one that originated at the time, was then passed on to subsequent generations of New South proponents, and now is enshrined in the literature. Even so, we must stay alert to ways in which the South could be "new" but still unlike the North. We also must be careful not to assume that either the new or the old was inherently "good" or "bad."

Not surprisingly, the First New South contained elements of both change and continuity, distinctiveness and similarity. Faced with often contradictory evidence, historians have tried to interpret this past in a way that makes sense to them and their readers. Some have therefore emphasized change, others continuity; some distinctiveness, others sameness. By acknowledging the mixture of the old and the new, the similar and the unique, in the pages that follow, I want to avoid the "either-or" trap that too many scholars have fallen into. But although I allow for the significance of shared characteristics and change in a region roughly defined as the former states of the Confederacy plus Kentucky, I also will argue for the more fundamental importance of distinctiveness and, to a lesser extent, continuity in evaluating this period of southern history. For by 1920, the South, despite often momentous instances of change, was more as it had been in 1865 (or even 1860) and less like the North than New South spokesmen had hoped it would be or claimed it had become. The experience of the Civil War, emancipation, and Reconstruction; the persistence of antebellum values, attitudes, and behavior; the unprecedented changes in the North; and, above all, the presence of large numbers of former slaves set the South apart from the rest of the nation. And the continuity between the old and new Souths would have been even greater had it not been for the positive impact of the Reconstruction experiment that white southerners almost unanimously condemned.

Despite the New South rhetoric, southern reality in 1920 meant widespread poverty, continued dependence on single-crop agriculture, limited industrialization and urbanization, and racial oppression. As a result, the South was economically the nation's most underdeveloped region, and politically and socially, its most benighted. The legacies of that reality still confront and confound us today.

CHAPTER ONE

The Economy

The antebellum southern economy had been based on agriculture, much of it market-oriented. Virginians, South Carolinians, and Kentuckians grew great quantities of tobacco for northern and overseas markets. Large plantations produced sugar in Louisiana and rice in coastal South Carolina. But it was cotton that was king. As soil was exhausted in South Carolina and Georgia, cultivation moved west into the Black Belt of Alabama, Mississippi, and, by the eve of the Civil War, Texas. Most of the cotton produced for market was, like tobacco, rice, and sugar, grown by black slaves. Plantations of twenty or more hands that contained the majority of the slaves took the lead, but smaller farms also participated in the market economy.

Most southern whites, however, were relatively untouched by the market. They toiled in the uplands of the coastal states or mountains of the interior, perhaps with a slave or two, but usually with none, producing grain and livestock primarily for their own use. Because of the region's still-primitive railroad system, they were likely to be isolated from the major commercial centers; hence they aimed at self-sufficiency, although an active wagon trade carried surpluses to nearby towns.

Industrialization and urbanization had begun to affect the southern economy, but in both areas the South lagged well behind the North, and during the 1840s and 1850s the gaps actually widened.

The end of the Civil War in 1865 and especially the overthrow of Reconstruction in the mid-1870s elicited claims of great change from white southern leaders. By the 1880s and continuing in the years that followed, those leaders proclaimed that the South had shed what they now viewed as its antebellum economic problems. Instead there had emerged a "New South," one characterized by rapid industrialization, significant urbanization, and a diversified agrarian sector that no longer was totally dependent on cotton. Allegedly responsible for these developments and fully committed to them was a new generation of white southerners.

Even by 1920, however, the rhetoric of New South spokesmen failed to square with the realities of southern economic life. Rather than becoming less of a factor in southern agriculture, cotton had increased its importance; railroad construction, urbanization, and industrialization, though making impressive strides, continued to lag behind the North; and the South had become an economic colony of the North. The South now was even more clearly the most poverty-stricken and economically retarded region of the country. Per capita income, which had been 72 percent of the national average in 1860 before slumping to 51 percent in 1880, was still only at 62 percent in 1920. The relative lack of success was due in part to spectacular advances in the North and that region's control of the country's new national market for industrial and agricultural goods. However, southerners contributed as well because they could not triumph over regional liabilities and had not totally shed the mind set of the past.

Agriculture

The most important point about postbellum agriculture and indeed about southern economic life in general is that the region became dependent to an unprecedented degree on cotton. Despite the virtual stagnation in the worldwide demand for southern cotton between 1860 and 1880, most whites who had grown cotton in the antebellum period continued to do so. More important, the majority of freed slaves and formerly self-sufficient whites (even in less fertile upland areas) now set aside more land for cotton than for foodstuffs. As a result, by 1880 the South no longer was self-sufficient in foodstuffs and for the first time became a net importer of grain and livestock. What the Gwinnett *Herald*, an upcountry Georgia newspaper, said about the local situation in 1881 applied to much of the rest of the rural South:

From all sections of the county comes almost a universal complaint of scarcity of corn, fodder, wheat, and in fact nearly everything that is necessary to sustain man and beast. For the first time in several years the farmers of Gwinnett will have to look to the West for corn, flour, and meat. . . . Gwinnett has always been known as a grain growing county . . . but within the last few years nearly everybody has abandoned the ways of their fathers . . . and caught the cotton planting mania.

Historians are divided as to the reasons for this dependence on cotton, but agree that the southern economy was driven by a one-crop mentality until at least 1920. Spurred on by the increasing use of guano as fertilizer, cotton output by 1879 had passed the 5.4 billion bales grown in 1859. Cotton occupied 42 percent of the tilled lands in Mississippi and 34 percent in Georgia. Despite a drop in prices from about 8 cents a pound during most of the 1880s to a low of 4.5 cents in 1894, southerners harvested 10 million bales in 1900.

Even with the continued advance of the cotton-devouring boll weevil, which entered Texas in 1892, some recovery occurred in the Cotton Belt after 1900. In the spring of 1904, prices went to 17 cents a pound, and by the following year, the same size crop as that produced in 1898 brought twice as much income. But the spread of the boll weevil and the onset of World War I, which curtailed cotton exports, brought prices back down to their 1890s level. Renewed calls for diversification by farm journals, the United States Department of Agriculture, and popular writers—echoing one New South advocate's earlier pleas to turn to "small grains, grasses, truck farming, fruit growing, stock raising, and dairy farming"—were undermined by a postwar cotton boom that brought thirty cents a pound in 1919 for an 11.2 million-bale crop. In that year there were 200,000 more cotton farmers in Mississippi, Alabama, Georgia, and South Carolina than there had been in 1899, and by the late 1920s cotton was an even more dominant factor in southern agriculture. As one agricultural editor put it, "When southern cotton prices drop, every southern man feels the blow; when cotton prices advance, every industry thrives with vigor."

Cotton's dominance obscured other changes for which it was partly responsible. During the early postwar years corn—produced both for human consumption and animal feed—remained the region's leading crop in terms of acreage, but the number of corn acres declined and production failed to keep up with population growth or with the spectacular expansion in the Midwest. By 1929 cotton acreage in the South exceeded corn by nearly 10 million acres, practically a total reversal of the situation in 1879.

Often overlooked because of the dominance of cotton were notable developments in the growing of other crops. Rice production, which had been concentrated in the coastal region of Georgia and the Carolinas, began to shift in the 1880s to Louisiana, and by the first decade of the twentieth century it had spread into Texas and Arkansas. Between 1879 and 1909 rice acreage declined in South Carolina from 78,000 to 19,000 acres; in the same period Louisiana increased its rice planting from 42,000 to 317,000 acres. Transformed by former midwesterners, who implemented extensive mechanization that included steam-powered threshing machines, the Gulf Coast rice industry became the nation's first agribusiness; by 1920 Louisiana had quadrupled South Carolina's peak-year prewar production. Tobacco, the third primary antebellum money crop, experienced comparable changes. In 1879 farmers in the former Confederacy grew 247,431 acres of tobacco, but with the spread of flue-cured bright leaf tobacco out of North Carolina into adjoining states, that figure had increased to 495,601 acres by 1909. By the turn of the century, Kentucky was still the largest producer, but more than 150,000 southern farmers outside the state were raising tobacco.

Other crops were locally important. As in the antebellum period, sugar cane production was confined mainly to Louisiana, although refining facilities now were brought closer to the fields. Elsewhere in the South some farmers sought greater diversification. Although their efforts were less important than they had been prior to the war, they produced small amounts of wheat, oats, and hogs, or raised peanuts, sweet potatoes, and other vegetables and a variety of fruits. Georgia peaches, for example, began to reach northern markets in the 1870s. Despite frequent complaints about the lack of regional self-sufficiency, however, only in Texas was the raising of beef cattle a major farm activity, and dairying made limited advances.

The South's climate and the effects of wartime devastation only partly account for the distinctive nature of the region's postbellum agriculture. For one thing, the region lacked the kind of marketing and transportation networks needed to support a system of diversified agriculture. According to a Department of Agricultural official in 1905, "there is no use in growing apples, oranges, or peaches commercially without an efficient system of safe and rapid distribution," an observation that held for a variety of other crops as well. Then, too, southern farmers had to contend with more than their share of diseases, such as Texas fever and hog cholera. Farmers also were plagued by low productivity on the nation's smallest farms, the lack of capital for machinery and equipment, inadequate exposure to the new scientific agricultural education, limited soil conservation efforts, and the relative absence of nonfarm opportunities that would draw surplus farm population out of agriculture and into other employment.

The lack of machinery contrasted dramatically with the North. As late as 1930, only 2 percent of farmers in Georgia and South Carolina were using tractor power, compared to 25 percent in Minnesota and 35 percent in Kansas. When it came to plowing, the more colorful mule was still indispensable. One farmer commonly shared a chew of tobacco with his mule in order to get him to work better; another found that Pepsi Cola did the trick. A third, who used "Whoa, Gee, and Haw" to direct his mules, reported that "They were right considerate about doing what I told them."

The absence of mechanization was not surprising, given the prevalence of cheap labor and small farms and, except for rice, the unsuitability of the region's basic crops for mechanization, as demonstrated most tellingly in the failure to develop a mechanical cotton picker. Even by the third decade of the twentieth century, the day-to-day process of farming in what had become, particularly for tobacco and cotton farmers, a "mule culture" had changed little since the 1870s, as the South continued to lag behind the rest of the nation. Even the most optimistic southerners could find little evidence that, as one early twentieth-century agricultural reformer claimed, "The day of reform is clearly dawning, and the sun-light of science will soon brighten with exuberant harvests, every cultivated field of the South."

The nature of southern agriculture, with its heavy dependence on cotton and absence of progressive farming techniques, was determined to a large extent by the development of the sharecropping system, which grew out of the social and economic effects of emancipation.

Blacks, as they had been before the Civil War, were the backbone of the cotton economy. Now, however, they performed their labor, not as slaves in gangs, but for the most part as tenants on white-owned land that was divided into family-sized units of between twenty and fifty acres (a single family could raise fifteen to thirty acres of cotton) and rented for a share of the crop or, less often, a fixed rent. By 1880, less than 10 percent of the tilled land in areas of the South that were most dependent on cotton was cultivated on farms that could be considered plantations. By contrast, over one half of the farms were operated by croppers and cash renters.

This change was reflected in the growth of the number of southern farms from 691,000 in 1870 to 1,253,000 ten years later. Observers at the time and early generations of historians believed that these farms were actually owner-occupied and represented the breakup of the old plantations, both in terms of ownership and as a system of production. This view was encouraged by the 1880 federal agricultural census, which failed to distinguish between owner and tenant in tabulating the number of farms. For one northern visitor in 1893, the multiplication of farms east of the Mississippi was a sign that "old-time plain people are now in possession of new estates and enjoying greater prosperity than before." That occasionally was the case, but in the South as a whole there was no basic change in the concentration of land ownership. The lands of former plantations were simply divided into small farms where tenancy was the rule.

Economists and historians have examined the varieties of tenancy, their origins, and how they operated. Everyone agrees that there was a period of experimentation after the war, from about 1865 to 1867. Initially planters sought to work freedmen in gangs for fixed wages or collective share wages. In the spring of 1865, in a contract with eight of his former slaves, Virginia tobacco planter David Shelton agreed to pay them "such part of the crops made on the farm . . . the present year . . . as any [one] white gentlemen of the neighborhood shall say is just and right." The workers were to do whatever tasks assigned to them "as they formerly did when slaves." Landowners were encouraged in this effort by Freedmen's Bureau representatives who sought to get freedmen to sign year-long contracts. But most former slaves resisted such arrangements because they were too much like slavery, even when a system of squad labor was used that paid blacks for working a specific area of a field that they did not live on. "I mean to own my own manhood," explained one South Carolina freedman in rejecting an offer of 25 cents a day, "and I'm going on to my own land, just as soon as when I git dis crop in." One South Carolina upcountry planter recalled that in 1868, "hands could not be hired for wages. . . . I had to yield or lose my labor."

Sharecropping thus emerged as a compromise between the laborer's pursuit of greater autonomy on his own land and the landlord's desire for a stable work force, his attempt to minimize risk, and his need to get around the chronic shortage of capital. Wage laborers still accounted for about 25 percent of the workers on larger cotton plantations in 1910 and remained the dominant form of labor in the more mechanized and less labor-intensive rice- and sugar-growing areas, but black demands—in addition to the nature of the crop—were clearly instrumental in producing cotton's dependency on sharecropping. As one planter put it in 1869, "a share in the crops is the universal ploy; negroes prefer it and I am forced to adopt it. Can't choose your system. Have to do what negroes want." He added in a bit of an overstatement, "They control entirely."

At first the contracts varied greatly. Though taking longer in some places than in others, the contract was finally standardized by the end of the 1860s so that the fraction of the crop received by the laborer who was supplied everything except food and clothing was increased to one-half the output, whether grain or cotton. This was known as working halves.

Some tenants could afford to rent for cash, but the major alternative to sharecropping was share tenancy. As in sharecropping, the landlord was required to supply the land, house, and (in most cases) fuel, but the tenant, unlike the cropper, provided his own work stock, implements, and provisions. For use of the land the tenant paid a standard rent of one-third of the corn (or other grains) and one-fourth of the cotton. Like cash tenancy, this practice was more common among whites than blacks because of the tenant's greater need for capital resources. Share tenants clearly were higher on the agricultural ladder than sharecroppers, enjoying greater status as well as the chance to make more money from their crop, but there also were significant differences that could have important legal implications. Laws varied according to time and place, but generally the tenant owned the crop and paid his share as rent; the cropper, however, was an employee who got paid in a share of the crop, which belonged to the landlord.

The facts of the tenancy system are relatively clear-cut, although historians continue to trace the variations in the system and its origins. What is in dispute, however, are the reasons for the centrality of cotton in the system and the effects on blacks.

Some scholars see sharecropping as an inefficient system in which the former slaves were trapped and exploited by merchants who initially peddled goods and then opened small stores that competed with the old plantation stores. Many merchants were northerners; others were former Confederates, farmers or even planters; but among the most successful were Europeans, particularly Jews. The merchants had limited capital and faced a lot of risks; they were further handicapped by high interest rates and unreliable sources of credit. In their stores the freed slaves and the mass of whites could purchase "luxury items" that might include chewing tobacco, cloth, and combs. Amid the decline in self-sufficiency and growth of a market economy, these merchants also became a source of such necessities as flour, meat, seed, fertilizer, and tools. In the cash-short rural South, the merchants turned to a two-price system of cash and credit that meant an approximate 60 percent markup for goods bought on credit, as most of them were.

The economists Roger Ransom and Richard Sutch argue in *One Kind of Freedom* (1977) that geographically dispersed merchants enjoyed "territorial monopolies" and forced blacks to raise cotton. Their evidence suggests that given a choice, blacks would have taken a different course. Immediately after emancipation, black women and children had largely withdrawn, if only temporarily, from the fields. Their absence, plus the fewer hours worked in the fields by the men, meant an estimated 28 to 37 percent drop in the labor supply. The withdrawal of female and child labor reflected to a certain extent the black male's assertion of the family authority that had been denied him under slavery and black insistence that their families should function more like those of whites. One dismayed Georgia plantation mistress, for example, reported that "Gilbert will stay on his own terms, but withdraws Fanny and puts Harry and Little Abram in her place and puts his son out to a trade. Cook Kate wants to be relieved of the heavy burden of cooking for two and wait on her husband." Together with the reduced activity of black men, such actions revealed an inclination towards subsistence farming rather than producing cotton for market. In making this decision, as they had on the South Carolina and Georgia Sea Islands during the war, blacks were acting very much like their counterparts in Jamaica following their emancipation thirty years earlier. Nevertheless, according to Ransom and Sutch, black desires were thwarted as they were dragged into cotton production by merchant demands. They had wanted to avoid white supervision, but they were unable to do so and their progress was blocked by racism.

But there is room in this scenario for other possible villains than white merchants. Jonathan Wiener and Jay Mandle, both of whom have studied the problem, agree that whites forced blacks into a ruinous concentration on cotton. They blame the planter, however, not the merchant. Relying heavily on a detailed study of five Black Belt Alabama counties, Wiener argues that planters were behind the division of the plantation into small tenant farms and the end of centralized management. Out of a desire to have the year-round labor supply that the planting, chopping, weeding, and picking of cotton demanded, they created a system of "bound labor" in which their own coercive actions and the enforcement of state vagrancy and debtor legislation helped restrict the mobility of labor, in contrast to the free-labor capitalistic agriculture found in the North.

Whether they focus on merchants or planters, critics of the tenancy system's dependence on cotton and inherent racism have been challenged by a group of free-market economists. Put simply, they ask whether raising cotton made economic sense, given the nature of the southern economy at the time. They are sometimes called neoclassicists, because they believe that market conditions govern behavior, or cliometricians, because they rely on mathematical models and statistical data to support their claims about history. Although often differing among themselves in emphasis or approach, they see postbellum southern agriculture responding to the same laws of supply and demand, division of labor, and rational choice that allegedly are found in all capitalist societies.

Rejecting the view of merchant monopoly or planter omnipotence, Robert Higgs, in *Competition and Coercion* (1977), sees the freedman as being able to work his way out of the system, play one landlord or merchant against another, and exercise mobility. As others have demonstrated, merchants rarely had the kind of monopoly accorded them by Ransom and Sutch, and few planters were in as total control as Wiener and Mandle claim. In South Carolina, for example, there was an increase of almost 150 percent in the number of stores in the low country, and new upcountry merchants thrived because of new railroad connections rather than a "territorial monopoly." In the Natchez District along the Mississippi and Louisiana border, where the number of merchants more than doubled between 1860 and 1880, a community was likely to have at least six suppliers with easy access to the same plantations.

Ignoring the seeming preference of blacks for self-sufficiency, Higgs notes that cotton, despite its problems, was the region's most profitable crop and it was therefore a rational decision to raise it. He especially plays down the force of racism in the marketplace, arguing that blacks made great strides after 1865; by 1910, 175,000 blacks owned the land they worked, and another 43,000 were part owners. Higgs acknowledges that full owners comprised less than 20 percent of all blacks (as compared to 52 percent of the whites), their average holdings were much smaller, and the mass of blacks were poor, but he argues that the comparative disadvantage resulted from the blacks' late start as free laborers, and, to a lesser extent, from the failure to give them land after emancipation.

The neoclassical argument is filled with insights. As compared, for example, to Mandle and Wiener's depiction of an immobile black labor force virtually imprisoned by a conspiratorial plantation culture, its emphasis on mobility and options is especially compelling. Even as slaves, blacks had negotiated with their masters, often successfully, for a degree of autonomy over their own labor and personal lives. Particularly in the rice- and sugar-growing areas, but elsewhere as well, slaves sought greater control over their tasks and more free time to tend their gardens, engage in worship, or visit friends and relatives. More highly skilled slaves might arrange to hire their own time or even work out the details for purchasing their own freedom or that of a loved one. But in the new postbellum world, former slaves now had the option to quit and move on, forcing planters to compete for their labor. Even the largest planters in the Mississippi Delta at the beginning of the twentieth century were complaining that blacks drifted from plantation to plantation or sought new delights in Delta towns.

It is also important to keep in mind the initial conditions facing blacks before we attribute their lack of progress simply to racial discrimination. As one planter put it, "I never yet, since the negroes were freed, had a negro or white man I employed that ever came to me with anything but the clothes they had on their back." And emancipation did bring increased economic benefits to blacks. Owning themselves, they now retained a greater share of the value of their labor, and market conditions at times gave them certain advantages in selling that labor.

Despite the valuable insights their viewpoint provides, neoclassicists generally ignore the presence of racism in the legal system and education. When they do mention it, they separate it from the market, thus loading the dice by picking up the story after discriminatory educational policies and the unequal dispensation of justice had helped limit occupational choices. The success of isolated individuals aside, the land tenure system plus the white racism that reinforced its liabilities seriously impeded black progress and indeed the region's economic growth.

Sharecropping would have been a good temporary system for an economy short of cash. The problem was that it became a permanent system and, when combined with the notorious crop lien needed to secure credit for the purchase of goods, it bound much of the South to cotton and blocked black as well as white upward mobility. Indeed, the crop lien was the chief evil in the system, though it too was a manifestation of the chronic shortage of capital and probably unavoidable. It gave an interest in the crop to the person, whether landlord or merchant, who sold supplies on credit to the tenant. The tenant would then have to pay off the debt from his share of the crop. If that share was worth less than the debt, the supplier could make up the difference by taking personal or real property. In the likely event that the cropper had none, the debt, despite laws that usually limited such debts to a single year, could be stretched into the following year and the borrower would have to grow what the merchant or landlord wanted. As one merchant-landlord put it, "If I say 'plant cotton' they plant cotton." Because the debt would include interest rates of between 40 and 70 percent, many croppers found themselves enmeshed by 1901 in a system akin to peonage. And because the only way out was to try to maximize production of a staple crop on a small plot of land, particularly in cotton and tobacco areas, the system took its toll on the soil as well, leading to even lower productivity.

By the end of the century, then, the sharecropping system had lost much of its flexibility and independence. There was little meaningful change in the ensuing years, though during the first years of the twentieth century there was the spread of new-style "tenant plantations" in Black Belt counties that, using a mixture of croppers, tenants, and hired labor, employed up-to-date capitalist organizational practices to rationalize the growing, processing, and marketing of cotton. By 1910, 43 percent of blacks were sharecroppers and 34 percent were share tenants. It is tempting to ascribe this tightening to increased racism, but the tenancy system affected whites and blacks alike. Though comprising a much smaller percentage of the white farm work force, white croppers by 1910 greatly outnumbered black croppers. More than 50 percent of all farmers in Arkansas, Louisiana, and Texas were mired in tenancy; in Alabama, Mississippi, Georgia, and South Carolina, the figure exceeded 60 percent. The combination of tenancy on small plots of land, reliance on the crop lien, and dependence on single-crop agriculture left the soil depleted and most farmers impoverished. A northern visitor in 1901 found that "as soon as one gets away from the towns, and ventures himself into the barren wastes of the unredeemed country about, the wretchedness is pathetic and the poverty colossal."

Although blacks justifiably have received the most attention, in certain respects the postbellum years brought the greatest changes for rural whites, especially the yeomen. Slavery and sharecropping were not the same, despite the claims of some authors; but whether as slaves or as croppers, the great mass of blacks continued to raise staple crops on land they did not own. The change for whites was much greater. For many, the postwar years brought a serious decline in their economic fortunes.

Until recently, historians have been most concerned with the fate of the former antebellum planter elite, especially with regard to land ownership. Everyone agrees that the individual farms on most plantation land had a common owner, but there is disagreement over how much was still in the hands of the antebellum owner. Some scholars, such as C. Vann Woodward, who asserted in *The Origins of the New South* (1951) that "the Civil War destroyed the planter class," argued that there had been a shift in ownership from the old planter class to a new middle class drawn from the ranks of business and the professions; others disagree. Wiener and Mandle argue that most antebellum planters retained ownership of their land and that "persistence" in landowning was the key to their continued economic and political power after the war. Another historian of three cotton-growing counties in northwestern Georgia concluded that "the large property holders of 1870 were for the most part, the same individuals and the same families as those of 1860." Yet further research will probably reveal more of a mixture between continuity and change in land tenure. In two counties in Virginia's central Piedmont, for example, there were high planter persistence rates in ownership of parcels of five hundred or more acres, but as a group, the planters held fewer acres and a smaller proportion of the land than they had before the war.

Unfortunately, much of the research has centered on the fate of cotton planters. The great sugar planters of Louisiana seem to have survived the war with their holdings relatively intact. South Carolina rice planters in the low country were hit harder by the effects of the war and emancipation, and had to confront the westward shift of the rice industry, but most retained control over their lands, albeit in less prosperous circumstances and often only after threats and violence by their former slaves (the most assertive and independent-minded in the South). A definitive answer to the issue of planter persistence awaits further local studies, but given what we now know, it is clear that claims of the disappearance of the antebellum planter class are unwarranted, particularly in the sugar and rice regions. As Gavin Wright has observed in *Old South, New South* (1986), given the extent to which antebellum planters had moved their slaves from plantation to plantation, emancipation affected the planters primarily by turning "labor lords into landlords."

Indeed, the continuity of individual landowning tells only part of the story. Although the war and emancipation left much of the prewar elite in positions of economic, social, and political power, many planters had an altered set of values and view of the world that make the question of continuity or change even more subtle.

Some scholars argue that southern planters retained not only their land, but also their antebellum values founded in precapitalist or indeed anticapitalist attitudes and behavior that embraced a paternalistic responsibility for blacks and opposed any economic forces that threatened the supremacy of labor-intensive, staple-crop agriculture in the southern economy. But such a view ignores the more complex reality of what happened to planters in the postwar world.

In the five counties of Mississippi and three parishes in Louisiana described by Michael Wayne in *The Reshaping of Plantation Society: The Natchez District, 1860–1880* (1983), change at first was the order of the postwar world. Some members of the old planter elite migrated to the North; others went to Brazil, where approximately four to six thousand whites from throughout the South settled. Of the majority who remained in the Natchez District, several leased out their estates to Yankees, and others attempted to attract immigrants, particularly the Chinese, to replace blacks in the fields. Faced with floods, labor difficulties, a high temporary federal cotton tax, and armyworms—"In a few days the fields were blackened like fire had swept over them"—most of the northerners got discouraged and left after 1866 or 1867.

As a result, by 1868, the district's agriculture was largely in the hands of the old planters. Some had lost their land, but most were operating their own plantations or renting to freedmen. Despite crop failures, increased debts, and the forfeiture of land for nonpayment of taxes, especially between 1873 and 1879, the gentry held on to their lofty economic status. As was often the case elsewhere, tax records reveal an increase in the ranks of farmers and small planters between 1860 and 1870, but large planters remained dominant. Even in Mississippi's Claiborne County, where they fared the worst, those planters who had owned at least 1,000 acres before the war saw their share of acreage decline only from 60 percent in 1860 to 51 percent in 1880, and their percentage of the county's real estate wealth decline only from 64 percent to 51 percent. In other counties the large planters continued to own more than 75 percent of the land. Given the smaller size of the new planter elite, wealth was arguably even more concentrated in 1880 than it had been before the war. As further proof of the absence of a "revolution" in land titles, over half the large planters in the district in 1880 could be traced directly to the antebellum aristocracy.

Even allowing for some leakage and the addition of new men from the ranks of former small planters and local merchants, this continuity is quite remarkable. Showing an ingenuity worthy of Scarlett O'Hara, planters got help from friends and relatives, undertook profitable marriages, transferred land to wives or children, and used their power and influence to see that land lost for taxes was bought back cheaply by friends or relatives at auction. Indeed the key to their success was the general deterioration in the real estate market. Conditions improved in the 1880s, but the district started to lose its preeminent position in the Cotton South. A significant number of planters moved to more fertile land in the Mississippi Delta, Arkansas, and East Texas, leaving behind land-poor members of the elite who were too burdened with debts to move.

Yet the planters could not hold on to their old values as change in the Natchez District went beyond the general decline in economic prospects. The persistence of the old planter elite within a changed economic and social environment created by emancipation meant, according to Wayne, "not the demise of the antebellum ruling class ..., but its transformation." There was, for example, a new attitude toward planting, as many began to direct surplus capital into other enterprises, including railroads and utilities, and a yarn mill, cotton mill, and ice company. Some planters began encouraging their children to go into other professions. "It is a pity to have these two boys grow up without any business habits," wrote one planter's wife to her husband. "If I had a home for them in New Orleans I should say put Tom in a business house & let him learn to make a living & learn to depend upon himself as soon as possible, & break him from the poluting [*sic*] society he is exposed to on a plantation."

The planters saw themselves as adopting new values—had they known of it, they might have used the term *bourgeois* to describe themselves. And here the new relationship to the ex-slaves is critical. At its core was the rejection of the attitudes and practices of the planters' former world. Forged in the antebellum years, that world, although it left a place for capitalistic practices, was built on paternalistic assumptions that posited a father-child model in the master-slave relationship. Yet if, as Wayne reminds us, "emancipation destroyed the social basis of paternalistic behavior, it did not alter assumptions about the character of the Negro." Despite the intervention of federal authorities and other northerners, the devastation and dislocation of the war, and the end of slavery, the planters expected the freedmen to remain on the old plantations, work in gangs, and be supplied with housing, food, and the like, by the planter.

Initially neither the planter nor the freed slave wanted to sacrifice the advantages each enjoyed under the old system. As they had in the antebellum years, blacks expected to receive gifts, have certain holidays, and enjoy weekend leisure time, and the planters at first continued many of these traditional practices. But the old paternalism soon collapsed as blacks embraced the freedom of the marketplace and planters ended the practice of "gifting" and turned over care of the elderly and infirm as well as law enforcement and punishment to local and state authorities. For one Louisiana planter, obviously disgusted with the new order, the issue was clear: "When I owned niggers, I used to pay medical bills and take care of them; I do not think I shall trouble myself much now."

In *Patronage and Poverty in the Tobacco South: Louisa County, Virginia 1860–1900* (1982), Crandall Shifflett demonstrated that planters in a very different part of the South also had to adapt if they were to survive in the new, more complex, postwar world. In 1860, Louisa County was a tobacco planter–dominated area in the central Virginia Piedmont in which 62 percent of the population were slaves. Although the war reduced the wealth of large estates and dissolved the major source of income (slaves), most of the 145 owners in 1860 who held 500 acres or more appeared in the county landbooks in 1870 with holdings that were almost the same size.

There was, however, a striking growth in the number of small landholders, despite considerable outmigration and population decline. Between 1870 and 1900 the number of black landowners increased from 22 to 314, making them 39 percent of all owners, although they owned only 11 percent of the land. Yet whether or not they owned land, blacks and most whites depended on the large landholders for their supplies and credit. Still, the planters could not control their former slaves to the extent that they would have liked. One planter spoke of "expecting trouble" from "his darkies" before the end of the year. As renters, they sought to renew their contracts, whereas he hoped they would "come and go to work—just as they used to do when they belonged to me."

The planters then had to negotiate with their former slaves; they also had to adjust to the new realities of commercial agriculture. But Louisa's planters, like most of their counterparts elsewhere in the South, if not in the Natchez District, had been acting as capitalists even before the war. The war had accelerated that tendency and forced the planters to learn to deal with the reality of free labor, with its wages and bargaining, but they retained control over the primary means of production. Even though tobacco remained the dominant crop through the 1880s, Louisa planters moved away from labor-intensive farming, introduced stock raising, and substituted machinery for tenant labor. One of the county's largest landowners wrote to a friend in 1869, "I am trying to raise corn, wheat, and tobacco, but have failed so that I am considering turning my Green Springs land into a grazing farm. I bought $150 of grass seed the other day." By 1876 he was selling lambs and mutton in Richmond, his main crop was grass, and he had a dairy that produced "lots of butter and milk." The milcher and washer at the dairy was the daughter of a slave, "who used to belong to me."

Thus members of the old planter class weathered the transition to the new postbellum world and remained a visible presence in large areas of the South, particularly in the Mississippi Delta and the rest of the Black Belt. They continued to own much of the land and, though forced into a new relationship with the former slaves, exercised a good deal of control over the latter's lives. But what of their relationship with the new merchant class that was becoming an increasingly important part of the new economy, particularly in cotton regions?

Prior to the Civil War, the marketing of staple crops was carried on largely by factors (agents) based in the major port cities of Charleston, New Orleans, and Norfolk. They disposed of the crop abroad or in the North and arranged for the purchase of imported manufactured goods for the planter class. The credit supplied by the factors and their marketing skills were indispensable for the creation of the antebellum planter class. One byproduct of the relationship was the creation of plantation stores in which local whites and blacks could purchase goods supplied to the planter by his factor. Plantation stores coexisted with the few country stores operated in the interior by a relatively small number of merchants.

Factors lost their privileged position in the postwar years. The war itself had disrupted the lucrative cotton trade and driven many factors out of business. The postwar penetration of railroads connected the countryside directly to northern markets, and the growth of interior cities, with their own merchants and bankers, further undermined the factor's position. But related to these developments was the emergence of rural merchants.

We have already seen how the merchant could influence the region's crop mix, particularly in cotton areas. Any assessment of the extent of that influence is directly related to how one views the relative power of the merchant and planter.

Such scholars as C. Vann Woodward, Roger Ransom, and Richard Sutch, maintain that merchants quickly wrested control over the countryside from planters. As agents of the new capitalist or bourgeois economy, merchants overcame opposition from the remnants of the weakened planter class. Other historians argue that the planters not only retained their former ...sures to with-

...d undisputed changing for- between them ..y between parts ....pper hand in most areas ... B(.............. ....ot in the less fertile northern part .e state; .... south Carolina upcountry planters were dominant in the lower Piedmont, their bailiwick in antebellum years, but less strong in the upper Piedmont.

Everywhere, however, planters were forced to accept the presence of the merchants within a credit-starved environment. There were few national banks, and port factors were closing down. Those factors still in business wanted mortgages on land or crops in exchange for loans. In the 1880s most planters in the Natchez District continued to rely on such factors or commission houses to market their cotton and handle their finances. But many turned over to the laborers the responsibility for getting their own provisions. As Michael Wayne points out, this meant that the storekeeper, once on the periphery of the plantation economy as a middle man between the planter and factor, now moved to center stage.

By the early 1870s local merchants performed numerous services for their customers, from paying taxes, lodge bills, and church dues to arranging for medical care and funerals. Such activities—secured by the crop lien—brought growing conflict with planters, with the lien system at the heart of the trouble. In Alabama, planters used that state's lien law to guarantee them the first claim to a tenant's crop. In Mississippi, however, an 1867 statute conferred a "prior lien" on those who furnished

materials "necessary for the cultivation of a farm or plantation." A landowner was not entitled to benefits of law unless
he also provided the essential supplies, as in fact many planters
did. Planters in Louisiana gained the upper hand in an 1874
statute that, like its Alabama counterpart, recognized the claim
of landlord over supplier. Advantage alternated back and forth
in South Carolina until the lien law of 1885 made the landlord's claim for rent superior to all other liens, however, the
merchant retained his lien for agricultural supplies.

In practice, however, planters and merchants regularly
ignored lien laws. Matters were decided in negotiations between parties in which power, influence, and social position
proved decisive. There often was a sharing of authority and
responsibility with, most commonly, the merchant continuing
to furnish the labor force and the planter serving as middleman
by providing a purchase order for the tenant. At the end of
the year the planter would pay the merchant and the tenant
paid the planter.

What had emerged, then, was a partnership between merchants and planters. Some planters even allowed merchants
to run a store on the plantation. The next step was for the
plantation store to be owned and managed by the landlord
himself. Meanwhile, some merchants used hard times to ac-
quire significant financial interest in land and plantations. In
Louisa County, Virginia, where more than half of the farmers
with over 300 acres sold off small parcels of their land, merchants were certainly among the purchasers. In the Natchez
District, merchants began to hold on to their stores even after
getting land. A select group in one Mississippi county, for
example, rose to the top of the planter economy, helping to
increase the acreage owned by merchants from 0 in 1861 to
16,054 in 1879.

Unfortunately, scholars have not considered whether the
merchant-landlord was more important than the landlord-
merchant. The key point, however, is that the absence of either
planter or merchant monopoly and the presence of a process
of negotiation often gave the tenant a choice of whom to do

business with, but little choice over the essential features of the credit transaction.

Although their relative dominance might vary from region to region or even from locality to locality, together planters and merchants helped shape the South's new postwar economy, particularly its growing dependence on cotton. Numerically, however, they were less important than the white middle-class farmers. This group, too, had experienced notable changes as a result of the war and the new demands of the postbellum economy.

The largest number of antebellum whites had been small farmers. Many continued in that capacity in the postbellum years. They augmented family labor with white and black hired hands and often rented part of their holdings to tenants or croppers. Yet such primarily subsistence-oriented farmers were increasingly drawn into the cotton economy. Railroads that penetrated once-isolated areas and loans for expansion or supplies often were dependent on guarantees of raising a cash crop, usually cotton. "The majority of the farmers are going to plant largely of cotton," reported the Jefferson (Georgia) *Forest News* in 1878, "as most of them are in debt, and cotton is the only thing raised on the farm that will command ready money in the fall." The decline in cotton prices, unfavorable weather, or crop disease might force farmers further into debt. Old methods of cultivation might produce further hardship through soil erosion and reduced productivity. Each year many farmers lost their farms and were forced to become renters.

Such exiles from the middle class swelled the ranks of the already growing class of renters, croppers, and day laborers. This class had existed during the antebellum period, but in far fewer numbers. In three representative upland Georgia counties, 14 percent to 24 percent of all farm operators had been renters, rather than farmers, in 1860. By 1880 the percentage of renters ranged from 26 percent to 29 percent, a change remarkably similar to the increase from 11 percent to 30 percent in nearby Edgefield County, South Carolina. At the same time, there was a sharp increase in the number of unskilled white farm laborers.

As important as the increase in numbers of white tenants was their changed status. Like the black croppers, they too saw their autonomy limited. In order to get credit, they had to agree to raise the market crop that the lender demanded, rather than achieve the self-sufficiency or "competency" they had prized. White renters in Louisa County, for example, used more fertilizer, grew more crops, hired day laborers, and thus produced a greater volume of products than black renters. But, like their black counterparts, they were forced to grow more tobacco and less foodstuffs than they would have liked. There is even some evidence that black renters were more likely to become landowners, perhaps because of the greater use of family labor or more reliance on credit. New laws further forced less-fortunate whites into the cash-crop nexus. Beginning in the 1880s, fence laws reversed the antebellum and early postbellum pattern in which farmers could let their livestock graze on open land, while neighbors had to fence in their pastures to protect their crops. Livestock owners were now forced to fence in their animals, often at what would be a prohibitive cost. One white tenant complained that "no poor man not a landowner could raise stock of any kind" except "at the mercy of the landlord." Another wrote that "This law will simply take rights away from the poor man and give them to the rich," denying poor men "the liberty that our forefathers fought for."

Laws originally aimed at limiting the economic options of blacks also bore especially hard on this class of whites. Trespassing laws and the establishment of hunting "seasons," though not uniformly enforced, forbade or limited the kind of hunting, fishing, and foraging that formerly self-sufficient whites had used to augment their small gardens. Proponents of game laws cited conservation needs as they sought to prevent the "wholesale and ill-seasoned destruction of deer, partridges, and wild turkeys by shooting, hunting, trapping, and other means," or the catching of fish through the use of poison or drugs. But by prohibiting hunting between spring and fall, the period of greatest need for agricultural labor, white land-owners revealed the primary motivation behind such efforts. And the denial of access to previously available hunting and fishing areas helped force many white tenants into the ranks of day laborer.

One of the most far-ranging effects of the transformation of the plantation was the elimination of the antebellum duality in the treatment of black and white laborers. Now the same means were used to control both black and whites—high credit prices, crop liens, mortgages, trespassing laws, and manipulation of the supply system. Thus, the principal means of controlling the behavior and restricting the opportunities of blacks were class-determined and also used against whites, helping to erode what historians have termed the "republican dual economy" (that is, separate slave and yeoman spheres) or "social economy" of the antebellum period.

The quality of life thus sharply declined for large numbers of the rural white lower, and even parts of the middle, classes. As a U.S. Senate committee reported in 1893, hard times excluded such farmers "from any enjoyment of the luxuries and elegancies of life, and prevents the education of their children. Leisure essential for the mental cultivation and social enjoyment accorded to the prosperous is wholly wanting." The decline was, of course, a gradual process, moving slowly through counties increasingly affected by railroad expansion and commercial agriculture. We also must be careful not to idealize the "sturdy yeoman farmers," whose antebellum lives were often quite difficult, monotonous, and unpleasant. But by the turn of the century, the transformation of the southern white yeomanry was close to complete. And contributing to that transformation was a particular kind of industrialization that depended upon a low-paid, submissive work force for whom agriculture had become a less attractive alternative.

Industrialization

As already noted, the South had lagged behind the North in industrialization during the antebellum period. Now a new generation of southern leaders, led by prominent newspaper editors such as William Mahone of the Richmond *Whig*, Henry Watterson of the Louisville *Courier-Journal*, and Henry Grady of the Atlanta *Constitution*, urged the region to catch up. Some felt that the lack of a solid industrial base had cost the South the war, but most looked to the future rather than the past. Industry would help end the South's overreliance on cotton, and a diversified economy would provide more jobs.

For too long, it was argued, the South had failed to make the most of its rich resources and depended upon the North for what it could have produced itself. "We have got to go to manufacturing to save ourselves," wrote the editor J. D. B. DeBow in 1867, echoing his antebellum statement that "no country that produces raw materials only can be prosperous." In his famous "funeral oration," Henry Grady wrote of the burial of a fellow Georgian:

They buried him in the midst of a marble quarry: they cut through solid marble to make his grave; and yet a little tombstone they put above him was from Vermont. They buried him in the heart of a pine forest, and yet the pine coffin was imported from Cincinnati. They buried him within touch of an iron mine, and yet the nails in his coffin and the iron in the shovel that dug his grave were imported from Pittsburg [*sic*]. They buried him by the side of the best sheep-grazing country on the earth, and yet the wool in the coffin bands and the coffin bands themselves were brought from the North. The South didn't furnish a thing on earth for that funeral but the corpse and the hole in the ground. There they put him away . . . in a New York coat and a Boston pair of shoes and a pair of breeches from Chicago and a shirt from Cincinnati, leaving him nothing to carry into the next world with him to remind of the country in which he lived and for which he fought for four years, but the chill of blood in his veins and the marrow in his bones.

After listing northern products, from toothbrushes to locomotives, that the South depended upon, the industrialist and editor of the Charlotte *Observer*, Daniel Augustus Tompkins, similarly concluded that "We do all this in spite of the fact that the South is the best country in the world for manufactures. Not only ought we to manufacture all these things for home consumption, but we ought to be pushing out and supplying the wants of other sections."

Yet New South advocates realized that the region was short of capital and what there was sought out agricultural rather than industrial investments. Outside capital was needed, as were workers interested in industrial pursuits. State governments initially led the way in seeking an influx of funds and workers. By the 1870s and 1880s, according to one historian, every southern Appalachian state had "established immigration bureaus and dispatched agents to New York and Europe to spread the word of southern opportunities." Commercial conventions in the North and abroad exhibited state resources, and by the turn of century state-supported geological surveys were used to market the area's mineral wealth. The *Manufacturers' Record* in 1906 could justly claim that in West Virginia, "the entire machinery of State government has been used to attract capital to the State to develop its railroads, its coal, and its timber interests. A succession of four or five governors ... were widely known ... in the financial circles of the East, not for their political activity, but for their activity in telling the Eastern people and the Eastern press about the undeveloped wealth and unbounded opportunity in West Virginia."

No other state could match West Virginia's zeal, but in 1869, Governor John Stevenson of Kentucky, while arguing that European immigration was necessary for a sufficient supply of labor, concluded that "our need does not stop there. We must look to Europe also for capital ... if we desire to increase our population and develop our industrial and mineral wealth." Two years later the Kentucky legislature established a bureau of immigration. Tennessee had done so in 1867, and by 1900 North Carolina, Virginia, and Georgia had followed suit.

As one historian has concluded, however, New South governments "were willing to encourage immigration to their states and to grant tax exemptions, liberal charters, and other special privileges to promote industrial growth, but they were reluctant to burden state treasuries with large publicity budgets." The brunt of the publicity campaign was thus borne by the private sector.

Led by Atlanta *Constitution* editor Henry Grady, New South advocates toured the North, seeking investment in cotton mills, iron foundries, railroads, and coal mines. They sought to attract northern dollars by listing the rich natural resources of the region. To Richard Hathaway Edmonds, owner of the *Manufacturer's Record*, the South was "Creation's Garden Spot," as nature had "more richly endowed the South than any other section of the country." Northern allies, such as Pennsylvania's William "Pig Iron" Kelley, dutifully identified specific places with "abounding supplies of materials for widely diversified manufactures."

There also were prospects of a favorable climate, a pliable work force free from unionization, and low taxes or other financial inducements. Drawing on the spirit of reconciliation that followed Reconstruction, Grady was especially good at suggesting that northern investment in the South would help heal the wounds of the Civil War, even while he told southerners that they must adopt northern ways so as to compete better against the former enemy. Grady was careful to flatter his northern listeners by suggesting that this New South had more to learn from the North than it did from its own past.

In a well-publicized speech at the New England Society of New York's 1886 banquet at Delmonico's restaurant, Grady announced that "words, delivered from the immortal lips of [former Confederate General] Benjamin H. Hill, at [New York's] Tammany Hall, in 1866" would be his text. "There was a South of slavery and secession—that South is dead," Grady quoted Hill as saying. "There is a South of union and freedom—that South, thank God, is living, breathing, growing every hour." According to Grady, these words were "true then and truer now." Hill had said no such thing; indeed, there is no evidence that he had even spoken at Tammany in 1866. But the northern businessmen present at Delmonico's were in no mood to quibble. They wanted to hear about what Grady called a "New South" eager to rejoin the union, a worthy South that took the North as its model for future progress and was ready to make the most of northern investment. Grady did not disappoint them as he reported:

We have established thrift in city and country. We have fallen in love with work. . . . The old South rested everything on slavery and agriculture, unconscious that these could neither give nor maintain healthy growth. The new South presents a perfect democracy . . . — a hundred farms for every plantation, fifty homes for every palace— and a diversified industry that meets the complex need of this complex age.

Despite such appeals, northern money never flowed in to the degree that New South advocates had hoped. That which did, together with indigenous sources, altered the industrial character of the region, though never to the degree hoped for or claimed by the proponents of industrialism.

Northern investment had its greatest immediate and long-term consequences in the area of railroad development. During the antebellum period, southerners briefly had been pacesetters in the use of railroads to promote urban growth. Seeking to make Charleston's access to upland cotton less costly, John C. Calhoun and Robert Y. Hayne had promoted a railroad from Charleston to Hamburg, South Carolina. Completed in 1833, the South Carolina Railroad covered 136 miles and was the first steam-powered railroad in the nation. In the two decades that followed, southerners sought to use railroads to free themselves from what one termed "commercial vassalage" to the North. Yet Charleston, along with New Orleans and Norfolk, among other cities, failed to accomplish ambitious plans to open up the West to trade. Only Baltimore successfully reached the West with the completion of the Baltimore and Ohio Railroad in 1853.

Although prewar southern planters and farmers showed a greater inclination to invest in railroad stock than is commonly acknowledged, land and slaves drew away potential funds. As a result, the South lagged well behind the North in total track mileage. More important, much of its trackage consisted of uncompleted lines that failed to contribute to a coherent rail network. The absence of such a network was a key factor in the South's defeat in the war, and the destruction wrought by the Union armies left the South's rail system in ruins.

Even before the beginning of Reconstruction, southern states, cities, and individuals sought to rebuild the region's railroads. Equipment was worn out and thousands of "Sherman's hairpins" (rails twisted around trees) bore testimony to the numerous gaps in the system. Nonetheless, between 1865 and 1868, lines were rebuilt and placed in operation and new projects were under way. Atlanta businessmen pressed the city council to subscribe to a number of railroads, and the first postwar city government in Montgomery bought $500,000 worth of stock in the South and North Railroad. Most cities, however, were content to lure railroads to town with more limited capital subscriptions, tax breaks, and free rights of way. Although the former Confederates anticipated the Yankees when it came to the use of bribery, phony companies, and watered stock in railroad promotion schemes, the new Republican Reconstruction governments certainly kept the process going. Corruption and waste could be expected, given the circumstances of postwar dislocation, but despite criticisms by southerners at the time and subsequent historians, there was no denying the tangible results.

This initial, largely southern-financed, postwar railroad boom collapsed in the wake of the Panic of 1873. Although the Panic and the subsequent six years of depression severely hurt the North, the South and its railroads suffered more because of the region's traditional shortage of capital. By November 1873, fifty-five railroads in ten states (Kentucky plus all the Confederate states except Arkansas and Texas) had defaulted on interest on their bonds. Within three years, 45 percent of the 127 major southern lines were in default of their bond coupons, and the figure was 50 percent or more in Virginia, Florida, Alabama, and Louisiana; in the rest of the country less than one-fourth of the lines were in default. Default usually led to receivership; together they greatly restricted the amount of new railroad construction. The depressed conditions of the 1870s thus accelerated the decline of the South's share in the nation's railroad mileage. That share had shrunk from nearly one-third of the total in 1861 to little more than one-fourth in 1865, and to one-fifth in 1873. By 1880, the 14,811 miles in the southern states constituted less than 16 percent of the national total. The shortage of funds also led to a decline in the quality of equipment, roadbeds, and service.

It was at this point that northern capital had its greatest impact. Many of the bankrupt locally owned southern railroads fell into northern hands. In 1870–71 only 19 percent of the traceable members of the boards of directors of forty-five major southern railroads were from the North, whereas by 1880–1881, 37 percent of the directors were northerners, and nearly half the railroads had northern presidents, compared to less than one-sixth ten years before.

The infusion of northern capital and capitalists helped pull the railroads out of the depression and thus aided local merchants and manufacturers who had been suffering from erratic service and high freight rates. Of crucial importance was the organization in October 1875 of the Southern Railway and Steamship Association. Open to any southern railroad south of the Ohio and Potomac rivers and east of the Mississippi, it had twenty-seven members in 1877. Thanks to the efficiency of this new pooling arrangement and the passage of time, freight rates to eastern cities declined between 1875 and 1887. Rates between Atlanta and New York, Boston, or Baltimore, for example, were reduced roughly one-third between 1876 and 1884. There was no new default among major railroads after 1878, and new construction increased in 1879 and 1880.

During the 1880s American railroads added more mileage than in any other decade in history. This time the South outpaced the nationwide growth; whereas the increase in mileage for the nation was 79 percent, the southern mileage more than doubled. During that decade Texas, already first in the South in total mileage, led the entire country in miles constructed; Georgia ranked second. Alabama's total trackage almost doubled, and Florida's almost quadrupled. Although Virginia, South Carolina, and Tennessee lagged behind, each built more new lines in the decade than all of New England. New construction slowed in the 1890s, especially after the depression that began in 1893, yet the southern rate of increase remained slightly greater than the national average, with Texas, Georgia, Louisiana, Florida, and Alabama in the forefront. Thanks largely to the efforts of northern financier Henry M. Flagler, Florida—described by a tourist guide in 1892 as "in the main inaccessible to the ordinary tourist, and unopened to the average settler"—had jumped from last in total trackage in the region to fifth by 1900; twelve years later Flagler's railroad and hotel empire reached Key West.

The last twenty years of the century also brought increased consolidation of the southern lines. Though coming later in the South than in the North, that process of consolidation was essentially completed by 1900. By 1900, three-fourths of the mileage in the South outside of Texas was controlled by five corporations: Southern Railway, Louisville and Nashville, Atlantic Coast Line, Seaboard Air Line, and Illinois Central.

It was no coincidence that these five railroads were in the hands of northern bankers. The expansion and consolidation of southern railroads had in fact been accomplished by a steady increase in northern capital and management. Of the big five, for example, all but the Illinois Central were under the control of the New York financier J. P. Morgan, who, beginning with the reorganization of the insolvent Richmond and West Point Terminal Company in 1894, combined shrewdness, skill, bribery, and stock jobbing and watering to engineer this remarkable era of consolidation. By 1900, over 60 percent of the directors of the South's major lines came from the North, as did 58 percent of the presidents. The extent of northern control was even greater than it seemed, for southerners operated only the shortest lines, over which the larger railroads exerted significant influence through leases, stock ownership, and other financial ties.

The expansion, consolidation, and infusion of northern capital greatly improved the southern rail system. Without consolidation and northern influence, for example, the switch by southern railroads to the northern 4-foot, 8½-inch gauge in 1886 would have been delayed several years. By 1900 there was better service, more efficient interchange of traffic, better equipment, and lower rates than there had been in the past, although in none of these areas had the southern railroads attained parity with the North. In the next two decades, the southern railway network grew from 59,600 miles to 84,600 miles. This 42 percent growth rate outpaced that of the nation at large and for the first time since 1861 gave the South about one-third of the nation's rail mileage, roughly the percentage it has retained to the present day.

Railroad penetration and industrial development went hand in hand, particularly after 1880; as in the antebellum period, southern industry continued to depend upon the processing of the region's rich raw materials. This can be seen especially in the development of the iron and steel, timber, tobacco, and cotton textile industries.

Coal and iron had been produced in the South since colonial times. Throughout the antebellum period both industries were centered in Virginia, although on the eve of the war Alabama and Tennessee coal fields began to have some impact. The war stimulated production, although both industries remained largely scattered in rural areas and considerably underfunded. The Tredegar Iron Works in Richmond, Virginia, which towered above other southern factories in producing iron for the war effort, was dwarfed by countless northern counterparts.

At the end of the war Tredegar and the rest of the iron industry lay in ruins. Conditions gradually improved, however, sparked by the development of new supplies of iron ore and coal in northern Alabama, eastern Tennessee, and western Virginia.

In 1871 two northern real estate speculators, attracted by the rich iron deposits of northern Alabama's Jefferson County, founded Birmingham in what had been a cornfield. Realizing the site's potential, the Louisville and Nashville Railroad built a line to Decatur, making a junction with an existing railroad near Birmingham. L & N officials invested in real estate and in the town's new iron mills, ran special trains for prospective investors, and provided lower rates for southern pig iron. The town was linked to Atlanta by rail in 1883, and a plethora of new lines soon connected the once-isolated community with the major cities of the North and South.

The industrial impact was immediate. In 1880 the southern states produced approximately one-sixteenth of the nation's pig iron. By 1890, thanks to Birmingham, along with Anniston, Sheffield, and Bessemer, Alabama was producing nearly one-tenth, and the South as a whole one-fifth, of the nation's pig iron. Southern iron was at first unsuitable for conversion into steel by the then-dominant Bessemer process, but during the 1890s conversion was achieved through the use of the open-hearth process. As in the case of southern railroads, a shortage of local capital meant that northerners rather than southerners brought the industry to its fullest potential. Again mergers were the order of the day, and once more J. P. Morgan was the key player.

The prize this time was the Tennessee Coal & Iron Company. Originating as a coal mining company in eastern Tennessee in 1852, it shifted its operations to Alabama in 1886, and by the turn of the century it had become the largest southern iron company. It became a part of Morgan's United States Steel Company in 1907 and was the largest iron and steel producer in the South until World War II.

Although the industry continued to expand, its growth could not match that of the North. In 1914 southern pig iron had dropped to 11 percent of the national production; southern steel amounted to only 6 percent of the national total. In part this was because of the absence of a large industrial market in the region's still primarily agrarian economy. However, a discriminatory pricing system known as Pittsburgh Plus, whereby southern iron was priced according to the Pittsburgh rate plus the freight charges from Pittsburgh (rather than from the closer southern production center) to its destination, also was responsible. Although the Federal Trade Commission banned the policy in 1924, southern iron continued to face freight-rate discrimination until it was ended by court action in 1948.

The area around Birmingham had been largely unsettled, so that industrialization, while bringing with it the benefits and liabilities of this new kind of life, did not transform the lives of a resident population. This was not the case elsewhere, particularly in Appalachia, where the expansion of the coal industry had a transforming impact similar in many ways to that of cotton elsewhere in the South.

Ronald Eller traces this transformation in *Miners, Millhands and Mountaineers* (1982), a study of 112 counties in the mountain areas of Kentucky, West Virginia, Virginia, Tennessee, North Carolina, and Georgia. Modernization did not pass the region by, as is often claimed; instead, the area experienced capitalist modernization that ruined the preindustrial economy and way of life. Although it is easy to romanticize the region's premodern period by presenting a pastoral picture of self-sufficient yeoman farmers without referring to the high death rates or frequent violence, it is important to note that the kind of progress that southern leaders sought had terrible effects.

Railroad penetration was again the key to development. In 1870 there was only one major railroad in Eller's 112 counties; by 1900 there were four. Land companies moved in, buying up farm land or using what were known in eastern Kentucky as broad form deeds to purchase the mineral rights under the land. Local elites served as brokers for land sales, most of which were voluntary, although there were cases involving chicanery. These sales eased the way for the entrance of outside capital.

Land ownership became concentrated in the hands of absentee landlords. Coal and timber companies built many of the railroads, and railroad interests bought much of the coal and timber land. Boom towns such as Middlesborough at Cumberland Gap were built with British and northern capital. By the end of the century, according to Eller, "the Appalachian South had become the economic colony of the urban Northeast."

Coal mining became especially important. Leases were easy to obtain and only limited capital was needed to open a mine. By 1900 bituminous coal production in the region had tripled, and in the next three decades it multiplied more than five-fold, coming to account for almost 80 percent of national production. The penetration of the Great Lakes markets by southern coal companies paved the way for the emergence of a coal boom in the mountains. By 1898 the southern operators began to challenge the division of territory that had confined them to eastern markets and transatlantic trade. Appalachian coal was of better quality than the northern product. In addition, it could be delivered at a lower price, because the relative accessibility of the coal seams meant easier and less expensive mining operations that required little machinery, railroads usually charged lower rates for long hauls, and, in the absence of unionization, mountain miners could be paid less than their unionized counterparts in the North.

Southern West Virginia was most affected by the increasing national demand for coal in the first decade of the twentieth century, thanks to the entrance of the railroads in the 1890s. There were many independent operators, but a few large companies, most notably U.S. Steel and the Pennsylvania Railroad, came to dominate the field. Kentucky, the second largest coal-producing area in the mountains, did not really hit its stride until around 1910, by which time southwestern Virginia and eastern Tennessee had built on less-extensive earlier antecedents. Between 1909 and 1910, the total number of mines in the country increased by more than a third, and the largest percentage increase was in the South, though many of the mines were only marginal.

World War I gave a great spur to the industry. Southern mines had an edge over northern competitors because they had a larger labor reserve, lower transportation costs to the Midwest-centered industries, and larger mine capacity, which led to the allocation of more railroad cars. The boom years continued until early in 1923, when bituminous coal production reached its height. A decline then set in because of overproduction, increased shipping costs, and a decrease in demand as oil, gas, and hydroelectric power became popular sources of energy.

Outsiders generally were in charge of the companies. Of 140 mine operators in southern West Virginia, eastern Kentucky, and southwestern Virginia between 1880 and 1930, 77.8 percent were born outside the mountain South. Over 46 percent were from the North, primarily Pennsylvania, and more than 31 percent were born in the nonmountain South. Most of the mountain natives were small operators or managers for absentee corporations. An estimated 80 percent of the operators in Tennessee and Alabama were nonmountain Southerners.

Most of the miners, however, were from the mountains, although there were large numbers of blacks from the nonmountain South and recent immigrants from southern Europe, especially Italy. Whatever their background, a larger percentage of the workers lived in mining towns than was the case in Ohio or Pennsylvania, and debt peonage kept many of the immigrants there against their will. The number of immigrants and blacks declined, however, with the impact of World War I and the migration of blacks to the North. Injuries and deaths in the mines were common as a result of unsafe conditions. On March 13, 1884, a coal dust explosion in the Pocahontas Laurel mine in Virginia killed the entire night shift of 114 men. With the increase in mechanization after 1900, such tragedies became more common. Between 1902 and 1927 mine explosions in the mountains killed over 2,400 men.

Even before coal mining, the timber industry had taken its toll in Appalachia. In the antebellum period, almost every mountain county had at least one sawmill, which usually was combined with a gristmill and located along the banks of a stream. But prior to the 1890s, the market for sawed lumber was localized, the technology was simple, and the amount of timber cut made only a slight impact on the region's resources. As late as 1900, over 75 percent of the southern Appalachia region remained in woodland.

Two major lumber booms soon transformed the area. Relying mainly on water transportation and the seasonal labor of mountain folk, the first stage of the new lumber industry, from 1880 to the early 1890s, involved selective cutting of choice black walnut, yellow poplar, and ash, trees that had begun to disappear from northern forests. More damaging was the second stage, from 1890 to 1920, spurred on by increased demand and financed by northern capital. Rather than depend on seasonal labor, owners moved mountaineers into timber camps and logging towns. Absentee landowners, whom the West Virginia State Board of Agriculture termed "alien owners," in 1900 owned between 40 and 75 percent of the saleable timber in four of the best counties. As was true elsewhere, they soon opened large tracts to cutting, built new sawmills, and took advantage of new rail lines in the area.

By 1900 the Southern Appalachian region contributed 30 percent of the hardwood cut in the United States; by its peak in 1909, the figure was nearly 40 percent. Conservation efforts were rare and matters were made worse by the introduction of machine logging after 1910. Pulp mills now began to take even the smallest trees. A reprieve of sorts came only after World War I, when deforestation caused the lumber industry to switch to Oregon and Washington.

The new labor-intensive, extractive economy not only meant absentee landlords and exploitation of the rich natural resources; it also had a negative effect on agriculture. In 1910, a local minister reported that "When I first started my work in these mountains, 30 years ago, the forests were untouched, the mountains were full of sparkling brooks and creeks which required a two or three weeks rain to make muddy; today, a few hours rain will muddy them . . . ; many of the mountain streams are dry throughout the summer and fall, while in winter, the waters descend in torrents and do vast damage, rendering worthless the bottom lands which used to be the most desirable for farming purposes." The average mountain farm had consisted of 187 acres in the 1880s, but was reduced to an average of 76 acres in 1930 and as little as 47 in some counties. The number of farms increased, but the total amount of farm land actually decreased by 20 percent. Farming went from being the primary income producer to parttime employment, with the major sources of income shifting to mining, logging, and textiles. This process was most pronounced in coal fields and other areas of intense economic growth. Modernization thus left in its wake the small marginal farm, poverty, and a pattern of underdevelopment akin to that found in the third world. By 1930, three-fifths of the mountain population was employed off the farm and many farmers engaged in parttime industrial work. Many of the remaining farmers worked farms that were classified as submarginal.

The transformation of displaced farmers into an industrial work force also was evident in the tobacco industry. This time, however, the driving force was a southern capitalist, James Buchanan Duke of Durham, North Carolina.

Although tobacco had spread from Virginia, the first commercial tobacco factories were concentrated in northern port cities. Between 1790 and 1860, they shifted to the tobacco-growing districts of the South to be closer to the raw material and to take advantage of surplus slave labor. By 1860, Virginia produced 56 percent of the nation's tobacco goods, with its chief competition coming from Kentucky, Tennessee, and Missouri. After the Civil War, the manufacture of smoking tobacco and cigarettes continued to be southern-based industries. Kentucky and Virginia remained important centers of production, but North Carolina took the lead after the installation of the first practical cigarette-making machine in the

Duke factory in Durham, North Carolina, in 1884. James Duke not only pioneered the use of new industrial techniques, but also was among the first to use extensive advertising to promote sales. His Durham factory became the nation's largest producer of cigarettes, and by 1890 Duke had merged with several competitors to form the American Tobacco Company. As he put it, "I said to myself, 'If John D. Rockefeller can do what he is doing for oil, why should I not do it in tobacco.'" At its peak, American Tobacco controlled 80 percent of all tobacco manufacturing in the country, with the exception of cigar making, which was still a small-scale handicraft industry centered in the North, although it was facing an increasing challenge from new plants in Tampa, Florida. But cigarettes were the wave of the future, and by 1920 they had replaced cigars in sales.

James "Buck" Duke was able to beat northern capitalists at their own game. Duke and his family provide strong support for assertions that the postwar southern business leaders were "new men" from middle-class backgrounds. Duke's father, Washington, had a farm near Durham where he began the home manufacture of bright-leaf smoking tobacco after the Civil War. In 1874, he sold the farm to concentrate on tobacco manufacturing, and his sons became full partners in W. Duke Sons and Company when it was incorporated in 1878. By 1884, James had moved permanently to New York to manage the branch factory there and subsequently transferred his company headquarters to the city. Well before the Supreme Court called in 1911 for the dissolution of American Tobacco Company in one of the nation's greatest antitrust cases, Duke had begun to diversify by investing in hydroelectric power (eventually leading to the Duke Power Company) and in what by then had become the South's leading industry—cotton textile manufacturing.

Although the cotton textile industry was centered in New England until the end of the nineteenth century, there had been small textile mills in the South since the colonial period. By 1850, there were more than 200 mills in the South, primarily in the Piedmont of Virginia, North Carolina, South Carolina, and Georgia. Two major figures in the industry were southerners William Gregg and Daniel Pratt.

Using this foundation and taking advantage of proximity to the expanding cotton supply and the availability of cheap, nonunionized labor, the industry grew rapidly in the postwar years. As late as the 1880s, however, the industry still had much in common with its more modest antebellum antecedents. But the number of spindles rose sharply in the 1890s and the amount of capital invested rose from $22.8 million in 1880 to $132.4 in 1900. By that year, the textile industry not only was the region's major industrial employer, but the South had surpassed New England to become the nation's textile center. By 1915, the South accounted for 60 percent of the country's cotton manufacturing.

The industry's expansion had its greatest effect on South Carolina, which by 1900 was second to Massachusetts in the number of spindles, and in which mill workers and their dependents were 12.6 percent of the white population. By 1910, after the rapid expansion of the mid-1890s, there were 147 corporations producing yarn and cloth, and 45,000 textile workers. The typical plant had more than 25,000 spindles. The state's spindleage had increased nearly forty-five times between 1880 and 1900, which, according to the leading historian of the process, reflected a "fundamental shift away from small factories producing primarily yarn for local sale to integrated cloth mills competing in national and international markets."

As late as 1890, with water power still the primary energy source, the mills were likely to be in isolated rural areas. After 1895, however, the demand for cotton textiles, along with railroad penetration, urban rivalry, and the development of cheap electricity, brought major expansion and the construction of mill villages on the outskirts of existing Piedmont towns. The Olympia mill in the Columbia mill district was the largest cotton mill under one roof in the world.

For southern leaders at the time and for early generations of historians, the mill was the symbol of the New South, and the "Cotton Mill Campaign" was undertaken by the region's elite (often led by planters) as part of a philanthropically inspired "community enterprise" to provide jobs for poor whites. In reporting the speech of a Salisbury, North Carolina, mill advocate, for example, one newspaper noted approvingly that he declared "the establishment of a cotton mill would be the most Christian act his hearers could perform." According to a journalist writing in the 1920s, "People were urged to take stock in the mills for the town's sake, for the poor people's sake, for the South's sake, literally for God's sake." Yet the reasons for the proliferation of mills and the nature of their development were often less altruistic than New South supporters were willing to acknowledge.

Scholars today find little support for claims of a benevolent motive or planter dominance behind the founding of the cotton mills. Although one study does argue that antebellum planters and their children developed North Carolina's postwar cotton textile industry, it concludes they did so more as a means of controlling than helping the state's poor white population and in order to place limits on capitalist expansion. The mills were envisioned as a plantation for poor whites. Most historians, however, stress the capitalist motives behind the enterprises and their break with the past. In *Mill and Town in South Carolina 1880–1920* (1982), David Carlton finds change especially evident in the origins of the industrialists and in the ways they conducted business. According to Carlton, the antebellum textile manufacturers carried on their business like local gristmillers—their postbellum successors were "modern industrial capitalists." To be sure, as others have argued, the textile manufacturers were overwhelmingly from South Carolina, with 88.2 percent from the Piedmont, 3.8 percent from Charleston, and 4.2 percent from the Northeast. But more important, a solid majority was from commercial backgrounds, whereas 20 percent were professionals and only 11.6 percent from agriculture.

Such men were part of a communitarian crusade, but "community" meant the middle class, and the profit motive was far more important than philanthropic, humanitarian, or social-control purposes. Note the quest of competitive-minded boosters in Raleigh, North Carolina, for a textile mill. "How about that cotton factory?" chided the *Raleigh Daily Constitution* in urging local businessmen to "awake from your lethargy" in 1875. "Wilmington has one, Charlotte is thinking about establishing one and Raleigh should not be behind the times." Thirteen years later, civic leaders still were trying to bring a factory to the city. "What is to become of Raleigh unless we do something to increase its business?" bemoaned the *State Chronicle*. So much for the philanthropic, noncapitalist motive for the cotton mill crusade. Raleigh finally got its mill in 1891 and two others soon followed.

But whoever was responsible for the mills and whatever their original motivation, the sad reality was that the desire for profits became paramount and the workers, as in the rest of the southern economy, paid the price. One mill employee reported that his "mill runs day and night. The day hands commence work at 6 o'clock in the morning and run till 7 o'clock at night. They stop at 12 o'clock for dinner and ring the bell at 12:30 o'clock. I contend that the hands are in actual motion 13 hours per day. The trade check system [wages paid in trade checks redeemable at the company store rather than cash] is used here, and is not as good as cash, at this place nor any other place. . . . This long hour system is destroying the health of all the young women who work in the mills. The employment of children in the mills at low wages keeps a great many men out of employment." In 1889 another worker complained that "Just so long as they give [trade] checks and pay once a month, they will keep us on the grind-stone, and we cannot get justice or give it in this condition." He added hopefully that "The day is coming when mill-owners will find out that if they give their hands good houses to live in, pay them cash, and teach them how to live and take care of their earned money, both parties will prosper and grow fat." But most employers did not believe that such a mixture of paternalism and capitalism was in their interest and, even thirty years later, this worker's expectations remained unrealized.

New South spokesmen were proud of the remarkable growth in the production of coal, iron, steel, timber, tobacco, and cotton textiles. There also was the evident success of other extractive-based industries, such as cottonseed oil, furniture, minerals, and leather tanning. Then, too, they could point to the burgeoning new industry that followed the opening of the Spindletop oil well in Texas in 1901. Yet the gilt of New South oratory obscured the core of Old South realities. C. Vann Woodward's assessment in *Origins of the New South* still holds: the South, by running fast, had, despite considerable progress, merely succeeded in standing still in its race with the North. In 1860 the South had 17.2 percent of the manufacturing establishments in the country and 11.5 percent of the capital; by 1904 the respective figures were 15.3 percent and 11 percent. The value of manufacturers rose only slightly, from 10.3 percent of the total value produced in the United States to 10.5 percent. In 1900, the proportion of people in southern states east of the Mississippi engaged in manufacturing was about the proportion in all states east of the Mississippi in 1850. Even the 99 percent rise in the number of production workers in southern industry between 1899 and 1919 did not appreciably close the gap between the South and the rest of the country. And, as historian Blaine Brownell correctly notes, southern industries "were often engaged in the first- or second-stage processing of agricultural products rather than in the more sophisticated types of manufacturing, and employed workers who were relatively unskilled when compared with those of the North."

Helping to account further for the region's economic failures as well as its (less significant) successes was the nature and degree of southern urbanization.

Urbanization

Urbanization traditionally has been treated as a relatively unimportant factor in southern history. Population figures for the era of the First New South would seem to support this assessment. Although the proportion of urban dwellers in the South grew from 7.2 percent in 1860 to 15.2 percent in 1900, the region was less than half as urbanized as the rest of the country. Furthermore, the South had no city with over 300,000 people and only three of the nation's twenty-seven cities with populations between 100,000 and 300,000. Urbanization increased noticeably during the first decade of the twentieth century, but as late as 1920, only 22 percent of southerners lived in communities of more than 2,500 residents, as compared with slightly over 50 percent in the nation at large. And, as had been the case for every census year since 1890, when New Orleans dropped out, there was no southern representative among the nation's ten largest cities.

Yet, as in earlier periods of southern history, the cities of the First New South were far more important than their limited share of the total population would suggest. Indeed, without the changes in urban development, southern agriculture, industrialization, and railroad expansion would have had a far different character. Urbanization did not produce these outcomes by itself; rather, a complex interaction was the key to what was new in the southern economy, as well as to what was old. As Don Doyle has suggested in *New Men, New Cities, New South* (1990), these developments and the new urban "business class" that helped bring them about served to "open the road to the modern South."

Before the Civil War, the ten largest cities in what soon would be the Confederate South were river or sea ports located on the perimeter of the region east of the Mississippi River and served mainly as export centers for the products of southern agriculture. By 1900, however, the top ten included such burgeoning new inland cities as Atlanta, San Antonio, and Houston, and Dallas and Birmingham ranked eleventh and twelfth. By 1920, Birmingham (3) and Dallas (7) had pushed out Charleston and Savannah, two of the remaining major prewar port cities, leaving only New Orleans (1) and Norfolk (10) in the top twelve.

Although individual cities might rise or fall in spectacular fashion, there was no sudden change in the overall hierarchy of cities. In part this was because the Civil War was not the watershed in urban development that some have claimed it to be. At first glance, comparative census data for the North and South support those who argue that the war seriously hindered postbellum southern urban growth. In 1860, the eleven Confederate states had 13.8 percent of the nation's 392 urban centers; ten years later the same states had 10.1 percent of the 663 urban centers. Yet this drop in the South's percentage of the nation's towns was part of a decline that began in the 1830s. The war merely accelerated a trend long under way.

The Civil War *was* responsible for the disruption of traditional trade routes, damaged agricultural hinterlands, ruinous inflation and speculation, the decline of public services, and the loss of men. But for most cities there were offsetting benefits, and for many the war definitely contributed to urban growth. Generalizations about what one former rebel termed a "prostrate South" are risky. Galveston and Houston were hurt by the Union blockade, but San Antonio flourished as a result of its secure inland position and its role as a military and supply center for the Confederacy. Charleston, Savannah, and Mobile lost a major share of the cotton trade, but the occupation of New Orleans and Memphis by Union troops in 1862 allowed cotton merchants in those cities to prosper.

As was the case for much of the agricultural sector, even some cities that experienced severe destruction and disruption quickly recovered. The outstanding example was Atlanta. Again we can see the antebellum roots of postbellum developments. During the antebellum period Atlanta, originally called Terminus, had emerged, according to one biographer, as "an incidental byproduct of a railroad system constructed to promote the prosperity of other towns." On the eve of the war it was connected by five railroads to major cities of the North, West, and South. By 1864, the city had doubled its 1860 population to over 20,000. As a military headquarters and manufacturing, supply, and medical center, it was among the three most important Confederate cities.

The much-publicized "destruction" of the city in 1864, immortalized in *Gone with the Wind*, did little to hinder its path to regional dominance, in part because the extent of the damage has been exaggerated. On arriving in the city in November 1865, northern journalist Sidney Andrews, surprised to find less devastation than he had expected, wrote, "the City Hall and the Medical College and all the churches, and many of the handsomer and more stylish private dwellings and nearly all the houses of the middling and poorer classes were spared." Less than a year after Sherman had left the remainder of the city in flames, all five railroads were in active operation. A local editor could rightfully claim in the fall of 1866 that Atlanta "is the radiating point for Northern and Western trade coming Southward, and is the gate through which passes Southern trade and travel going northward."

The task of postwar recovery was greatest for the older port cities, especially New Orleans and Charleston. Even before the Civil War, these cities had seen their once-lofty positions challenged by competing towns and especially by the intrusion of railroads that opened new markets to inland farmers. Their comparative decline continued in the early postwar years. Along with Mobile, both cities were plagued by obstructions still blocking their harbors. Charleston also suffered from the destruction of the 104-mile rail link to Savannah that remained out of operation until March 1870. But these port cities were hurt most by changes in the cotton trade that undermined the role of their factors.

In the first decade after the war, the new rail links, which greatly expanded the small overland trade to the North by way of Memphis, seriously hurt the Gulf ports. The growth of east-west railroads south of the Ohio River also drew cotton to the Atlantic ports. Although Charleston and Savannah continued to be destinations, they already were being challenged by Norfolk. Norfolk greatly benefited from the swift repair of its two major railroads, which by 1874 had made it the third cotton port, behind New Orleans and Galveston.

The postwar railroad recovery spurred the growth of interior towns and altered their economies. Between 1860 and 1870, such cities as Montgomery and Selma (Alabama), Augusta (Georgia), and Shreveport (Louisiana) grew by at least 20 percent, and Little Rock's population more than tripled. In 1870, Dallas was a sleepy Texas town in the middle of nowhere with a population of 2,960. Then in 1872 the Houston and Texas Central Railroad came to town, followed the next year by the Texas and Pacific Railway. By 1880, Dallas had over 10,000 people. Interior towns attracted merchants and bankers who eventually took over the credit and supply functions of the port factor. Dallas, for example, opened its first bank in 1868; by 1872, Atlanta had ten banks, none of which had existed at the end of the war. And, of course, their merchants, such as the Lehman brothers in Montgomery, began to purchase local cotton themselves.

Clustered around railroad stations, lesser-known towns of between 5,000 and 10,000 people proliferated as locations for the new technology that would help transform life in the countryside and rearrange the urban hierarchy. Larger cotton gins drew ginning from the plantation to towns, where powerful cotton presses and cottonseed-oil mills processed the crop. Cotton presses were especially important to the economy of interior towns because newer and larger presses meant tighter packing of cotton, which allowed more cotton to be sent by rail directly to the North or to inland transhipment centers such as Dallas, Birmingham, or Atlanta, thus bypassing the port cities.

These larger interior centers benefited from northern financing, but southern urban leaders also played an important role. Known for their fervent boosterism even then, Atlantans, for example, were not content to simply let prosperity come—they went out and grabbed it. Indeed, one can trace the roots of the famous "Atlanta Spirit" to these years. "Chicago in her busiest days could scarcely show such a sight," observed a somewhat overly impressed Sidney Andrews. Seeking to retain the wagon trade of nearby upcountry farmers, Atlantans quickly rebuilt the public market in 1866 and began to stage the annual Georgia State Agricultural Society fairs in 1870. In order to wrest the state capital from Milledgeville in 1868, they promised to provide free of charge for ten years any necessary state buildings. Flushed by their manufacturing success during the war, they actively sought to encourage industry. The Atlanta Rolling Mill was back in operation by 1866, and within five years after the war there were more manufacturing establishments than ever before, producing goods valued at over $2 million annually. Sparked by an impressive construction boom, Atlanta real estate more than tripled in value between 1860 and 1870. To celebrate their recovery and proclaim their receptivity to outside investment, local businessmen even announced plans to construct a monument to honor Abraham Lincoln!

Other southern cities drew on their wartime experiences and memories of the antebellum industrial crusade in the hope of diversifying their basically commercial economies. Urban boosterism was thus a prime factor in the New South movement to industrialize. Nevertheless, from 1865 until the Panic of 1873, manufacturing ventures were less important than an unprecedented building program that sought to improve the quality of urban life by providing residents with needed services.

Much of this activity was financed directly by the cities. The major expenses in Houston were for streets and bridges; in Atlanta, they consumed 32 percent of the budget between 1868 and 1873. Other large chunks of money went to new public buildings. Montgomery, Atlanta, and Houston were among the many cities that rebuilt or erected new public markets and city halls. Montgomery and Atlanta, like Norfolk, also constructed municipal waterworks. And by 1873 almost every southern city had inaugurated a public school system, a further contribution to local construction booms.

The private sector also contributed to the postwar building surge. In addition to impressive new commercial buildings, there were great hotels, such as Atlanta's six-story Kimball House, and theaters, such as New Orleans's Grand Opera House. Everywhere private gas companies received charters and began tearing up the streets to lay their pipes. But most important to urban life was the appearance of horse-drawn streetcars. Only New Orleans and Mobile had streetcars prior to 1861. The Civil War delayed the installation of systems in the other large cities, but did not seriously interfere with their subsequent adoption. Most major cities had street railways by 1866, and all had them by 1870.

There were still complaints about muddy streets, inadequate water, insufficient police protection, and high freight rates, but clearly there was much ground for optimism. The Panic of 1873, however, produced an economic downturn that continued until the end of the decade. This meant a period of belt tightening to pay for the heady expansion of the early postwar years. Cities had increasing difficulty in maintaining municipal services and in paying the interest on their bonded debt. The collection of property taxes (since 1860 the chief source of regular income) became even more difficult than in the past. In an unsuccessful effort at social pressure, newspapers listed the names of residents who owed taxes, but even city officials such as Nashville Mayor Thomas A. Kercheval could be found among the defaulters.

At the same time that the slower population growth and rising unemployment of the 1870s weakened the tax base and forced city governments to cut basic services, private companies also were failing to live up to the requirements of their franchises. Streetcar, water, and lighting companies went out of business or failed to maintain or extend their services. Most streets remained unpaved—this was true of all but three of Atlanta's one hundred miles of streets in 1880—as "retrenchment and reform" replaced "enterprise and progress" as the slogan of the day.

For several cities the economic troubles of the 1870s were made even worse by the ravages of disease, almost a constant fact of life in southern cities well into the twentieth century. In 1873, for example, epidemics of cholera in Nashville and yellow fever in Montgomery drained city finances and interfered with trade. Already hurt by altered trade routes, New Orleans's economy was further damaged by yellow fever epidemics in 1873 and 1878 that left thousands dead and caused other cities to close their doors to New Orleans trade lest the disease be spread.

The importance of a healthy environment to urban growth was even more evident in Memphis, which, unlike New Orleans, had been prospering in the postwar period. Blessed by a choice river location and the coming of the railroads, the Bluff City saw its population grow from 22,623 in 1860 to 40,226 ten years later. Through the early 1870s it looked as if nothing would impede the city's rise to regional dominance, but in 1878 its longtime disregard for sanitation and the poverty of its growing lower-class population finally took their toll. The city had endured frequent yellow fever epidemics, but in 1878–1879 the dreaded disease killed approximately 5,800 people. The wealthy fled, many settling permanently in St. Louis. Unable to meet its financial obligations, the battered city lost its corporate status, and its legal name was changed to "Taxing District of Shelby County." By 1880, the population had shrunk to 33,592, and the following year the New Orleans *Picayune* entitled a gloating editorial "Is Memphis a Pest House?"

The trouble of the 1870s was largely forgotten in the boom years that followed. The period from 1880 to 1892 was one of rapid urban growth throughout the country, and this time the South led the way. Whereas in 1880, 8.7 percent of southerners qualified as urban, by 1890, the figure stood at 12.8 percent. Urban growth continued during the 1890s, although it was less marked because of the Panic of 1893 and the economic hard times that followed. By 1900, 15.2 percent of southerners were urban, as compared to 39.7 percent of the nation as a whole.

Twenty years later, the region's urban population finally neared 25 percent.

Urban boosters were delighted with the increase, but not with one of its major causes. One of the consequences of emancipation and the end of the war had been a marked movement cityward of large numbers of rural blacks, even though, as we have seen, the great majority remained in the countryside. This migration threatened to reverse the antebellum trend towards the thinning out of black urban populations. In 1820, 37 percent of all southern town dwellers were black; by 1860, as a result of the growing demand for black labor in the countryside and white concerns over their ability to control urban blacks, less than 17 percent of urban residents were black. Drawing on that antebellum experience, the *Montgomery Daily Ledger* wrote of urban blacks in 1865, "Our advice to them is to go into the country and cultivate the soil, the employment God designed them for and which they must do or starve." The editor added that the city was "intended for white people."

The postwar influx destroyed any illusions that the urban black population would continue to decline. According to census data, between 1860 and 1870 Atlanta's black population grew from 1,939 to 9,929, and the blacks' percentage of the total population rose from 20 percent to 46 percent. In 1860, Richmond's 14,275 blacks constituted 38 percent of the city's population; ten years later, 23,110, or 45 percent, of the residents were black.

As sizable as were these gains, the federal census did not reveal the full extent of what was happening. The 1870 census greatly underestimated the number of urban black southerners, and by that date there already had been some filtering back to the countryside. Whatever the true extent of the migration, the increase of black residents marked a change in the composition of southern urban populations and, as we shall see, affected every aspect of city life, despite the claims of those historians who see only unremitting continuity between antebellum and postbellum urban life.

Rural blacks came to the cities for a variety of reasons. For some the cities as headquarters for the federal forces represented safety from the violence and intimidation of the countryside. "They leave the country in many instances because they are outraged, because their lives are threatened; they run to cities as an asylum," testified black leader Henry M. Turner at the congressional hearings investigating the Ku Klux Klan in 1871. Others came for the welfare and educational services provided by the army, the Freedmen's Bureau, and northern missionary societies. Still others were drawn by the attractions of city life—what one uneasy white Atlantan called "the inherent love of the negro for a crowd, for shows, for amusements, and for opportunities of making a precarious living by occasional jobs when they may be idle at other times"—an explanation particularly favored by whites who denied charges of mistreatment in the countryside and believed that that was where blacks "naturally" belonged. No doubt many former slaves came simply to test their new freedom of movement. Whatever the motivation, most knew that in the antebellum period the cities had been better places for blacks than the rural areas. Even in 1908 the black leader W. E. B. Du Bois could rightfully claim that the "country was . . . the seat of slavery, and its blight still rests . . . heavily on the land . . . but in the cities . . . the Negro has had his chance."

Although individual blacks moved in and out of the cities, the absolute number of blacks generally increased, so that by 1890 roughly 15 percent of southern blacks lived in cities, comprising almost a third of the region's urban population and almost 70 percent of the nation's black urban dwellers. Their numbers would not begin to thin until the first wave of migration to the North around the first decade of the twentieth century and the even greater movement associated with the Great Migration of the World War I era. Even so, in 1920, when the South remained home to 85 percent of the nation's black population, blacks constituted one-third of the southern urban population.

The great majority of black males held menial jobs, and black women, unlike their white counterparts, formed a significant part of their race's work force. Blacks were hindered by their lack of skills, but, given the indispensable role that slave and free black artisans had played on antebellum plantations and in southern cities, many blacks clearly were confined to low-paying, unskilled jobs solely because of their race. In 1870 in Atlanta, for example, 76.1 percent of black males aged sixteen and over were classified as unskilled workers, as compared to 16.8 percent of their white counterparts. An English visitor to the city in 1876 reported that local whites believed that "if the Negro is kept in his place and is made to work, he does very well, but he is not fit to rise higher; he has no judgment and does not make a skilled mechanic." Out of Nashville's work force of 8,100 black males in 1890, 1,017 were employed as servants and 3,811 as unskilled laborers. Yet of the white male work force of 14,847, there were only 56 servants and 676 laborers. Although there were 991 white carpenters and joiners, only 198 blacks were in those skilled positions. Of the 6,609 employed black women, 2,465 were laundresses and 3,372 were servants; of the 2,989 employed white women, 104 were laundresses and 378 were servants. Outside of the cotton mills, from which they were excluded, blacks throughout the urban South comprised a large part of the unskilled factory workers and were in great demand as day laborers for such hazardous occupations as well digging or sewer building. The streets, docks, and rail yards throughout the urban South were filled with black workers.

At the same time that the ranks of unskilled black workers were increasing, there emerged a small urban black professional and business class, comparable in some ways to the most successful landowning blacks of the countryside, but a more important factor in black life. There already were prosperous blacks in the 1870s, many of whom, like the Atlanta barber Robert Yancy or the dentist Frederick Badger, had a white clientele. By the end of the century, however, a black elite of doctors, lawyers, teachers, ministers, self-employed craftsmen, grocers, undertakers, and barbers who had primarily a black clientele had risen to prominence in southern cities. Black business districts along Raleigh's Hargett Street or Nashville's Cedar and Cherry streets (now Fourth and Charlotte avenues) announced their presence.

Yet as an 1899 survey of black businessmen in the South suggests, the range of occupations was limited. More than 40 percent were grocers, general merchandise dealers, or barbers, all of whom had $500 or more invested; the next two highest groups were printers and undertakers. Groceries comprised more than one-third of Atlanta's sixty-one black businesses of sufficient size to be counted. Nevertheless, a group had emerged that was on the other end of the economic scale from the mass of blacks. As of 1891, Richmond blacks owned real estate valued at $968,736; four years later, there were six blacks who owned more than $10,000 worth of property in the city's largely black Jackson Ward. By 1886, the combined wealth of Nashville's black population was approximately $1 million, with seventeen individuals worth more than $10,000. More than half of that $1 million was owned by forty-four families.

The economic prospects of urban blacks and whites alike continued to depend heavily on the railroads. Indispensable in the immediate postwar years, after the 1880s they had remained, as in the rest of the country, an essential factor in urban growth and economic expansion. According to one scholar, the perfecting of the rail network meant that "by 1900 important towns were aligned along the principal railways like beads on a string." New lines enhanced Atlanta's position as the "Chicago of the South," and helped swell its population from 37,400 to 65,533. The expansion of the Norfolk and Western Railroad into the rich Virginia and West Virginia coal fields had by 1885 allowed coal to replace cotton as Norfolk's chief export and helped increase the city's population from 21,966 to 34,871, well above the percentage increase for other coastal cities. By 1900, the penetration of Florida by rail had led to the founding of Miami in 1896 and almost quadrupled the population of Jacksonville from its 1880 figure of 7,650, while Tampa had grown from 720 to 15,839.

Most noteworthy was Birmingham, which, as we have seen, owed its existence to the Louisville and Nashville Railroad's interest in the area's mineral wealth. Because of a cholera epidemic and the effects of the Panic of 1873, growth was slow: there were only 3,086 inhabitants in 1880, nine years after its founding. But spectacular growth followed in the wake of improved rail connections. By 1890 the population was 26,178, and ten years later it had climbed to 38,414, on its way to the almost unbelievable figure of 132,685 in 1910. In addition to carrying the products of local mills, machine shops, and foundries, the city's eight railroad lines also helped distribute the output of more than fifty different kinds of noniron manufacturing enterprises.

Despite the high hopes and rich rhetoric of advocates of industrial expansion, of the ten largest cities in the South in 1900, only Memphis approached Birmingham in the transforming effects of manufacturing. The addition of seven new railroads in the dozen years after 1880 not only helped increase Memphis's population from 33,592 in 1880 to 64,495 in 1890, but also triggered a sharp increase in the rate of investment in manufacturing that sparked its recovery from the yellow fever catastrophe. Lumber production was the city's major industry until the turn of the century. Second largest was the manufacture of cottonseed products, which began in the 1880s. Additional manufacturing included beer, snuff, printing and publishing, and drugs and pharmaceutical supplies.

Such growth, as urban boosters proudly trumpeted, depended on a cheap labor force. A local editor boasted in 1904 that "Memphis can save the northern manufacturer ... who employs 400 hands, $50,000 a year on his labor bill." Industrial proponents were likely to applaud rather than condemn the regional pattern in which the real wages of southern workers not only lagged behind those in other regions, but actually declined after 1914. Nor did anyone seem terribly alarmed that by 1914 northern capital controlled two-thirds of the city's cotton mills.

Throughout the South, other communities sought to build their post-1880 economies around industry. Richmond initially was the tobacco capital of the nation, with more than fifty factories in operation by 1880; its rich hinterland also provided resources for its flour mills and iron and steel foundries. Steamboats ran regularly between Richmond and Norfolk, New York, Baltimore, and Philadelphia. It was the terminus of six railroads, nearly all parts of trunk lines that connected Richmond with principal markets throughout the country. But just as Birmingham took Richmond's place in the production of iron, and cities such as Norfolk challenged its flour milling leadership, by the end of the century the new tobacco towns of North Carolina had replaced Richmond, using production of what King James I once called a "stinking weed" to catapult themselves from obscurity to urban prominence. From 1880 to 1900, Winston grew from 443 to 10,008, and the Dukes of Durham pushed their town's population to 6,679 after it had been entirely omitted from the census of 1870. To the south, Tampa had grown, in the words of its biographer, "from an isolated gulf coastal town of sandbeds, small merchants and cattlemen to a thriving commercial port city" after the beginning of the cigar industry in 1885.

As in the case of Memphis, which became the nation's leading producer of cottonseed oil, much local manufacturing throughout the South centered around cotton. Montgomery was typical of many of the medium-sized interior towns. One local firm produced cottonseed oil, another manufactured cotton presses and other machinery, and a third operated a cotton press. The first capital of the Confederacy also had a textile mill.

The expansion of the cotton textile industry that we have already traced owed much to the efforts of urban promoters. The Atlanta International Cotton Exposition held in the fall of 1881 was especially important in attracting attention to the industry. Still pushing in 1909, organizers of Atlanta's automobile exposition used as its symbol a bale of cotton framed in an automobile wheel. Although initially concentrated in rural areas, the mills eventually helped increase the populations of numerous North Carolina towns: between 1880 and 1900 Greensboro grew from 2,105 to 10,035; Charlotte from 7,094 to 18,091; and Gastonia from 236 to 4,610. By employing as textile workers the wives of men who worked in the city's furniture factories, High Point, unlisted in the 1870 census, grew to 4,163 by 1900.

As we have seen for the region as a whole, however, the much-vaunted "industrial revolution" can be described more realistically as "industrial evolution." Because so much of the industrialization occurred in the countryside or in small towns, and because so much of the finishing, distributing, and taking of profits occurred in the North, it is not surprising that the largest southern cities were even less affected by manufacturing than the region as a whole, as local businessmen preferred the more attractive rewards of commerce and railroad speculation.

Just as cotton remained king in the countryside, so, too, was commerce still king in the cities. Such cities as Memphis and Augusta sought manufacturing to encourage growth, but their respective economies clearly depended on their positions as the first- and second-largest inland cotton markets in the country. The value of manufactured goods in Memphis, for example, had increased to $18 million by 1900, but during the 1890s the city's annual trade was estimated at $200 million. The production of cigars helped Tampa, but without the trade of its growing agricultural hinterland, the export of phosphate discovered nearby in 1883, and its role as the major embarkation and supply port during the Spanish-American War, its growth would have been minimal. And, as was true of sugar refining in New Orleans, tobacco manufacturing in Richmond, meat packing in Fort Worth, or furniture making in Memphis, manufacturing was itself commerce-related.

The success of trade, the stimulus of manufacturing, and the general return to prosperity in the nation after 1880 allowed the southern cities to return to the task of extending and mod-

ernizing municipal services. "I wish they would finish Atlanta," complained a local resident who found his city's building boom too disrupting. But southern city administrations
clearly were less inclined than their northern counterparts to
spend public funds for urban improvements. In 1902, every
southern city over 25,000 had a tax levy per capita that was
at least one dollar below the national average of $12.89 for the
160 cities with that population. Although some of the gap in
public spending between the North and South resulted from
the great number of poor people in southern cities, particularly
blacks, it was due more to the twin desires to keep spending
low and to give tax breaks to manufacturing concerns.

Within the confines of limited budgets, the municipal governments sought to improve their urban plants. By 1902, six
southern cities had joined the fourteen northern cities with
more than 25,000 people that had erected municipally owned
electric light plants. Three of them, Jacksonville, Galveston,
and Fort Worth, had also constructed municipal waterworks.
Other cities purchased the private companies that had been
supplying their cities (poorly) with water. Nevertheless,
throughout the urban South at the turn of the century, most
citizens still depended upon cisterns and wells, there was insufficient water pressure with which to fight fires, and pure
water was still a goal rather than a reality. A letter writer in
Nashville described his town's drinking water in 1890 as
"warm and thick," and visitors unaccustomed to it were ad-
vised to flee to the suburbs for a purer version.

Businessmen in such towns as Mobile, Memphis, and
New Orleans had learned the economic costs of disease and
took the lead in urging improved sanitation measures. Their
counterparts in healthier cities, such as Atlanta, sought improvements in public health in order to maintain prosperity
rather than to regain it. Local governments strengthened
boards of health and made efforts to improve disposal of sewage and waste. New sewers were built, as in the case of Memphis, which between 1898 and 1901 added ninety-eight miles
to its system. In New Orleans, however, it took the deaths of

almost four hundred people from yellow fever between 1897 and 1899 to force the city to purchase the franchise of the dormant sewage company and to begin laying sewer pipes in 1903. Mobile was not to learn its lesson until it was hit by a yellow fever epidemic in 1905.

Together with the installation of sewers, the paving of streets received the bulk of municipal expenditures. But despite significant advances in paving over the previous twenty years, by the turn of the century few southern cities had more than half their streets paved. As one historian concluded, "Southern cities still maintained a rural casualness about their physical appearance." By 1902, New Orleans had more than doubled its mileage of paved streets, but that still left almost 500 of the city's 700 miles of streets unpaved. As was generally the case, it was the downtown and the better residential areas that avoided the dust and mud that plagued most urban residents.

The private companies that controlled the financially troubled water companies and most utility and all streetcar operations also affected the economic life of the cities and region. By the turn of the century the "natural monopolies" of telegraph and telephone, which had arrived in most southern cities by the late 1870s, were largely under the control of the northern-based Western Union and Bell System. Likewise, the twenty-year competition within the gas and electric light industries had left one company in each field in control of a given city. As we have seen for so many other areas of southern economic life, the loser was frequently a local outfit; the winner, either northern owned or northern financed. New Orleans, for example, chartered three electric light companies, two of them owned by local residents. By 1897, the northern-owned Edison Electric Company had absorbed one of its local rivals and had driven the other out of business.

The most significant franchised enterprise of the closing twenty years of the century was the street railway. Thanks to a highly decentralized system, telephones remained in the hands only of the rich and successful (there were 1,641 phones in New Orleans in 1898). Electric lights illuminated only the downtown areas and the homes of the very rich, and many urban residents had neither gas nor water, because companies cared more about profits than service. But for all but the very poor, the streetcar was an indispensable part of urban life.

As in the rest of the country, the period from the mid-1880s until the Panic of 1893 witnessed the installation of the first streetcar systems in such cities as Raleigh, Natchez, and Baton Rouge, or the reinstallation in such cities as Montgomery, where systems had failed during the hard times of the 1870s. Installations were especially frequent in towns of fewer than 10,000 residents, for which streetcars became a symbol of urban maturity. And in one of its few instances as a pacesetter, the South took the lead in the electrification of the lines. The first electric streetcar in regular operation appeared on Montgomery streets in 1886, and two years later successful service on hilly Richmond streets convinced most of the remaining doubters that the new invention was practical. By 1890 several southern towns were among the fifty-one cities with electrified lines, although New Orleans and Norfolk were among those that lagged.

As with the other utilities, the rapid expansion of the streetcars during the 1880s and 1890s attracted northern financiers. During the 1890s, the Memphis streetcar network expanded from thirty to seventy miles through the consolidation of the different lines into the Memphis Street Railway Company. Consolidation also meant a shift from mule power to electricity. Then in 1905 the system was sold to a northern syndicate. Representing associates in Omaha, Nebraska, E. A. Allen and O. M. Carter purchased Houston's two streetcar lines and converted them to electric power in 1891. Ten years later, after several receiverships, the Stone-Webster syndicate of Boston assumed control.

The electric streetcar and the "dummies" (steam-driven, with their engines disguised as passenger cars) that also appeared on southern streets after the mid-1880s greatly affected the lives of city residents and would continue to determine the shape of the urban landscape until displaced by the automobile after 1920. As in the North, they not only provided needed construction jobs, but also contributed to the sorting out of the population by race and income and, through the creation of economic subcenters, helped to usher in the golden age of the downtown. The entry of the lines into previously isolated areas of the city sparked a housing construction boom. Housing advertisements now identified neighborhoods in terms of their proximity to the streetcars. As early as 1882, the *Nashville Banner* observed that the six-month-old Fatherland Streetrailway had "brought into prominence that hitherto comparatively inaccessible but most beautiful portion of the city known as the East End." Even those who were too poor to ride the cars regularly to work could take them to pleasure grounds such as Atlanta's Ponce de Leon Springs or Nashville's Glenwood Park that the lines opened to increase their ridership.

The streetcar's greatest impact was on the boundaries of the metropolitan area. The expansion of the lines resulted in the development of numerous streetcar suburbs on the rim of the city. Outside Norfolk, for example, Ghent was transformed from farmland into one of the city's most exclusive residential neighborhoods. In 1890, the *Nashville Banner* carried a full-page advertisement for the sale of lots in "Waverly Place, the Suburban Gem." Located about twenty miles from the heart of the city, Waverly offered to the "wealthy and professional classes" as well as the "man of moderate means" "all the quiet of the country with the advantage of proximity to the business center of a big city, by means of quick motor transportation." And as in the North, operation of the street railway and suburban land development were often directly connected. O. M. Carter and his American Loan and Trust Company of Omaha purchased the Houston City Railway to ensure that his suburban community, Houston Heights, would be linked by rapid transit to the city.

For the same reasons we hear today, cities sought to annex the surrounding areas. Proponents urged annexation so as to achieve better sanitation for the entire metropolitan area, raise the city tax base, and make suburbanites pay for the use of such city services as street maintenance and police protection. "In plain words tax dodging through the use of a trolley line should be abolished," said the *Birmingham Age-Herald* in 1900. "Suburbs should not be built up at the expense of cities. ... If one avails himself of the advantages of a city in the earning of his daily bread, he should share the burdens of that city." Urban boosters also called for annexation so that the federal census would show a great increase over the previous decade. In typical New South spirit, the *Nashville Banner* pointed to Chicago and Cincinnati on the eve of the 1890 census to argue that "the bigger the town the stronger it draws people and capital." By taking in the "populous suburbs," Nashville would have "the population of a great city." The failure of this effort left Nashville boosters feeling like their unsuccessful counterparts in Birmingham after the temporary defeat of their "Greater Birmingham" campaign in 1899. "The city," the *Age-Herald* said, pointing to the forthcoming census, "stands before the world belittled by cramped confines."

Suburban dwellers were divided on the issue of annexation, but by the 1890s they were more attracted by improved city services—water, schools, sewage, etc.—than repelled by an expected increase in their taxes. Following smaller annexations in 1873, 1883, and 1889, Birmingham, for example, had grown from 1.4 to 3 square miles, after which opposition prevented more ambitious efforts until the city expanded to 48 square miles and took in 72,000 people in time for the 1910 census. Few cities made as spectacular use of annexation as Birmingham, but throughout the South these annexations contributed greatly to the growth in urban population. Even a smaller city, such as Knoxville, could use a five-and-a-half-times increase in area between 1900 and 1920 to more than double its population.

The horizontal expansion of the cities, which kept pace with the developments in the North, was not matched by a vertical expansion. The less expansive economies of southern

cities and their relatively uncongested cores meant that downtown skylines were still of human scale. In 1900 the Memphis
business district consisted mostly of old four-story buildings.
The highest structures were the eight-story Randolph Building
and the eleven-story Porter Building. Neither Nashville nor
Norfolk had a building over seven stories, though plans were
soon announced for a thirteen-story building in the former
and a twelve-story building in the latter. Significantly, they
were to be banks. But in 1900, large office buildings did not
dominate the skylines. Rather, the new railroad stations, hotels, theaters, YMCAs, government buildings, and churches
were preeminent. On business streets such as Nashville's Second Avenue or Montgomery's Commerce Street, one could
enjoy the finest period of American storefront architecture—
two- and three-story commercial buildings erected between
1880 and 1900 with concern for scale and design that was
sorely lacking in subsequent years. In a further concession to
the urban aesthetic, most cities during the first decade of the
twentieth century began placing utility wires underground.

Such progress continued during what has been termed an
"urban boomlet" in the wake of American entrance into World
War I in 1917. The South got its first taste of what would later
become a major source of growth as federal government contracts stimulated local economies. Seaports benefited from new
naval construction and textile towns worked overtime to fill
orders for uniforms and other war material. New skyscrapers
appeared in what the southern journalist W. J. Cash would
later derisively cite as another attempt to "out Yankee the
Yankee." Atlanta entrepreneur Joel Hurt constructed the
South's first skyscraper, the Equitable Building. Also in Atlanta, Rich's Department Store attracted no fewer than five
streetcar routes to its front door, and Peachtree Street began
to emerge as one of the South's great commercial and financial
centers. The old downtown of Memphis gave way to several
skyscrapers and an impressive new city hall.

By 1920, then, southern cities had more to offer their residents in terms of services, attractions, and economic well-

being than they had in the immediate postwar years. Yet they still lagged well behind cities in the rest of the nation, and the fruits of what progress had taken place were not equally distributed. The primary beneficiaries were what Blaine Brownell calls the "commercial-civic elites," who made sure that the downtowns and residential areas in which they lived received the lion's share of urban improvements. Members of the working class and especially the poor, as we will see more clearly in the next two chapters, often suffered from the low priority given their needs.

Some historians view the attempt to fashion an urban South in the image of the North as a complete failure that led to greater exploitation of the majority of the population while increasing southern dependence on the North, further contributing to the region's new colonial status. C. Vann Woodward concluded that "the sum total of urbanization in the South was comparatively unimportant." David Goldfield, the leading student of southern urbanization, asserted in *Cotton Fields and Skyscrapers* (1982) that "By 1920, the South was relatively less urban and less prosperous in comparison with other regions than it had been in 1860."

Such judgments seem too harsh and a too simple brief for unremitting continuity in southern urbanization. There had been real change of significant importance that should not be discounted. The founding of Birmingham and Miami meant that by 1900 every one of today's major southern cities had been established; their arrival, plus the growth of the young Texas towns, spelled the end of the hierarchy of cities that had existed in 1860. Only two, (three, if you include the increasingly nonsouthern city of Louisville) of the region's ten largest cities in 1860 still enjoyed that status in 1920. And this was more than a "geographic change," as Goldfield calls it, for it reflected a new economy in which the railroad, dependence on cotton to an unprecedented degree, and ties to the North had rearranged the face of the region. The new trends may have perpetuated old injustices, and we might not like the results, but there is no point in denying the changes.

Similarly, the northern financiers did bring a degree of "progress," however costly, without which future improvements could not be achieved. Besides, in manufacturing, as in so much else, southern cities looked bad only when judged against what was happening in the expansive North. Indeed, those who see nothing but continuity tend to confuse continuity and distinctiveness. Continuity was more significant than change in southern urbanization, but comparisons with the North often say more about the spectacular changes in that region than about what happened in the South. And if urban services and amenities still left much to be desired, southern cities had at least made noteworthy strides toward the day when the bluster of urban boosters would match the reality of southern urban life. For many cities and a new generation of leaders, that time was just over the horizon in what one historian calls the industrial take-off of the 1920s, and from which another dates the emergence of an "urban ethos."

New South advocates failed to achieve their goal of a diversified, balanced economy that had a strong enough manufacturing base to free the South from dependence on the North. And the southern masses—both black and white—paid the price in terms of increased poverty for the kind of unbalanced economic development that did take place. Yet economist William Parker reminds us that, although it may be tempting to do so, it is not enough to ascribe the South's relatively weak economic position to "exploitation, a skewed income distribution, or a drain of agricultural profits to the North." As he and fellow economist Gavin Wright argue, too much of what happened in the New South was determined by the decisions and the resources (limited capital and entrepreneurial expertise, largely unskilled labor force, and agricultural and mineral abundance) of the Old South. In this sense, despite the remarkable evidence of change in specific areas of southern agricultural, commercial, and industrial activity, continuity in terms of the region's past and relation to the North remained more important. Given the drag of the past and the North's growing economic and political power, which together limited indigenous options, it is unlikely that the South could have avoided its status as the nation's most economically troubled region even without the Civil War. And as we shall see next, the South's political and social systems reinforced the economic imbalances.

CHAPTER TWO

Politics

Despite beliefs that originated in the Revolutionary Era about the evils of political parties, white southerners made the antebellum South a stronghold of two-party politics. Throughout much of the First Party system, which lasted from the mid-1790s to the second decade of the nineteenth century, Jeffersonian Democratic–Republicans engaged in heated combat with Hamiltonian Southern Federalists. Following the death of the Federalist party and a brief interlude of nonpartisan but factional politics, the Kentuckian Henry Clay's Whig party emerged in the mid-1830s to challenge the Democratic party of Tennessean Andrew Jackson and South Carolinian John C. Calhoun. Until the Whig demise as an organized party in the early 1850s, the two major parties fought to a virtual standstill, electing roughly equal numbers of congressmen and, despite the fact that each enjoyed a virtual monopoly in some states, evenly dividing the region's state and local offices. Even during the political realignment of the 1850s, when the Democratic party increased its regional support, southerners gave a large share of their presidential vote to candidates of the American and Constitutional Union parties.

In addition to a strong two-party tradition, the antebellum period bequeathed upon the South a variant of the coalition politics found throughout the country as emotional and tangible issues blurred divisions within what has been called a "herrenvolk democracy" of white male voters. In general, the more commercially oriented Federalists and Whigs supported greater governmental intervention in the economy, especially by the federal government, that included support for internal improvements and a protective tariff. The "states rights" Democrats were more likely to oppose such policies. At times, however, both sides shifted positions for reasons of self-interest and, as slavery came to dominate both national and state politics, political consistency became even more difficult to discern. Nevertheless, during the Second Party system, from the 1830s through the mid-1850s, Whigs were most likely to draw their support from sugar planters and certain large Black Belt cotton planters and their urban allies, whereas Democrats used their common-man rhetoric to forge an alliance between the remaining planters and the great mass of white yeoman farmers, particularly in the upcountry. Again, patterns changed from state to state or even by area within states, and although these divisions were minimized temporarily by the formation of the Confederacy, they persisted throughout the Civil War and in varying degrees came to influence postbellum southern politics.

Following their surrender in April 1865, the eleven Confederate states were reorganized according to the minimal requirements of Presidential Reconstruction, a policy initiated by Abraham Lincoln in Louisiana and other federally held areas during the war, and applied more broadly, and some would argue even more leniently toward the defeated whites, by his successor, Andrew Johnson, after the war. In a period that lasted until March 1867, which historian John Hope Franklin dubbed "Reconstruction: Confederate Style," the southern states were pretty much allowed to conduct their own reconstruction. They responded by electing wartime officials and Confederate military heroes to federal, state, and local offices.

The new administrations, chosen by a white-only electorate, acted as if the South had not lost the war—aside from rather perfunctorily repealing their ordinances of secession—and sought to minimize the effects of emancipation. New black codes, for example, included harsh penalties for vagrancy for blacks, prohibitions against blacks owning guns and possessing liquor, and restrictions on courtroom testimony by blacks. Legislation limited opportunities for mobility of blacks in the countryside, where neither state nor local officials protected blacks from white violence. Urban governments established curfews for blacks, dispensed unequal justice that filled city chain gangs with black prisoners, and took other steps to discourage potential black migrants. On one occasion in 1866 that was widely reported in the North, Nashville officials permitted two local whites to take from the workhouse approximately fifty black "vagrants," including a few women and several boys, and transport them secretly to northern Mississippi to work on cotton plantations.

The mistreatment of blacks and the prominence of former Confederates angered the victorious northerners. Especially galling was the election to Congress of Alexander Stephens, the former vice-president of the Confederacy, who now had the effrontery to describe himself as part of Georgia's "Union element." In addition to such principled resentment, Republican partisanship and growing hostility towards Johnson led Congress in March 1867 to assume supervision over Reconstruction. Except for Tennessee (about which see below), the former Confederate states were denied reentry to the Union and their representatives were refused admission to Congress. The South was divided into five military districts, each under the control of an officer who was at least a brigadier general in rank, until the ten states had adopted new constitutions. These new constitutions had to provide for universal manhood suffrage and ratify, as had Tennessee, the Fourteenth Amendment (which, among other things, made blacks citizens of the United States, guaranteed every person equal protection of the law, repudiated the Confederate debt, and disfranchised Confederates who had broken a previous oath of allegiance to the United States). Once they did so, the commanding generals would call new elections in which blacks could vote and the resultant new governments would then be readmitted to the union.

These new Republican-controlled Reconstruction governments (or Radical, or black and tan governments, as opponents at the time and later derisively called them) included black officeholders and, until recently, have been roundly condemned by generations of unsympathetic scholars. In fact, these governments gave the Southern states their most democratic constitutions, established the first systems of public education, expanded services for the indigent, secured passage of the Fourteenth and Fifteenth amendments (the latter protected black access to the ballot), and helped rebuild the southern economy. Most of all, together with the federal government these Republican state governments guaranteed the end of slavery that had been proclaimed by the Thirteenth Amendment.

Republican city governments implemented the new state legislation and paid greater attention than had their Confederate predecessors to the needs of local blacks. Black councilmen throughout the South used their considerable influence to secure schools and greater relief aid for blacks and to provide improved services for black neighborhoods. In Montgomery and Raleigh, they also pressed successfully for the appointment of black police officers and the establishment of black fire companies. Few other cities had black policemen during Reconstruction but, with the notable exceptions of Atlanta and Richmond, most cities had black firemen.

Yet despite the impression fostered by movies such as *Gone with the Wind* or *Birth of a Nation,* this was not a period of vindictive "Africanization." Only in the South Carolina constitutional convention of 1868 and in that state's first Re-

construction legislature was there a black majority; although
P. B. S. Pinchback served briefly as acting governor of Louisiana, there was no elected black governor; and only fifteen
black representatives and Mississippi Senators Hiram Revels
and Blanche K. Bruce served in Washington. On the local
level, no black served as mayor of a major city, and although
most Reconstruction city councils had black members, no
council ever had a black majority.

Despite the claims of hostile, earlier generations of historians and the beliefs of many white southerners today, these
Republican governments were not in power for long. Crippled
by divisions among themselves, Republicans were unable to
overcome a Democratic counterattack that combined gerrymandering (the manipulation of district boundaries), restrictive voting laws, and the less subtle means of vote fraud, intimidation, and outright violence. In Tennessee, which had
skipped Radical Reconstruction, the Republicans were ousted
in 1869. Virginia's Reconstruction government was defeated
prior to the state's readmission to the Union in January 1870.
Former Confederates were in control of the state governments
in Alabama, Arkansas, Georgia, North Carolina, and Texas by
1874; Mississippi was recaptured in a bloody election in 1875.
Only in Louisiana, Florida, and South Carolina did Radical
rule approach the ten-year mark that critics of Reconstruction
for so long claimed was the norm throughout the South.

Using the techniques that had worked so well on the state
level, though with less dependence on violence, southern
whites sometimes took longer to recapture control of their
cities. Native whites spent as much time, energy, and newspaper space trying to "redeem" their local governments from
the control of white "carpetbaggers" (northern-born Republicans who came south carrying their possessions in carpetbags,
allegedly to plunder the region), "scalawags" ("traitorous"
white southerners who supported the Republican "invaders"),
and their "ungrateful," "illiterate" black allies as they did in
trying to rebuild their cities. Often the two problems went
together, as when the *Montgomery Daily Advertiser* urged the

defeat of the local Radical administration for fear that otherwise the Democratic state government would move the Alabama capital to another city.

In the first popular elections under universal manhood
suffrage, many cities, including Norfolk, Savannah, Memphis,
and Richmond, immediately came under Democratic or Conservative (as the opponents of the Republicans frequently
styled themselves) control, while, in Atlanta, an independent
Democratic mayor elected with Republican support confronted a Democratic-controlled city council. In New Orleans
and Nashville, brief periods of Republican hegemony had
ended by 1873. The Republicans were not ousted in Houston
until 1874, and in Raleigh and Montgomery until 1875. In a
handful of other cities, including Jackson, Mississippi, and
Chattanooga, Republicans continued in power until the late
1880s.

Meanwhile, a northern electorate, troubled by hard times,
tired of trying to defend the results of Reconstruction, and
increasingly inclined to believe that the freedmen could never
achieve equality with whites, helped turn over the national
House of Representatives to the Democrats in 1874. As *Les-
lie's Newspaper* put it, "the white North cannot avoid sym-
pathizing with the white South." Although the Republicans
still controlled the Senate, the Supreme Court, and the pres-
idency, the Democrats now had an effective veto over Reconstruction legislation, and there was growing support at any cost
for President Ulysses S. Grant's plea, initially made in accepting the Republican nomination in 1868, to "Let Us Have
Peace."

The presidential election of 1876 between the Democratic
governor of New York, Samuel Tilden, and the Republican
governor of Ohio, Rutherford B. Hayes, opened the door for
the final defeat of Republican Reconstruction in Louisiana and
South Carolina, where the last of the South's Republican governments depended upon federal troops to keep them in power
following contested state elections. The electoral votes of those
states plus those of Florida and one of Oregon were in dispute,

and a constitutional crisis was threatened as the Democratic-controlled House of Representatives filibustered to prevent the counting of the electoral votes after an electoral commission had awarded all of the disputed votes to Hayes. After a period of political maneuvering between Tilden forces and Hayes forces, Hayes agreed to recall federal troops to their barracks in the South, conceding "Home Rule" and thus enabling Democratic governments to take power in Louisiana and South Carolina, in return for the end of the filibuster and peaceful acceptance of his election. The "Wormley House Bargain," as that deal was called because of the hotel in which it was struck, can be viewed as constituting the official end of the national government's first attempt to reconstruct the South and protect black rights.

But because Hayes had already hinted that he would withdraw the troops, something that Tilden in any case would have done, some questions remain about the resolution of the crisis. In *Reunion and Reaction: The Compromise of 1877 and the End of Reconstruction* (1951), C. Vann Woodward dismissed the Wormley House Bargain as only a "minor element" in the "Compromise of 1877." He argued that economic concessions by the Republicans that included support for federal subsidies to the Texas and Pacific Railroad and other internal improvements in the South were more important. There also was a "political plan" in which Hayes would name a southerner to his cabinet, and southern Democrats would help the Republican minority in the House elect James Garfield as Speaker. This political aspect was part of the economic deal, because the southerners involved in the settlement sought Republican support for federal funding for the region's infrastructure that northern Democrats and some southern Democrats were likely to oppose.

Although Woodward's version of the story has been widely accepted, recent research has reopened the issue. In fact, claims for the economic and patronage deals depend on unreliable alleged participants, and even Woodward admitted that much of his argument was based on circumstantial evidence and that there was no indication that Hayes had ever given prior approval to the elaborate plan. Southerners in Congress were stronger backers of the filibuster than were northern Democrats and there was no significant correlation between southern support for subsidies and opposition to the filibuster. Indeed, the man most responsible for ending the filibuster was a northern Democrat, Speaker of the House Samuel Randall of Pennsylvania.

In the end, none of the alleged compromise elements took place, except for the appointment as postmaster general of Democratic Senator David Key of Tennessee. There was no Texas Pacific bill, opposition to federally financed river and harbor improvements remained, and the House was not organized for Garfield. Despite the claims of Woodward's critics, the fact that these things did not occur does not "prove" that there was no deal in the first place, but their absence has turned attention away from coalition-minded southern Democrats and back to the Wormley House Bargain.

Based on what we now know, it seems that Hayes was able to assume office primarily because the northern Democrats, including Tilden, who was willing to accept defeat, realized that the power of legality and force were in Republican hands and that it would have been dangerous to impede Hayes's selection further, especially after the electoral commission had given the disputed votes to the Republican electors. On the other side, the key ingredient was Hayes's determination to bring about the supremacy of the reform wing of the Republican party, which required peace in the South to undermine the regular Republicans' emphasis on southern white resistance to Reconstruction. Hayes believed that he could build a new Republican party in the South based more on white than black support. Such a prospect, he thought, was most likely to bring about both racial and sectional peace. For these reasons, he would probably have recognized the new governments even without the filibuster threat, but he was perhaps bluffed by Democratic threats of a renewed Civil War.

The Aftermath of Reconstruction

Historians customarily divide post-Reconstruction southern politics into three distinct periods. First are the years from 1877 to about 1890, which can be termed the Bourbon, Redeemer, or as I prefer, Conservative Era. This period marked the return of former Confederate leaders to power and the emergence of the so-called Solid South as the region cast one resounding vote after another for the Democratic candidates in state and national elections. In a sharp break with the past, and despite pockets of Republican resistance in some urban areas and in mountain regions of eastern Tennessee and western North Carolina, the South became a bastion of one-party politics. This period was followed during the 1890s by an eruption of agrarian protest that had its roots in the earlier period, but was capped by the so-called Populist Revolt. Finally, there was the Progressive Era, which began with local and state reform efforts around the turn of the century and culminated in the return to power on the national level of southern politicians during President Woodrow Wilson's two Democratic administrations.

The division is fitting and useful, but only if one remembers the underlying continuity of the years between 1877 and 1920. For throughout this period, having ousted the Republicans, representatives of the old planter and new urban elite waged a continuing battle to control or even eliminate the votes of blacks and lower-class whites. They were especially successful in eliminating the former, and, though suffering occasional setbacks, they were almost as successful in disciplining the latter. The other side of this effort, of course, was the attempted resistance of the proposed victims. The resultant conflict made southern politics far less tranquil and monolithic than New South spokesmen or some subsequent historians pictured it to be.

The Conservative Era

At the center of post–Civil War politics were the men who ran the initial southern state and local governments between 1865 and 1867, and then in state after state had by 1877 overthrown the Republicans. These men were popularly known as "Bourbons" (referring to the French royal family of whom it was said on their return to power after Napoleon's downfall that they had "learned nothing and forgotten nothing") because they allegedly sought restoration of the Old Order. Although some historians have continued to call these leaders Bourbons, most now commonly refer to them as Redeemers.

The term Redeemer was coined by C. Vann Woodward in his *Origins of the New South* (1951). Woodward felt that this first generation of post-Reconstruction leaders was looking, not to the past, but to the future. This is not surprising, because in Woodward's view they were, for the most part, not representatives of the Old Order who wanted to resurrect the Old South, but rather "new men," interested in producing a "New South." Because they themselves spoke of "redeeming" the South from Republican rule for the forces of white supremacy, Woodward called them Redeemers, and concluded that ". . . it was not the Radicals nor the Confederates but the Redeemers who laid the lasting foundations in matters of race, politics, economics and law for the modern South."

There is more than a semantic difference here. For contemporaries and early generations of scholars, these veterans of the Civil War were heroes. They represented the reemergence of the old planter elite and therefore the best of the Old South. As one southerner wrote of two postwar leaders, they "stood as striking types of the most cherished sentiments and practices of our ante-war civilization." Such men had expelled the allegedly corrupt carpetbagger and Negro-dominated regimes, reestablished white supremacy, and ended military occupation. Critics of Reconstruction then and in the years that followed viewed them as saviors, and celebrated their war records, courage, honesty, and sincere devotion to good government.

According to Woodward, however, who identified with their enemies and did not like these men or what they stood for, the Redeemers did not constitute a return to power of the old planter elite. As he had done in the case of the economic leaders, Woodward emphasized the discontinuity between the political leaders of the Old and New South. Although he acknowledged that some true "Bourbons," such as U.S. Senators Robert Toombs in Georgia, Isham Harris in Tennessee, and John Reagan in Texas, continued to hold office and resisted the new capitalist order, they were exceptions and usually were losers in larger intraparty battles and a minority in the Conservative or Democratic party. The dominant figures were capitalists rather than agrarian aristocrats; rather than being traditionalists, they were forward-looking and often urban-based. They also were likely to be former Whigs rather than the Democrats who had come to dominate the region's politics on the eve of the war. Thus, "In the main, they were of middle class, industrial capitalistic outlook, with little but nominal connection with the old planter regime."

Indeed, according to Woodward, a number of these "new men," that is, former Whigs who sought to build a New South modeled economically after the North, played the critical role in putting together the economic and political deals that made Hayes president.

Woodward's analysis seemed to work best for Georgia. The so-called Bourbon Triumvirate of Alfred H. Colquitt, John B. Gordon, and Joseph E. Brown controlled Georgia politics into the 1890s. "Triumvirate" certainly fit, but as for "Bourbon," Woodward believed that "no group of Southern rulers less deserved that much-abused epithet, with its implications of obstinate adherence to the old loyalties and abhorrence of the new." During the first eighteen years after the overthrow of Reconstruction, either Brown or Gordon was in the U.S. Senate, and after 1883 Colquitt held the other seat. Neither Brown nor Gordon, who was commander-in-chief of the United Confederate Veterans, had planter backgrounds; both engaged in a variety of railroad, mining, and other speculative ventures. And although Colquitt had been one of the largest planters in the state, he quickly adopted the New South agenda by joining Gordon in investing in "two Southern railroads, a

New England textile mill, and a Tennessee fertilizer factory, and in coal mining."

Elsewhere in the South, there was significant evidence in the postbellum Democratic party of what historian Thomas Alexander dubbed "persistent Whiggery." Many former Whigs, who remained pro-Union, antisecession and pro–economic development, had stayed politically active after their party died in the early 1850s by supporting the American party and Constitutional Union party, which sought to hold the union together by trying to downplay the slavery issue in the 1856 and 1860 presidential elections. Other Whigs backed Stephen Douglas, the more moderate of the two Democratic candidates in 1860. Many former Whigs defied this simple trajectory, but several who achieved prominence in the Confederate government became the strongest critics of President Jefferson Davis, to the point of resigning from his cabinet.

As one traveler put it about North Carolina in the fall of 1865, "the old parties are both alive, and neither of them a whit older or less pugilistic than it was twenty years ago." Taking advantage of the opprobrium attached to lifelong Democrats following the Confederacy's defeat, former Whigs enjoyed notable electoral success in the first postwar elections. Although the Whig party had practically disappeared in the Confederate states by 1860, the 1865 elections produced at least eight governors who had been Whigs, eleven senators, and thirty-six (as compared to only thirteen Democratic) representatives. Whig success in constitutional conventions and legislatures was even more overwhelming, especially in Tennessee, Virginia, and North Carolina. Many of these Whigs ran on the Democratic ticket or, as in Alabama, on that of "the Democratic or Conservative party." Yet old rivalries remained so strong that in Virginia the new coalition was referred to simply as "the Conservative party" until 1878.

Many of the future debates within the triumphant party that ended Republican rule, whatever its name, would continue to be grounded in antebellum animosities. But such continuity should not obscure an equally sharp break with the past because, as Woodward and Alexander remind us, former Whigs enjoyed a new influence in Democratic circles. Their role was most evident in the United States Senate. The office of senator was not only the choicest political plum, but also still was filled by state legislatures and thus was reflective of broader Whig strength. From 1867 through 1886, for those whose antebellum affiliations are known, former Whigs among primarily Democratic southern senators outnumbered life-long Democrats by more than two to one.

Yet such a picture of Whig triumph and "new men" is too neat. As historian William Cooper has demonstrated, the old Democratic planter elite in South Carolina, for example, easily weathered the storms of Civil War and Reconstruction. All of the leaders who ousted the Republicans had been antebellum Democrats and most were "over fifty years old and the scions of planters." Former slave holder and war hero Wade Hampton, whose violence-marred, victorious gubernatorial campaign in 1876 signaled the end of Reconstruction in the Palmetto state and who was later sent to the U.S. Senate, certainly was not a "new man" from a "new class."

Other antebellum planters, such as Mississippi congressman and author of his state's ordinance of secession Lucius Q. C. Lamar, or North Carolina's Confederate Governor Zebulon B. Vance, also cannot easily be dismissed as "losers" like Toombs, Harris, or Reagan. Lamar was a powerful postwar U.S. congressman, senator, secretary of the interior, and associate justice of the Supreme Court, and Vance served as governor and U.S. senator. And what is one to make of the fact that Vance was both a planter and a former Whig?

Upon closer examination, it even turns out that two of the Georgia Triumvirate, Brown and Gordon, had been antebellum Democrats, not Whigs. Indeed, one historian has estimated that at least nine of the thirty-one public men Woodward identified as typical "Redeemers" were prominent antebellum Democrats, not former Whigs. And both John Reagan and, especially, Isham Harris had more influential postbellum careers than Woodward suggests. Harris, Tennessee's

Confederate governor and a military veteran, once praised a man "chiefly because he belongs to that class of old fashion hard shelled, strict construction democracy for which I have always fought." He helped make the state's rights, agrarian-oriented Bourbons the dominant force in Tennessee politics during the 1880s and served in the U.S. Senate from 1877 to his death in 1897.

The region's political life owed much to the past in other states as well. One study of 656 prominent ex-Confederate leaders who survived an appreciable length of time after the war revealed that many occupied political office and only seventy-one failed to recover their previous position and prestige. Although the antebellum planter elite's economic and political power in postwar North Carolina and Alabama was less pronounced than some historians claim, its continued influence was evident in significant legislation that affected lien law, taxation, industrial and agricultural policy, and voting rights.

Nor should the new power of former Whigs in Democratic clothes cause us to overlook other instances of continuity between antebellum and postbellum southern politics. After all, the persistence of the Democratic planter elite in South Carolina and Texas is not surprising, given that the Whig party had almost been nonexistent in both states before the war. On the other hand, in such states as North Carolina and Tennessee, Whigs had been the dominant antebellum party, so the presence of former Whigs in power similarly does not represent discontinuity with the past.

It is now clear, then, that Woodward overstated the break with the past in terms of the political or even economic and social origins of the South's postwar leaders. So-called new men also were apparently not as crucial as he claimed in manipulating national politics. Upon closer examination, the allegedly key southerners in the Compromise of 1877 often turn out to have been antebellum Democrats, not Whigs, and were neither pro-industry nor pro-North. Andrew J. Kellar of Tennessee, for example, had worked to undermine the Redeemer elite in his state and belonged to the agrarian wing of the

Democratic party. And fellow Tennessean and Postmaster General David Key was a lifelong Democrat rather than a former Whig. Further undermining Woodward's position is the fact that between 1873 and 1897, southern Democrats in Congress aligned themselves with agrarian-minded western Democrats, rather than with the industrial-oriented northeastern wing of the party, to support inflationary currency proposals, low tariffs, taxation policies that favored agriculture, and business regulation, although they did break with the West on the kinds of public works issues that had first alerted Woodward to the possibility of a northern Republican and Redeemer alliance.

But if one explanatory model has been weakened, no convincing comprehensive alternative has yet emerged. More research is needed on the state and local level, where the degree of variation among leaders is greater than any standard formula would seem to permit. How one views the extent of discontinuity remains very much a matter of emphasis, given the mixed nature of the postwar leadership. Part of the problem, of course, is that it is never entirely clear which was more important—their nonplanter or their Whig origins—in defining a "Redeemer." In other words, were "new men" defined by a new economic viewpoint or an old party affiliation?

This brings us back to nomenclature. Because the postwar Democratic party was a coalition both within and across state lines of old and new men, life-long Democrats and former Whigs, and planters and urban figures, it would seem that neither "Redeemer" nor "Bourbon" accurately describes its members' origins. In politics as in economics, the planter class was still a force to be reckoned with, particularly in a region where, as we have seen, urbanization and industrialization still lagged behind the rest of the country. But that planter class now had to share power to an unprecedented degree with mercantile and industrial interests. The old planter aristocracy that had been such a major force within both the antebellum South and the nation, although it had not been destroyed, had gone from being perhaps the strongest agrarian class among western nations to being the least powerful.

A more important question, therefore, is what the men who overthrew the Reconstruction governments, whatever their origins, sought to do with their political power and what kind of governments they ran. And in answering it we will again discover both continuity and discontinuity. In some respects these men looked to the past; in others, to the future. More often there was a combination of the old and the new, though not necessarily in the ways that they claimed. Those in search of grand themes and easy answers might consider Roger L. Hart's *Redeemers, Bourbons and Populists: Tennessee 1870–1896* (1975). Hart found the Volunteer State's politics so muddled that he concluded, "The Redeemers and Bourbons were not disciplined, cohesive factions, but loose connections based more on patronage and symbolic issues than on conflict among sections or classes with different economic interests. Any attempt to trace continuing factions in the careers of individual politicians ends in a labyrinth of inconsistencies, reversals, and contradictions." Because again neither Redeemer nor Bourbon accurately describes the region's governments, it seems most reasonable to stop using both terms and to call these men Conservatives, or Conservative Democrats. Until we have a better idea of who they were and why they acted as they did, it is better to call them what they called themselves than to use terms invented by either contemporary or latter-day partisans. To call them Conservatives rather than Redeemers or Bourbons is also to acknowledge the coalition nature of the era's political leadership, which, like the First New South itself, was a mixture of old and new.

When it comes to assessing what these men actually did in office, there is refreshing unanimity concerning the alleged honesty and purity of their regimes. No scholar today would endorse historian Philip A. Bruce's claim in *The Rise of the New South* (1905) that "The incredible waste and robbery of the Reconstruction Era was followed as soon as that era ended by the most careful methods in the handling of the public funds. Nowhere has there been so little peculation and defalcation on the part of officials in charge of the public treasuries." In fact, Reconstruction governments were never as corrupt as critics then and later alleged, and corruption outside the South at the end of the nineteenth century was rampant and bipartisan throughout the United States, whether in Boss Tweed's New York or in the Santa Fe Ring's New Mexico. And, as Woodward reminded us, Conservative state treasurers as a group were unsurpassed in their inability to balance their books or to stay around long enough to explain their shortages.

The Georgia and Virginia treasurers during the 1870s initiated an era of generally unpunished malfeasance by trusted longtime officeholders. Their Tennessee counterpart, a Confederate veteran and the nephew and adopted son of former President James K. Polk, disappeared in 1883 with his funds $400,000 short; three weeks later, Alabama's three-term treasurer escaped to Mexico leaving a default of $233,000. The same pattern reappeared in Arkansas ($295,000), Kentucky ($229,00), Mississippi ($315,600), and Louisiana ($1,777,000). This last state was equally famous for its corruption-ridden state lottery, the personal fiefdom of the absconding treasurer, Major A. E. Burke, one of the most notorious "new men," who had done his best to bring about an economically profitable conclusion to the Hayes-Tilden election. In short, only partisanship (surely it was not sound historical judgment) could have led New South defender and respected historian Holland Thompson to argue in 1921 that "No governments in American history have been conducted with more economy and more fidelity than the governments of the Southern states during the first years after the Reconstruction period."

The Conservative regimes not only were filled with scandal and dishonesty, but, in addition, their probusiness, penny-pinching approach to government produced unresponsive administrations that were unsympathetic to the needs of the majority of citizens. They sought industrial development at all costs, slighted agricultural reform efforts, and cut basic public services such as education. In contrast to the Reconstruction governments, which spent unprecedented amounts of state funds establishing the region's first systems of public education and founding or expanding institutions for the care of the indigent, mentally ill, blind, and deaf, the Conservative governments severely cut appropriations. Blacks suffered most from this retrenchment, but poor whites were not spared. In a further attempt to protect their limited financial resources, all of the former Confederate states except Texas and Mississippi defaulted on or readjusted Reconstruction Era bonds and became more cautious in issuing direct subsidies or new bonds. But generous land grants and low taxes or outright exemptions for railroads, mines, and factories drained the public purse. In the first year of Conservative rule in Mississippi, for example, the total expenditure of state government was only $547,000, a figure that was steadily reduced in succeeding years.

Most odious was the notorious convict lease system. State convicts, most of them black, were leased out to politically connected owners of plantations, mines, railroads, and sawmills, who profitably used their labor under brutal and unhealthy conditions. One critic of the Alabama system wrote that state warden (and future U.S. Senator) John H. Bankhead "grew rich in a few years on $2000 a year." He added that "The 'penitentiary ring' is a power in the party, and it is a corrupt power. One of the State officers is a lessee of convicts, and has a brother who is a deputy warden." Treatment of convicts in Mississippi was typical. A grand jury investigation of the penitentiary hospital revealed that inmates were

. . . all bearing on their persons marks of the most inhuman and brutal treatments. Most of them have their backs cut in great wales, scars and blisters, some with the skin peeling off in pieces as the result of severe beatings. . . . They were lying there dying, some of them on bare boards, so poor and emaciated that their bones almost came through their skin, many complaining for want of food. . . . We actually saw live vermin crawling over their faces, and the little bedding and clothing they have is in tatters and stiff with filth.

Although granting that there were many abuses in the Conservative regimes, some historians have begun to question the totally negative assessment that has become enshrined in textbooks. Modern-day defenders of the Conservatives do not dispute the facts of retrenchment—some even find the cutbacks warranted. They emphasize, however, that the Conservatives were also responsible for such positive actions as increased railroad regulation, piecemeal improvements in education and welfare, and even some progress in reforming the hideous convict lease system. Mostly, however, they find that the Conservatives paid careful attention to the needs of agriculture. In "Redeemers Reconsidered: Change and Continuity in the Democratic South, 1870–1900" (1978), James Tice Moore argues that the Democrats "may have retained control of their region by representing—not obstructing—the interests of the rural areas." He notes that farmers held most of the seats in Mississippi's state legislature throughout the 1870s and 1880s and that other states had comparable agrarian strength. And Charles Flynn, in "Procrustean Bedfellows and Populists: An Alternative Hypothesis" (1989), complains that historians have "overstated the emphasis on industrial development and underestimated the heavy emphasis on agricultural interests in the New South Creed." But although there is no denying that Woodward exaggerated the destruction of the planter class and the ascendancy of a new urban, industrial, professional elite, the important question is not merely whether more attention was paid to agricultural or industrial interests, but what kinds of agricultural interests were favored and how this compared to previous policy.

Conservative help for the agricultural sector was indeed significant. The favorable environment for railroad expansion, after all, did not benefit only European, northern, or southern bondholders, or, for that matter, the region's growing cities. Farmers benefited perhaps the most, and two of the region's most agrarian states, Florida and Texas, were in the forefront in providing aid to railroads. Then, too, Mississippi officials sold large amounts of Yazoo Delta land to developers in the 1880s in the hopes that industrial and commercial expansion would help reduce levies on agricultural land. And drawing on a growing body of work, Moore correctly concludes that Conservative governments "affirmed their commitment to the countryside by establishing state commissions of agriculture, subsidizing state fairs, sponsoring the development of experimental farms, encouraging fish culture in the region's rivers and streams, and employing chemists to inspect fertilizers and conduct soil surveys."

The agrarian sector certainly was not neglected. But the chief beneficiaries of Conservative policies were large landowners and those farmers seeking to maximize production of staple crops for the market. Market-oriented, capitalist agriculture was indeed an important element in the New South creed and was not incompatible with commercial and industrial expansion. Yet here again one must not exaggerate the break with the past, for as we have already seen, by the eve of the Civil War southern agriculture had moved in the direction of capitalism. Entrepreneurial elements were important among antebellum planters, many of whom also supported urban development. But even if most planters wanted to resist the new capitalist forces in their midst, and that is doubtful, they no longer had the power to do so.

Urban politics during the Conservative Era is easier to decipher than state politics, in part because it was more narrowly based, but also because continuity was of greater consequence. In most cities the first postwar elections had returned the wartime city officers to power. These same men or their supporters also were the ones who finally defeated the local Radicals. Because the cities had been strongholds of antebellum Whiggery, it is not surprising that many of these men were former Whigs. Nor is it surprising that, as we saw in chapter 1, they revived their earlier policy of urban boosterism that focused on economic development. Although manufacturers were an important part of postwar urban political leadership in such cities as Birmingham, men active in commerce, including some small businessmen, and representatives of the professions, especially lawyers, came to predominate. At a time when urban politics was being transformed in the North by the emergence of immigrant-based political machines, the commercial-civic elite retained control in most southern cities either directly, through officeholding, or, more commonly, from behind the scenes. New Orleans and Memphis became the most noteworthy northern-style machine-dominated exceptions after the turn of the century.

Distaste for their Radical predecessors and their return to power amid the hard times connected with the Panic of 1873 made urban Conservatives as addicted to financial retrenchment as were their counterparts in state government. The combination of national depression, overspending, and tax evasion forced Houston's leaders to arrange compromises with that city's creditors in 1875, 1881, and 1888. They were able to fund a consolidated debt at a lower interest in return for cutting expenditures and raising taxes. Even small towns such as Greensboro, North Carolina, exhibited the new preoccupation with cost cutting. In 1874 Mayor Cyrus Mendenhall was elected to the first of three consecutive terms in response to pleas for better services. Under Mendenhall, Greensboro adopted charter amendments that tripled the property tax and increased the poll tax from $2 to $3. As other cities had done prior to 1873, the city under Mendenhall constructed a new market house, set up a mayor's court, improved the streets, gave free vaccinations, and levied new taxes to support a public school system. But by 1877 hard times had reached Greensboro, and a taxpayer revolt defeated Mendenhall. Silas Dodson was elected on a platform promising retrenchment and economy. Reelected annually from 1877 to 1882, Dodson cut taxes in half, producing substantial declines in city income and services.

As we saw in chapter 1, southern city officials were far less willing than their northern counterparts to spend money on urban problems. And when they did, as in the effort to improve streets and sanitation, they neglected those parts of the city where the mass of residents lived, concentrating instead on the downtown and nearby residential neighborhoods that contained their (and their supporters') businesses and homes. Similar neglect was evident in other urban services as well. In education, there was a sharp increase in the number of schools—now city-owned rather than rented—and every town with over 25,000 residents had at least one high school. However, when compared to northern cities of comparable population, southern cities were still far behind in the percentage of children enrolled, number of schools and schoolrooms, and number and salaries of teachers. In 1902, only Dallas, Houston, Fort Worth, Covington (Kentucky), and Wheeling (West Virginia) spent more than $3 per capita on schools at a time when the national average was $4.37 among communities with more than 25,000 population. Similarly, although law enforcement and fire protection hired more men, achieved a higher degree of professionalization, and benefited from new technological advances, low funding meant that southern cities probably were less adequately protected than their northern counterparts. The cities did better in increasing the amount of publicly owned parkland, but even here the gap with the North was still sizable. And as was true for streets and sanitation, the chief beneficiary of any improvements in fire and police protection or parkland was the commercial-civic elite, a group that often avoided the liabilities of southern public education by sending their children to private schools.

Blacks were hurt most by Conservative neglect of urban problems. Black areas of the cities shared even less than the poor white enclaves in the expansion of municipal services during the 1880s and 1890s. Water mains, sewer lines, paved streets, and regular garbage collection rarely reached into black neighborhoods. Neither electricity nor gas illuminated their houses. In Richmond, Virginia, the fire chief pleaded unsuccessfully for a fire station to protect the mostly wooden homes of Jackson Ward, and in Atlanta, Spelman Seminary's Union Hall burned down because fire engines had a two-mile run over rough roads to get there. Major black institutions such as Atlanta University were not served by streetcars. When streetcar service existed, it was unsatisfactory. Richmond's Jackson Ward had twenty-minute service on a single-track line; nearby white areas had five- and ten-minute service on double-track lines. In Algiers, a heavily black section of New Orleans, mule cars were still running in 1907, fourteen years after the rest of the city's lines had begun to be electrified. As we will see in chapter 3, separate but unequal treatment was the best that blacks could hope for in a range of other services, including welfare institutions and schools.

The worsening conditions for blacks were directly related to the reduction in their political power that the overthrow of Reconstruction had achieved. The Conservative triumph in such places as New Orleans, Atlanta, and Montgomery meant the end of black officeholding in nonfederal jobs until well into the twentieth century. In a number of other major southern cities, black politicians remained active in city government, but no longer were able to help their black constituents to the extent that their counterparts had during Reconstruction. Although the cases were certainly atypical, blacks were elected regularly to city councils in Nashville and in Jackson, Mississippi, until the late 1880s, and until the turn of the century in Richmond and Raleigh, where gerrymandering prevented Republican control but guaranteed council seats for blacks. During the 1890s, fusion movements (combinations of anti-Conservative elements) also returned white and black Republicans to office in a number of North Carolina cities; this also had happened in Jacksonville, Florida, in 1887.

Even though their power was limited, as revealed by their assignment to unimportant committees or to none at all, some black councilmen did have a positive impact. Nashville's leading black politician, J. C. Napier, was instrumental in the opening of new black schools and the hiring of black teachers; another black councilman in the early 1880s secured free water for some Negro neighborhoods and pushed through the organization of a regular black fire company, of which he immediately became captain. Thanks to four black councilmen in Jacksonville in 1887, almost half of the police force was black, as were the municipal judge and one of the three police commissioners. Richmond's black councilmen secured improved streets and better lighting in the heavily black Jackson Ward, the dispensing of coal to the black poor, the opening of the first black night school, the appropriation of money for the black militia companies, and construction of a separate armory.

A few blacks also still could be found in most state legislatures, and although there was no black senator after Mississippi's Blanche K. Bruce completed his term in 1881, several blacks were returned to the U. S. House of Representatives. Black congressmen served a total of twenty-four terms between 1869 and 1879, but only fourteen between 1879 and 1901. South Carolina led the way by electing six black officials to a total of thirteen terms during Reconstruction, and three more for a total of six terms afterwards, whereas Virginia sent its first and only black representative in 1889. However, one of the four blacks elected from North Carolina's famous "Black Second" District after 1877—George White, who was elected to his final two-year term in 1898—was the last southern black congressman until the 1970s.

Black legislators at the state and national levels could do even less to improve conditions for blacks than their local counterparts. Except for the eleven who served in the 1897 North Carolina legislature during the brief period of Populist-Republican control of state government, black state legislators in bodies dominated by Democrats typically were part of a small Republican contingent that had little say on important issues. They spent most of their time doing small favors for constituents, making speeches decrying the treatment of their state's blacks, and introducing bills that, if they made it to the floor, were quickly tabled or defeated. Although as Republicans they were more likely to be members of the majority party in the U. S. Congress, black congressmen were equally frustrated in their efforts to help southern blacks.

Conservatives at the local and state level cited the continuation of black voting and black officeholding to defend their treatment of blacks to northerners at the same time that they decried the persistence of such participation and its abuses to each other and their white supporters. Indeed, despite frequent expressions of support for the idea, the Conservatives were not comfortable with blacks exercising a free ballot. After all, blacks might use it to support the hated Republican party; worse still, they might encourage white Democrats to compete for their vote and thus destablize a political system that the Conservatives had worked hard to build. With typical New South rhetoric designed to assure skeptical and perhaps guilt-ridden northerners, Wade Hampton, the new governor of South Carolina, asserted in the spring of 1877, following the violence-ridden campaign that brought him to power, that "we . . . will secure to every citizen, the lowest as well as the highest, black as well as white, full and equal protection in the enjoyment of all his rights under the Constitution." The following year he told a black audience, "The best friends of the colored men are the old slaveholders. . . . They will defend your right to vote because it gives to the South infinitely more power than we ever had before." Yet President Hayes summed up the sad reality following the 1878 elections: "By state legislation, by frauds, by intimidation, and by violence of the most atrocious character, colored citizens have been deprived of the right of suffrage . . . and to the protection to which the people of those States have been solemnly pledged."

The prospect of black voting was acceptable to the Conservatives only as long as that vote could be controlled and used to support their regimes. Even a modicum of officeholding could be accepted if it did not threaten the status quo. The black vote, however, took on new importance with the growth of independent political movements that culminated in a widespread agrarian uprising.

Already in the late 1870s in Hampton's own South Carolina, disgruntled representatives of middle-class farmers charged that the Conservatives were using the black vote to deny elective office to opposition whites. In state after state during the late 1870s, and especially in the 1880s, so-called Independent candidates emerged to challenge Democratic candidates. Usually former Democrats themselves, these Independents appealed to certain white agrarian elements who felt neglected by Conservative policies. Typically they called for a "free vote and fair count," pledged full support for public education, and, less centrally, even appealed for black votes.

Georgia was especially rife with what the Conservatives saw as troublemakers, as one northern hill district sent William H. Felton to Congress in 1874 and another four years later sent Emory L. Speer to join him. Both Independents were elected in what the *New York Times* called "nothing less than a family struggle for power and the desire for office," despite ruthless opposition from the Triumvirate. Senator John Gordon felt threatened enough to write Mississippi Senator Lamar, "We want you to come to Ga., . . . & help us kill Independentism, which is . . . threatening us with the loss of our state." Arkansas, Alabama, Texas, and Tennessee were similarly afflicted, but it was Virginia that most frightened the Conservatives. There, under the leadership of William Mahone, a tavern keeper's son who became a Confederate war hero and then a failed railroad magnate, the so-called Readjusters captured control of the state at the end of the 1870s on a platform calling for the "readjustment" (that is repudiation) of about a third of the state debt. In addition to reducing the debt, the Readjusters lowered the tax rates for farmers, encouraged black voting and officeholding, increased appropriations for both black and white education by 50 percent, and significantly increased the taxes on railroads. Elected in 1881 to a U.S. Senate evenly divided between Republicans and Democrats, Mahone assured his own future defeat and that of his movement by aligning with the Republicans in order to gain control of Virginia's black vote and the state's federal patronage.

The controversy over funding debts incurred under the Reconstruction governments and even under antebellum and postbellum Democratic administrations disrupted politics in other states as well, as did Greenback-Labor party tickets (which advocated reissuing a paper currency unbacked by gold or silver) that emerged and enjoyed sporadic success in the late 1870s and early 1880s. The greatest challenge to Conservative hegemony, however, was the Populist movement.

The Populist Revolt

In February of 1892, a convention of reformers in St. Louis that included members of the Knights of Labor, Greenbackers, Prohibitionists, Single-Taxers, and Nationalists, but was dominated by delegates from the National Farmers' Alliance and Industrial Union, founded the People's party. The party held its first national convention in Omaha, Nebraska, on July 4, 1892. Deprived of its strongest candidate by the death of North Carolina's Leonidas L. Polk, the president of the Farmers' Alliance, the party nominated former Union general James Weaver of Iowa for president and ex-Confederate general James G. Field of Virginia for vice-president and adopted the famous Omaha Platform. Drawing heavily on the "Ocala Demands" that were drafted by the National Farmers' Alliance at its 1890 meeting in Ocala, Florida, the platform summed up sixteen years of agitation by a variety of third parties. Its preamble eloquently expressed the sense of urgency, self-righteousness, and commitment to reform: "We meet in the midst of a nation brought to the verge of moral, political, and material ruin. Corruption dominates the ballot-box, the legislatures, the Congress, and touches even the ermine of the bench. The people are demoralized."

After declaring the interests of rural and urban labor to be the same, the platform presented a wide-ranging collection of planks under the three broad headings of finance, transportation, and land that included the nationalization of the railroad, telephone, and telegraph lines, a graduated income tax, and "free and unlimited coinage of silver" at the ratio of sixteen grains of gold to one grain of silver (far more than silver was worth on the open market and thus an inflationary move that would make it easier for farmers to pay their debts). An "Expression of Sentiments" called for women's suffrage, the eight-hour day, and the direct election of U. S. senators by the people (rather than by state legislatures, as was then the case). After making a surprisingly strong showing in the 1892 national elections (Weaver won the electoral votes of Idaho, Nevada, Colorado, Kansas, and one of North Dakota's) and in subsequent state and congressional elections, the party declined following its endorsement in 1896 of Democratic presidential candidate William Jennings Bryan, who was soundly defeated by the Republican William McKinley.

For many years historians neglected the South's contribution to the People's party, or Populism, as the movement it fostered was commonly known, preferring instead to concentrate on the midwestern roots and development of the party and treating the South as the junior partner in the alliance of South and West against the industrial East. In *Origins of the New South*, however, C. Vann Woodward restored southern Populism to its rightful place in the partnership, arguing that, if anything, southern Populism was more radical than the midwestern version. It also was more persistent, continuing into the early twentieth century, long after midwestern farmers had returned to their traditional home in the Republican party following the end of drought, a rise in corn prices, the expansion of the gold supply, and the return of prosperity. And Woodward, as has been true of most historians subsequently, was sympathetic toward the Populists, whom he depicted as genuine reformers dedicated to improving the lives of white and black southern masses.

Conservatives in the 1890s, however, saw the Populists as a bunch of malcontents and threats to the New South they had forged, a view echoed by their early defenders among historians. In a typical reaction to the founding of the new party, the Tarboro *Southerner* denounced two of the founders of one North Carolina county's People's party as "anarchists" because, "With Messers. Cutchin and Battle, whatever is is wrong. To pull down without building up is anarchy, nihilism. A man does not have to preach murder and arson to be an anarchist." In Georgia, the Augusta *Chronicle*, expressing a fear perhaps even greater than that of anarchy, claimed that the Populists were "aiding the Republicans in their nefarious schemes" to supervise federal elections in the South.

Conservatives had good reason to fear the new movement. Southern Populism was so strong because it was not simply a reaction to national economic issues, but grew out of antagonism towards the unresponsive Conservative regimes. Indeed, Populism was a continuation of the earlier Independent movements that had evolved into the Greenback-Labor and especially the Farmers' Alliance movement that had spread out of Texas and Arkansas in the 1880s. By the end of the 1880s and the beginning of the 1890s, Alliancemen had taken over the Democratic party in many counties and several states. They captured control of the Alabama and Florida legislatures, claimed a majority of the congressmen in Virginia, Kentucky, and North Carolina, and in Georgia, according to one historian, "chose the governor, wrote the platform, named three-fourths of the senators and four-fifths of the representatives." But to many agrarians it seemed that, once in power, the Alliance leaders were co-opted by the Democrats and that a true third party was necessary.

Meanwhile, economic conditions worsened and no one seemed to be doing anything to help. Following a tour of the Georgia cotton belt in December of 1891, the editor of the *Southern Farmer* wrote that "the farmer has about reached the end of his row." Cotton was selling at the lowest price since before the Civil War, and "hundreds of men will be turned out of house and home, or forced to become hirelings and tenants in fields that they once owned. . . . The doors of every courthouse in Georgia are placarded with the announcements of such [sheriff's] sales. Hundreds of farmers will be turned adrift, and thousands of acres of our best land allowed to grow up in weeds through lack of necessary capital to work them. . . . The roads are full of negroes begging homes." There was "an epidemic of distress and foreclosures of mortgages now sweeping over our state."

Many Populists had been particularly dismayed at the failure of the Democrats to embrace the subtreasury that many viewed as the key part of the "Ocala Demands" and the Omaha Platform. The idea of C. W. Macune, a northern-born Texan who served as president of the southern Alliance, the subtreasury would free farmers from dependence on grasping middlemen by allowing them to keep their nonperishable crops temporarily in federal warehouses and grain elevators until sale prices became more favorable. In return they would receive loans in greenbacks or negotiable treasury notes at 1 percent interest equal to 80 percent of the value of their stored crop. They would pay back the government when they sold the crop.

Democratic fraud and the presence of a former Union general at the head of the Populist ticket probably cost the party victory in a number of southern states in 1892. "I told them go to it, boys, count them out," admitted Governor William C. Oates of Alabama. "We had to do it. Unfortunately, I say it was a necessity. We could not help ourselves." Conservative efforts to justify such actions as needed to prevent "Negro domination" only added to Populist resentment. "It is no excuse, to say that these iniquities are practiced to 'preserve white civilization," declared a Virginia Populist paper in 1893. "In the first place it was white men who were robbed of their votes, and white men who were defrauded out of office." Conservative hypocrisy even extended to padding their returns from Conservative-controlled Black Belt plantation counties, allowing them to overcome the results from white majority counties. Black voters were bought, intimidated, or simply counted for the Democratic ticket. And there was violence as well. One southern Populist leader reported, "The feeling of the Democracy against us is one of murderous hate. I have been shot at many times. Grand juries will not indict our assailants. Courts give us no protection."

Nevertheless, during the 1894 state and congressional campaigns, the new party did especially well in Georgia, Alabama, and Texas, and, through fusion with the Republican party in the 1894 and 1896 elections, won the governor's office and a majority of the legislature in North Carolina. Buoyed by their successes and by animosity towards the Democrats, southern Populists became the core of the "Middle of the Road" (no compromise) faction. This group sought to deny Bryan the Populist endorsement, hoping that by running their own candidate they would help destroy the Democratic party and attract its free-silver wing, leaving the Populists as the only alternative to the Republicans.

It is tempting to turn the Populist-Democratic struggle into a morality play. On one side are the noble, heroic Populists representing the southern masses; on the other are the wealthy, corrupt entrenched Conservative regimes. Based on especially detailed research into Texas Populism, the region's most radical manifestation, Lawrence Goodwyn's *The Democratic Promise* (1976), argued that southern Populism not only was the heart of the national movement, but also represented the only true version of Populism. Except in Kansas, midwestern Populism allegedly became mesmerized by the free-silver issue and was part of a "shadow movement." Real Populism, according to Goodwyn, grew out of the producer and consumer cooperative efforts ("the cooperative idea") of the Farmers' Alliance movement. And at its heart was not free silver as the cure for the nation's constricted money supply, but a commitment to the federal government's reintroduction of even more inflationary greenbacks and adoption of the subtreasury plan.

Goodwyn's Populists, then, were seeking a radical change in the economic structure of America in addition to pushing for meaningful political reform. Because they also were committed to racial justice—the chairman of the Texas party said "If he [the Negro] has a friend it is we, and he can be our friend . . . and he is a citizen just as much as we are"—Goodwyn saw them as "the last democratic mass movement in the United States." Their defeat meant the triumph of "corporate capitalism." And although economics played a part, the Populist vision of America was not the product of class consciousness, because landowners and tenants experienced the same problems of credit shortage, inelastic currency, and low crop prices. That vision instead was the product of a "movement culture," a self-generating communal network and expression of "collective hope" forged at frequent campground meetings and by efforts to organize cooperatives that provided its real staying power.

For some Populists, threats to an old way of life seem to have been at least as troubling as specific economic problems. In Georgia, the other hotbed of southern Populism, Steven Hahn's *The Roots of Southern Populism* (1983) and Charles Flynn's *White Land, Black Labor* (1983) found that many small landowners and tenants were drawn to Populism in reaction to the attempts of larger landholders to pass the stockman laws requiring the fencing in of animals (described in chapter 1). Hahn and Flynn argue that this was a great burden for the mass of whites, who resented the challenge to their traditional rights, and the campaigns to defeat the new laws prepared the way for identification with the Populist cause. As one upcountry newspaper put it, the People's party "is composed of the yeomanry of the country. The small landed proprietors, the working farmers, the intelligent artisans, the wageworkers, men who own homes and want a stable government." Taking such claims at face value, Hahn concludes that the Populists reflected "a nineteenth century producer ideology" marked by "sensibilities at odds with the tenets of bourgeois individualism and the free market."

But this view of Populism as a democratic movement of distressed farmers responding in rational ways to the abuses of capitalist-oriented Conservatives distorts the complex nature of southern Populism. There is no question that the Southern Populists were more democratic than their Conservative enemies. They also were more enlightened, at least initially, in reaching out to blacks, and they were moved to action by legitimate political and economic grievances. And, in general, southern Populists were more radical than their midwestern cousins. But the movement was less monolithic and had more in common with its enemies than is commonly acknowledged. It was one thing to attribute to Populism an alternative vision for America; it was quite another to consign to the "shadow movement," as does Goodwyn, those Populists who deviated on specific issues, such as support for greenbackism and the subtreasury plan. For one could still be a Populist without completely embracing the Omaha Platform or the "Ocala Demands," in the same way that one can still be a Democrat or Republican today without accepting all of the party's tenets.

In fact, individual Populists and indeed the movement as a whole were seriously compromised by what Goodwyn termed "the received culture." As Bruce Palmer notes in *"Man Over Money": The Southern Populist Critique of American Capitalism* (1980), Populists were divided between the greenback-subtreasury advocates, who were driven by a "crude class analysis," and the "financial reformers" of the free-silver persuasion, who favored a sectional interpretation (South and West vs. North) of the South's problems. It is true that Populists combined the Jeffersonian belief in small government, the importance of yeoman farmers, and a simple market economy with the Jacksonian antimonopoly thought that made room for small businessmen and labor and the Greenback/ Farmers' Alliance program. But their commitment to these older values was undercut by acceptance of basic mainstream American values that favored private property, industrial growth, and progress. Indeed, many individual Populists were well-off farmers and prominent small-town businessmen. Certainly there were more of them among the leadership than representatives of either the tenant or the wage laborer element. Populists in Georgia and Texas were the staunchest defenders of the Omaha and Ocala principles, but those in Alabama and North Carolina were infiltrated by the silver wing of the Democratic party and got swept up in the free-silver fervor that fatally weakened the movement. Yet supporters in the four states all were "Populists." In the end, most Populists placed their greatest hopes on free silver, enthusiastically endorsed Bryan, and left the dwindling subtreasury-greenback faction to tilt against windmills in "the middle of the road." Given the few Populists who remained committed to the Alliance principles, one is tempted to conclude that it was they who constituted "the shadow movement," especially in light of studies that have found little correlation between the strength of Populism and the presence of cooperatives. Not only were the southern Populists largely middle-rank farmers with mainstream economic values, most white Populists also believed in the doctrine of white supremacy and were never entirely comfortable with their black allies. This is not surprising, because the Farmers' Alliance that produced so many Populists had banned black members.

Few Populists thought of challenging the proliferating system of racial segregation. Individual Populist leaders, such as Georgia editor and politician Tom Watson, the son of affluent slave holders and a former cotton and fruit farmer, might shake hands with blacks or intervene to prevent the lynching of an innocent black man. But even Watson was outspokenly against miscegenation and "social equality" (the nineteenth-century equivalent of integration that would lead to miscegenation). "The question of social equality does not enter into the calculation at all," said Watson in 1892 as he emphasized the political and economic benefits that would result from a white-black alliance in the Populist party and sought to undermine Conservative appeals to white supremacy. "That is a thing each citizen decides for himself. No statute ever yet drew the latch of the humblest home—or ever will. Each citizen regulates his own visiting list—and always will." Rank-and-file members had no trouble agreeing with Watson about social matters, but few truly accepted his claim that "the accident of color can make no difference in the interests of farmers, croppers, and laborers."

Even Texas Populists, the most racially enlightened in the South, could go only part-way in recognizing black rights. The leading black Populist, John B. Rayner, the "silver tongued orator of the colored race," was appointed to the state executive committee and was a very visible speaker, and the state platform expressed support for "equal justice and protection under the law to all citizens without reference to race, color or nationality." Yet the party refused to endorse black officeholding or jury service. And even the right of blacks to vote was to be protected only when the vote was cast to help Populist candidates. The attempt at Populist-Republican fusion in Texas in 1896 failed primarily because of what two historians termed the "racial stigma attached to Republicanism" by the mass of white Populists, who refused to support the fusion ticket. At one stop during the campaign, Rayner ridiculed the idea of "negro supremacy" before a predominantly white audience in Austin. "A Democrat goes to bed at night and dreams he sees a nigger with the courthouse on his back running off with it," he told them. "The idea of 8,000,000 blacks, most of them ignorant and nearly all poor, gaining supremacy over 64,000,000 intelligent voters. Do you white men here believe it?" The white men in the crowd reportedly were not reassured. That would not have surprised P. W. Carter, a black Georgian Republican who charged in 1892, "many who are now Populists were the strongest kind for the [white-only] primaries because it shut the 'nigger' out."

What, then, can we say about southern Populism? Clearly the movement consisted of radicals, moderates, and conservatives; some Populists looked to a more self-sufficient, cooperative past, whereas others embraced the new commercial-industrial order; there was a similar range in Populist racial attitudes. And what one thinks of the Populists also depends on one's assessment of their predicament and the nature of their opposition.

Given such considerations and the actual complexity of southern Populism, historian Robert Durden perhaps summed it up best in *The Climax of Populism: The Election of 1896* (1965) when he referred to the Populists as "angry agrarian capitalists." For whether Populists had willingly sought out the cash nexus or been dragged into it and exploited by conspiratorial merchants, planters, and politicians, given the depressed state of the region's new economy in the 1890s, their primary need was immediate economic relief. Most believed that a free-silver quick fix would do the job without necessitating a basic restructuring of the American economy. In the tradition of most American reformers, they called for equal opportunity, opposed special privilege and political corruption, and would use government power to achieve those ends.

Although emotional factors prompted by the farmer's declining status in American society played a part, the movement emerged primarily in reaction to the very real economic and political abuses of both state and national administrations, whether Democratic or Republican. Yet southern Populists reserved their harshest criticism for the southern Conservative governments and what they perceived as the insensitivity of the national Democratic party, represented by President Grover Cleveland, a staunch opponent of free silver. Spurred on by hard times, the declining cotton prices of the early 1890s, and the Conservatives' increasing penchant for violence, fraud, and deceit as they tried to retain control, the Populists sought to drive the rascals out of power and trim the edges of American industrial capitalism so that they could get a bigger share of the nation's wealth.

Contrary to claims by some historians that the Populists aimed far beyond mere economic relief, it was no coincidence that a rise in cotton prices accompanied a declining fervor among the movement's supporters. Going even beyond Palmer's assertion about the degree to which Populists adopted mainstream beliefs, Barton Shaw, in *The Wool Hat Boys* (1984), demonstrates that even in Tom Watson's Georgia, rank-and-file Populists shared Conservative views on politics, race, and the economy. Despite anti-Conservative Populist rhetoric, both sides produced remarkably similar platforms that neglected state problems to address national issues—the only major differences involved Populist guarantees of a "fair count"—and were primarily concerned with the needs of commercial agriculture. Even the fence law issue looks less like a struggle between rich and poor, landlord and tenant, or defenders of a "moral economy" against the market's intrusion, than one between owners of small farms and large ones. One recent study of Georgia demonstrates that tenants and wage laborers would have been unaffected by the laws, but that small landowners would have had to reduce the size of their herds and take cotton land out of production if the stock law had been passed. The Populists did react in innovative and often enlightened ways to real problems. Still, one could argue that southern Populists failed, not because they were too radical, but because they were not radical enough. Because Conservatives and Populists had so much in common, on one level the fight between them was simply over access to political office—the Populists were out of power and doing everything they could to get in, and the Conservatives were in power and doing an even better job at staying in. But at a more principled level, the fight also was over whether the national Democratic party or a new national party was better able to convert the federal government to views shared by most Populists and Conservatives. Thus a charter member of North Carolina's Edgecomb County Populist party asked whether a Democratic rather than a Populist administration would "give greater impetus to the development of the South?—the extension of our railroad mileage—the opening up of our mining interests, the increase of manufacturing plants, the building up of villages, towns and cities? Will it infuse new life in the rural districts, by enhancing the value of realty and personalty? Will the price of products be enhanced? Will labor command better prices? Will the average man realize the difference?" The answer for him and others clearly was no.

But in order for the Populists to triumph, they had to do more than overcome Conservative violence, fraud, and appeals to white supremacy. They somehow had to convince voters to leave the Democratic party, the party that had overthrown the Republicans and had become the symbol of loyalty to the South. If the programs of the two parties were so similar in most states (the Texas Populist platform, with its eight-hour workday and a redemption law that would allow Texas residents to recover lands lost under forced sale, was the major exception), why should a Democrat switch? This was especially true once the hated Cleveland had given way to Bryan as the Democrats' standard bearer in 1896 and the party had endorsed free silver. In South Carolina, where Populism attracted little support, the same struggle was fought within the Democratic party, as Populist-like elements coalesced around Benjamin R. Tillman, the farmer son of a successful planter, who hypocritically took on the upcountry mantle of agrarian radical against the Conservatives. Tillman was elected governor in 1890, the same year he denied Wade Hampton reelection to the Senate, but neither he nor his supporters differed much in office from their Conservative predecessors, except in their virulence against blacks, further suggesting that specific issues mattered little in what was a struggle between personalities and generations, rather than classes or cultures. Typifying the resentment against Cleveland, Tillman promised during his successful senatorial campaign to take his pitchfork with him to Washington to prod "the old bag of beef in his old fat ribs," thereby earning the nickname "Pitchfork Ben."

The Populist challenge and its eventual defeat greatly affected relations among whites, but had an even greater impact upon blacks. As we have seen, neither Conservatives nor Populists were entirely happy with having to solicit black votes. Elements in both camps came to believe that without the black vote, white voters would be free to decide on issues without contamination by racial considerations. Tom Watson, the presidential candidate in 1904 and 1908 of the by-then decimated Populist party, personified the new political environment. A longtime defender of black voting rights, he was, by 1904, calling for "a change in our constitution which will perpetuate white supremacy for Georgia." Disillusioned by his party's defeats, he explained that "the white people dare not revolt so long as they can be intimidated by the fear of the negro vote." Without the "bugaboo of negro domination, . . . every white man would act according to his own conscience and judgment in deciding how he shall vote." Removing the black vote would also eliminate the incentive for the Democrats to steal it or for their opponents to solicit it.

Even before the emergence of Populism there had been growing interest in minimizing or eliminating black suffrage.

In the early post-Reconstruction years, some success had been achieved in negating the effects of the black vote by a mixture of gerrymandering, manipulation of election laws, fraud, and intimidation, and by turning what had been locally elective offices in heavily black areas into appointive positions filled by Democratic governors or Democratic-controlled state legislatures. Yet the black vote proved crucial in the Readjuster victory in Virginia and helped greenbackers and assorted independents gain office. Rural areas and state governments as a whole were affected, but urban whites felt most threatened by black voters.

Although the black vote most visibly helped elect Populists in North Carolina cities during the 1890s, blacks previously had increased their influence temporarily in other cities by combining with such groups as the Knights of Labor in Richmond, Mobile, and Jacksonville during the mid-1880s. But whites came to be more concerned about the role of blacks in statewide prohibition and local option campaigns, which were fixtures of local politics in the late 1880s. Liquor was an emotional issue that divided communities as well as the Democratic party. Even in Atlanta, where the white-only primary election to choose the party's nominee for office (tantamount to election in the one-party South), the poll tax, and white manipulation of the election procedures prevented blacks from winning public office, the issue of prohibition made blacks a pivotal force in municipal politics. From 1885 to 1888, Atlanta witnessed a series of referenda or electoral campaigns in which prohibition was the chief issue. Blacks sought to play off "the wets" against "the drys" to win concessions, but the victors never kept their promises to aid blacks, and the net effect was to increase white desires to eliminate the black vote. During Richmond's local option campaign of 1885, one newspaper editor feared that prohibition would be "forced upon white men by negro votes"; three years later a "race war" in Jackson, Mississippi, was attributed to bad feelings generated by a local option election.

The bidding for black votes in prohibition campaigns or when independents challenged incumbent Democratic administrations severely troubled local elites. The only remedy was to remove the black voter, because containment, though largely successful, was not enough. As they had done during Reconstruction, the urban dwellers turned to the state legislatures for help. And help soon came. Jackson (Mississippi) Democrats, who finally ousted their Republican mayor in 1888, secured an amended charter in 1890 that included, according to one newspaper, "changes [in the] wards so as to give perpetual control of the board of alderman to the white people." The same year, the state's new constitution incorporated the "Mississippi Plan," with its poll tax, secret ballot (a more complex ballot that had to be deciphered without assistance, thus penalizing the functionally illiterate), and literacy test—the first clear-cut statewide disfranchisement program in the nation.

Tennessee, however, had initiated the two-decade-long wave of systematic disfranchisement efforts that replaced the earlier piecemeal attempts to eliminate black influence at the polls. In 1889, largely in response to heated debate over prohibition, the legislature passed new voting and registration laws that applied only to Nashville, Memphis, Chattanooga, Knoxville, and their counties in order, according to a Nashville newspaper, "to practically exclude the vote of illiterate negroes." The key measure was adoption of the "Australian ballot," which was printed by the local or state government and listed candidates from all parties arranged by office or alphabetically. This replaced the different-colored ballots printed by each party that contained only the names of that party's candidates. This law (which prohibited help in reading the ballot), plus tighter registration requirements and a $2 poll tax enacted in 1890, reduced the number of black voters to fewer than 250 in the 1890 Nashville municipal election. But even after the passage in Florida in 1889 of an Australian-ballot, multiple-ballot-box system (modeled after South Carolina's 1882 measure, which required the voter to match his ballot for each individual office with one of up to eight separate ballot boxes), a poll tax, and other restrictions, blacks still were being elected to the Jacksonville city council after the turn of the century. By then, however, with the notable exception of Memphis, where "Boss" Edward H. Crump effectively incorporated blacks into his political machine, the passage of disfranchising legislation throughout the South had largely eliminated urban and rural black voters as factors in elections.

As the Mississippi, Tennessee, and Florida examples demonstrate, the disfranchisers were not called into being by the Populist threat to the Democratic party. Yet their efforts were given new urgency by the movement's appearance and the fear of future challenges to traditional Democratic control. Such views also were compatible with the increasing racism in the country at large, and the North's decision to let the South handle its "Negro Problem" after the defeat in 1890 of legislation sponsored by Representative Henry Cabot Lodge of Massachusetts that would have mandated federal supervision of southern elections. And in all of this there was the curious argument that the only way to eliminate vote buying, vote stealing, and voting fraud was to disfranchise the victims. As former governor William Oates admitted at the Alabama disfranchising convention in 1901, "White men have gotten to cheating each other until we don't have any honest elections." For the president of the Mississippi convention, black disfranchisement was required because "Fourteen years of fraud excited nausea."

Although certain states, such as Georgia, did not complete their efforts until the end of the first decade of the twentieth century, most disfranchisement legislation was passed in two earlier clusters. The first, from 1889 to 1895, was largely in response to the threat of renewed northern Republican intervention associated with introduction of the Lodge Bill; the second, between 1898 and 1902, was more a response to the Republican and Populist successes of the 1890s. Whether by resorting to constitutional conventions, as in Mississippi (1890), South Carolina (1895), Louisiana (1898), and Alabama

(1901), or by simply amending existing constitutions through referenda, as in North Carolina (1900), Texas (1902), and Georgia (1908), southern states incorporated a variety of measures that sharply reduced their electorates.

The disfranchising techniques included a mixture of new devices and old devices put to new uses. Because of the Fifteenth Amendment's declaration that the right to vote "shall not be denied . . . on account of race, color, or previous condition of servitude," the states could not simply abolish black suffrage. The poll tax, an old device, was the most common way to get around this prohibition. Ever since the antebellum period, a one- or two-dollar head tax had been used generally to support education, but collection was haphazard and payment was not required in order to vote. Now not only was payment required to vote, but receipts had to be presented at registration—itself a relatively new practice also aimed at reducing the electorate—and often again on election day. And in most states payment was cumulative, which meant that payment had to be made for at least some or, as in Georgia, all of the years missed in order to vote. Because poor people might move a couple of times a year and had no safe place to store receipts, providing proof of payment obviously was difficult for them. But that, after all, was the point, and registrars or election officials might choose not to ask for proof that the tax had been paid—an occurrence that was far more likely if the voter was white.

The second most common disfranchising device was totally new. Pioneered by Mississippi, the literacy test required the prospective voter to prove that he could read. Again the registrars had great latitude in administering the law. After the United States Supreme Court declared the Mississippi Plan constitutional in *Williams* v. *Mississippi* (1898), the literacy test and poll tax became staples of the second wave of disfranchisement legislation. Five states also instituted a property requirement for the franchise, and to discriminate further against illiterates, seven used the Australian ballot. As was the case with the literacy test, poll tax, and property requirements,

election officials, who increasingly were white Democrats, enjoyed broad latitude in enforcing the new requirements or deciding whether certain voters deserved special help. Such discretionary power also was extended to detection of conviction
for petty crime, which was more common among blacks and
was grounds for disfranchisement in several states.

There also were more formal loopholes to protect white
voters. Several states copied Mississippi (1890) and permitted
illiterates to vote if they could "understand" the state constitution. Whether they passed, of course, was at the discretion
of the official. Asked whether or not Christ could register under
the "understanding" clause, a leader of the Alabama convention replied, "That would depend entirely on which way he
was going to vote." Louisiana (1898) gave the other southern
states the famous "grandfather clause." Often mistakenly included among the disfranchising tools, it actually was a loop-
hole meant to allow otherwise unqualified whites to vote. Even
if a voter could not meet the other criteria for the franchise,
he could vote if a member of his family had been eligible to
vote prior to March 1867—that is, before blacks were enfranchised. An occasional freedman might get in by pointing to a
free black ancestor who might have voted (free blacks could
vote in Tennessee until 1834 and in North Carolina in 1835).
A black man also conceivably could claim the right to vote
by virtue of having a white forebear, but that was not a wise
course to pursue. Alabama (1901) and Georgia (1908) also
included a "good character clause" that could be resorted to—
far more easily by a white voter—if all else failed.

Disfranchisement had an immediate effect on the South's
electorate. On January 1, 1897, 103.2 percent of Louisiana's
white adult males were registered to vote (a figure suggesting
the need for some genuine reform), as were 95.6 percent of
the adult black males. On January 1, 1898, after the state's
new registration law went into effect, the respective figures
were 46.6 percent and 9.5 percent. By January 1, 1904, under
terms of the new constitution, the figures were 52.5 percent
and 1.1 percent, respectively. Turnout in North Carolina's gub-

ernatorial race declined from 75 percent in 1900 to less than 50 percent following passage of the disfranchisement referendum. Following Georgia's disfranchisement legislation in 1908, black registration dropped from 28.3 percent of adult males to 4.3 percent. By 1908, Jefferson County, Alabama, with 21,408 literate adult black males, had 376 registered black voters; Montgomery County, with the next largest number of literate blacks (8,265), had 69 registered black voters. It should be noted that many white voters who could not meet the property or literacy requirements were too embarrassed to register under the legal loopholes available to them.

There still is disagreement over disfranchisement's impact on Southern politics itself and, most basically, over just who were the primary targets of the disfranchisers.

Southern politics certainly became less fraudulent and less marked by violence, though both tendencies persisted. Blacks certainly were "put in their place." But were the new disfranchisement statutes really needed to keep the Democrats in power? In his classic *Southern Politics* (1949), political scientist V. O. Key argued that the new laws simply recorded a *fait accompli.* That is, the laws came after Populist suppression, the appropriation of Populist slogans by the Democrats, the reaction against black voting, and the consolidation of the one-party system. C. Vann Woodward, however, correctly noted that the earliest disfranchisement efforts actually preceded the rise of Populism and thus, for example, help to account for the weakness of Populism in Mississippi. These laws, then, were of more than symbolic importance—they truly altered the balance of southern politics.

The laws were especially important for the maintenance of Democratic power because, as J. Morgan Kousser demonstrated in *The Shaping of Southern Politics* (1974), Republican and Independent strength had been greater than previously realized. And rather than the constitutions being crucial factors, as was often claimed, the new legislative requirements for registration and voting had already produced the restricted electorates that assured adoption of the new constitutions or passage of disfranchising referenda.

Kousser also challenged long-held beliefs about the targets of the disfranchisement campaigns. Most scholars agreed that the new laws and constitutions sought to eliminate black voters. Even when they acknowledged that many lower-class whites were disfranchised and even were the target of some Black Belt planters, they argued that disfranchisement was primarily an expression of antiblack sentiment and listed lower-class whites, including disaffected Populists, among its chief supporters. Kousser, however, argued that the upper and middle classes, particularly in the Black Belt, were primarily responsible for the legislation and directed it as much against poor whites as blacks, which united them with "reformers" who sought to use registration laws, secret ballots, and other measures to limit the impact of the lower classes and immigrants in northern cities. As Louisiana's U.S. Senator Samuel D. McEnery put it after adoption of his state's new constitution, "The bestowal of political power upon mere numbers—the impersonal mass—cannot be justified." Edward McCrady, Jr., the author of South Carolina's 1882 election law, which paved the way for adoption of the state's 1895 constitution, was even more direct. He favored disfranchising "the dense mass of ignorant voters of both races."

Although such statements remind us that the coalitions of planter and urban elites were not averse to minimizing possible white support for challenges to the status quo at the same time that they claimed to be protecting the status of all whites by disfranchising the blacks, the evidence does not support the extreme claim that poor whites and blacks were coequal targets. Had this been the case, North Carolina's 1900 legislation, for example, would not have extended the grandfather clause until 1908, a time by which the state's education governor Charles B. Aycock and his supporters fully expected all *whites* to be able to pass the state's literacy test. The period of time for the grandfather exemption was shorter in Louisiana and elsewhere, but such measures were necessary to attract white support in those states where referenda had to be adopted. Few members of the elite would have minded if there had been a sizable drop in the white electorate, but that was a bonus and not their prime aim. Besides, poor whites might have been targets for reasons of political affiliation rather than class. McEnery and McCrady were exceptions in terms of their forthrightness, but they also probably were exceptions in their aims; more typical was North Carolina's Senator Furnifold Simmons, who recalled that in 1900 "[Governor] Aycock . . . and I decided that the Democratic Party must go forward educationally, industrially, and morally, but in order to do [that,] what we had first to make certain [was] that the negro can never come back into politics again." There certainly were white Democrats in North Carolina who hoped to bar poor whites from the ballot box, especially if they had voted Republican or Populist, but they tended to be Cleveland Democrats and were not the ones who wrote the disfranchising legislation.

The disfranchisers had argued that with the blacks out of the way, the remaining whites could divide freely over fundamental issues. This did not happen. Instead, as the Conservative generation began to fade from the scene after the turn of the century, a new set of issues and personalities emerged to keep conflict stirring in southern politics amid renewed charges of fraud and intimidation. This time, however, the struggle was framed more in terms of urban-rural conflict. And now the balance of power began to shift cityward. In part this was due to urban growth, but it also occurred because large landowners no longer had a black vote to manipulate to get greater representation in the legislature and because literacy tests took their greatest toll among whites in the countryside, where schools were far fewer and the demands of the agricultural calendar pulled whites as well as blacks away from those that existed.

Progressivism

After the turn of the century, southern politics and society reflected a new national trend that historians call Progressivism. Moved to action by mounting immigration and rapid industrialization and urbanization, progressives sought to attack the political, economic, and social ills that had been left to fester during the late nineteenth century. As in the case of Populism, historical accounts of the movement initially overlooked the South. After all, foreign immigrants had largely avoided the region, and, as we have seen, the South's degree of urbanization and industrialization lagged far behind the rest of the country. Influenced by visions of a permanently benighted, unchanging South and the popular argument that Progressivism emerged out of Populism, most scholars concentrated on the more visible western, midwestern, and northeastern manifestations of the movement. But as the reality of southern Populism sank in, historians began to look as well for examples of Progressivism in the South.

To some extent, the presence of southern Progressivism was obscured by the emergence around the turn of the century of the first generation of what two authors have termed "Dixie Demagogues." Appealing to rural resentment of entrenched interests and fueled by racial prejudice, these demagogues triumphed in gubernatorial and congressional races throughout the South. Mississippi's James Vardaman (governor, 1904–08; senator, 1913–19) and Theodore Bilbo (governor, 1916–20, 1928–32; senator, 1934–47); Florida's Sidney J. Catts (governor, 1916–20); South Carolina's Coleman "Cole" Blease (governor, 1910–14; senator, 1924–30); Georgia's Tom Watson (the embittered and tormented antiblack, anti-Catholic, anti-Semitic remnant of his heroic period [senator, 1920–22]); Alabama's Tom Heflin (representative, 1904–20; senator 1920–31); and Arkansas's Jeff Davis (governor, 1900–06; senator, 1906–13) were among those held up to ridicule as buffoons and hatemongers by their enemies, but embraced lovingly by their devoted followers. Davis, a rural lawyer who enjoyed playing the hick against urban "high-collared roosters," unrelentingly regaled his unimpressed Senate colleagues with the statement that "the only things Arkansas ever had on the free tariff list were possums, sweet potatoes and acorns." Vardaman, a rural editor who pitched his campaigns to white small farmers after being rejected by Mississippi's conservative Democratic leaders, helped perpetuate racial hatred in the state. Admitting on one occasion that as governor he *might* send troops to protect a "negro fiend," he was quick to add, "if I were a private citizen I would head the mob to string the brute up, and I haven't much respect for a white man who wouldn't."

But although they shared a common style and often relied heavily on race baiting, several of these demagogues advocated a variety of "progressive" reforms. Vardaman, for example, as governor, strengthened railroad regulation and abolished the remnants of the convict lease system. A failure in the Senate, Davis used his gubernatorial years to limit the power of Arkansas's corporations. Catts, a charismatic insurance salesman and Baptist minister who used anti-Catholic hysteria to gain election on the Prohibition party ticket, fought for labor and prison reforms and endorsed women's suffrage. About Bilbo, whose name became synonymous with race baiting, one historian concluded that "No other leader of the plebeian masses in the teens had either a program or a record to equal his." His innovations included the abolition of public hangings, and the establishment of a highway commission, a pardon board, a state tuberculosis sanitarium, aid to small farmers, and educational reform legislation that benefited both blacks and whites.

The impact of these men, whether positive or negative, can be easily overstated, however, because they usually had to share power within their state's Democratic party with both more traditionally conservative and progressive elements. What historian George Tindall called "plebeian-respectable divisions" came to dominate southern politics. The result was a series of crazy-quilt alliances that changed from election to election or deal to deal, but that often produced reform legislation worth taking seriously. Thus Vardaman and Bilbo, as well as Mississippi's aristocratic John Sharp Williams, who spent thirty productive years in Congress, all favored states rights, a lower tariff, direct election of U.S. senators by popular vote, and regulation of trusts.

Given these facts, Arthur Link, in his 1945 Ph.D. dissertation and in a series of articles, and C. Vann Woodward, in *Origins of the New South*, argued that historians had wrongly assumed that there was no Progressive movement in the South. The South, in fact, they claimed, frequently took the lead in pushing certain Progressive reforms, even if there were comparatively few of the kinds of people reform-minded historians felt comfortable calling progressives.

Progressivism had its greatest effect on southern politics, while itself benefiting from earlier political changes. Disfranchisement proved to be the cornerstone of the movement, although progressives and conservatives alike promoted its adoption. The new restricted electorate and tighter registration laws, it was claimed, would eliminate the fraud, intimidation, and violence that had plagued southern politics since the Civil War. A more informed electorate would elect better men and intelligently weigh the merits of policy alternatives. The white primary, which first had appeared in such southern cities as Atlanta during the 1870s, was now adopted in most states and used, not simply to exclude the few remaining black voters, but also to open up the Democratic party by weakening the hold of conservative party bosses. By using the white primary for the election of Democratic candidates, states such as Mississippi actually pioneered in the direct election of U.S. senators. Several states added the initiative, referendum, or recall to their constitutions. Others passed laws against corrupt practices and against lobbying that further aimed at cleansing politics. On the local level, Galveston, Texas, following a devastating hurricane in 1900 that overburdened the existing administration, became the first city to adopt the commission form of government; eight years later, Staunton, Virginia, became the first to try the city manager system. Both deviations from the allegedly corrupt and inefficient mayor-council alternative soon spread throughout the South and then to the rest of the country.

As was the case with their northern counterparts and the federal government, southern states took positive steps to regulate big business. States reorganized or strengthened their railroad commissions and established new commissions to regulate banks, public utilities, and insurance companies, though, as was true elsewhere, they often were staffed with commissioners who were overly sympathetic to the objects of regulation. Cities established their own local boards and city councils sought to tighten the terms of franchises granted to streetcar, gas, electric, and telephone companies. As we saw in chapter 1, city governments increased the number of municipally owned waterworks and purchased private electric and gas works. Local chambers of commerce took the lead in city planning efforts that challenged some aspects of private and corporate disregard for the public interest, as did the passage of antipollution ordinances.

Intervention in other aspects of the economy brought less change. State agricultural societies were revitalized in an effort to help commercial farmers. States established agricultural experiment stations that together with the new agricultural colleges, sought to spread the ideas of "scientific farming." Demonstration farms under the direction of Seaman H. Knapp of the U.S. Department of Agriculture enlisted "cooperating farmers," who received special instruction on the value of crop rotation, improved seeds, and proper use of fertilizer and then tried to get their neighbors to learn these new ways of cultivating the soil. However, the force of old habits and tradition, the continued shortage of capital and skills, and a widespread suspicion of "book farming" meant limited progress. There was little to substantiate the *Southern Cultivator*'s claims that every day more and more farmers were trying "new and better methods of farming."

A few states passed child labor laws, and others sought to regulate hours and working conditions for adult workers, particularly in coal mines and textile mills. More than a quarter of the workers in the textile industry in 1900 were under sixteen years old. One reformer charged that there were "not less than 60,000 children under fourteen employed in the cotton mills of the Southern states . . . most of them being little girls." Employers used intimidation, bribery, and deceit to undermine reform efforts, but progressives, as well as some historians, often overlooked the resistance to child labor laws by parents who were dependent on their children's income. Even when they believed there should be some limitations on the ages of child workers, parents usually drew the line below the ages of their own children, and in any case thought that they had the right to make such decisions about their children's employment. When her underage daughter was denied work at the local mill, Mrs. S. J. Vaughn of Sampson mill village complained to Governor Cole Blease, who was especially good at using mill parents' opposition to impede child labor reform in South Carolina. "There are children workin in all the Mills that are not a bit over 9 years old, & as I told you I am a widow & my little girl is 13 years old & they will not let her work at all[.] [I]t is awful to go in the mills & see the little tots in there & awful to hear the Parents tell a lie about their ages." Yet Mrs. Vaughn argued that her child should be allowed to work. "I have no way to make a living only be keeping howse for people & I have to take her around with me[.] I thought she could work in the mill while I kept howse & we could make a good living."

Progressive social legislation included efforts at both social control and social justice. As will be discussed more fully in the next chapter, one state after another institutionalized the largely custom-based system of segregation that already was evident during Reconstruction, a preoccupation with race that distinguished southern progressives from their counterparts elsewhere. Southern progressives, such as Alabama's Braxton Bragg Comer and Georgia's Hoke Smith, however, shared with many other progressives a desire to eliminate the manufacture and sale of alcohol. Prohibition campaigns sharply divided Democrats and even many reformers in states such as Texas, Tennessee, and Alabama, helping to create a bewildering set of alliances. Georgia was the first to adopt statewide prohibition in 1907, but it had been joined by every former Confederate state except Louisiana by the time the Eighteenth Amendment authorizing national prohibition was ratified in 1919. Kentucky, although still wet, had been among the first states to ratify the amendment in January 1918.

Southern advocates of social justice legislation were less successful. Together with laws regulating working conditions, there were some improvements in public education, particularly in North Carolina, where a succession of progressive governors, beginning in 1900 with Charles Aycock, conducted vigorous educational campaigns. There also were efforts to eradicate such public health menaces as hookworm and malaria. Georgia, Texas, Mississippi, Louisiana, and Arkansas abolished convict leasing, and other states made long-overdue improvements in their penal systems. Suffragists, in what was after all as much a movement for social justice as for political rights, enjoyed the support of a few leading progressives and mavericks, such as Sidney Catts, but only Tennessee among the states of the former Confederacy ratified the Nineteenth Amendment that enfranchised women. Broader demands for women's rights were even less favorably received. When Belle Kearney, a Mississippi temperance and suffragist leader, told her planter father she wanted to be a lawyer, he responded that, "No woman had ever attempted such an absurdity, and any effort on my part in that line would subject me to ridicule and ostracism."

There is widespread agreement as to what the progressives did, but considerable disagreement over the origins of the movement and its relative impact on southern society.

One view, expressed most forcefully in Arthur Link's "The Progressive Movement in the South" (1946), sees southern Progressivism as the natural product of long years of agrarian discontent. According to Link, there was a steady progression from the Grangers to the Alliancemen to the Populists to the progressives, augmented by crucial input from the agrarian wing of the Democratic party. After 1900, however, reformers became more interested in structural political concerns than in agrarian ones as leadership shifted from the hands of farmers to progressive editors, politicians, and other urban groups.

In fact, the movement owed a relatively small debt to the rural South. As C. Vann Woodward has argued, southern Progressivism was essentially urban and middle class in nature, an assessment that, ironically, undercut his own claims about the unimportance of southern urbanization. Rather than there being a continuum from Populism to Progressivism, the collapse of Populism had made change respectable again and allowed it to be championed by a very different set of men within the reform wing of the Democratic party. The widespread adoption of the direct primary had then enabled such individuals to gain power.

Link and Woodward also represent different ways of assessing the impact of the movement. In Link's view, the South actually was in the forefront of many progressive reforms, at both the state and national level. This was especially true in the areas of railroad regulation and the democratization of politics. More concerned with establishing the South's positive contributions to early twentieth-century reform, Link briefly noted that there was no attack on farm tenancy, and, almost in passing, admitted that the movement constituted "progressive democracy for the white man." Although Link acknowledged the extent to which the New South remained antiquated and backward, he urged readers to appreciate what had been accomplished, especially the extent to which the "masses" were powerful and were represented by demagogues as well as progressives, both of whom challenged the conservatives and the reactionaries.

Woodward, however, argued that its racial policies were central to southern Progressivism. Link had noted that nothing was done *for* blacks, but ignored what progressives helped do *to* blacks in terms of disfranchisement, legally enforced segregation, and weak opposition to lynching. For Woodward, such positions were so crucial that he entitled his chapter on the movement "Progressivism—For Whites Only." In addition to disfranchisement, Woodward emphasized prohibition, a second topic that Link had ignored. Just as progressives elsewhere had sought to tighten requirements for voting—although in the North and Midwest the targets were recent immigrants—so, too, had they favored either the containment or elimination of liquor. But, if anything, as was true of their pursuit of a "pure" electorate, southern progressives pursued the war on booze even more vigorously than their counterparts elsewhere.

Unlike Link, Woodward was more interested in drawing attention to southern Progressivism's failings or limitations than to its achievements. For if Link emphasized change and improvement, Woodward, while acknowledging all the examples of change, emphasized how much further the South had to go. As in his assessment of late nineteenth-century southern politics and economy, Woodward found evidence of significant advance that nonetheless left the region far behind the rest of the nation. Blacks were excluded, "reform" was conservative, especially in social matters, and, as witnessed by the popularity of the Bleases and Watsons, nothing really was done to help the downtrodden.

Since the early 1950s, the seminal assessments by Link and Woodward have governed the nature of the debate over southern Progressivism. Although only Sheldon Hackney's *From Populism to Progressivism in Alabama* (1969) has thoroughly examined the relationship of the two movements in one state, most historians agree that, with the possible exceptions of North Carolina and Texas, the sharp differences between Populism and Progressivism in Alabama accurately reflect conditions elsewhere in the South. Not only was Alabama Progressivism led by such urban types as Braxton Bragg Comer of Birmingham, who was elected governor in 1906, but, in addition, former Populists were among the strongest opponents of progressive legislation that included expansion of state power to control the railroads. Rather than the issueless and provincial "class of superfluous farmers and ineffectively organized workers" of Populism, Alabama progressives were program-oriented urban members of the middle class and Black Belt planters who challenged the northern-allied railroad and Birmingham steel interests.

Although there is a growing consensus on the origins of southern Progressivism that, like Woodward's view, emphasizes its separate urban roots while not denying some agrarian component, most historians evaluate the movement's accomplishments in terms closer to those of Link, despite the harsher assessments of some dissenters. George Tindall's *The Emergence of the New South 1913 to 1945* (1967), for example, presented a synthesis of the two earlier views. Tindall's progressives were small businessmen and agrarians who shared ideas that were "traditionalistic, individualistic and set in a socially conservative milieu." Like Woodward, he found the social justice wing of southern progressives to be very much in the minority, but he was less impressed than Woodward with the similarities between northern and southern progressives. Like Link, he downplayed the lily-white nature of southern Progressivism and preferred to emphasize the "modernization" of southern governments, although he acknowledged that by 1920 they still lagged considerably behind the rest of the country. According to Tindall, southern Progressivism, "an amalgam of agrarian radicalism, business regulation, good government and urban social justice reform, becomes in the end a movement for positive government."

Given the contradictions and halfway measures of the movement, any final assessment of southern Progressivism will depend on whether one decides to emphasize its failures or its achievements. Such a judgment, in turn, is linked to how one views the entire era between 1865 and 1920. Put another way, regardless of whether the glass of progress looks half full or half empty, Progressivism was the culmination of the First New South. Unlike Henry Grady and the early advocates of a New South, most progressives chose to stay at home and many did not like to make speeches. But their aims were similar. Although more concerned than Grady's generation with "social uplift" and their responsibilities to the masses, progressives were as determined to promote industrial growth, diversified agriculture, and at least the appearance of enlightened race relations, and sought to close the economic gap between North and South. Dewey W. Grantham accurately summed up the era in the subtitle to the most extensive treatment of the subject, *Southern Progressivism: The Reconciliation of Progress and Tradition* (1983), although from my perspective the subtle might as fittingly have been the reconciliation of change and continuity.

Thus southern Progressivism within individual states grew naturally out of the developments of the previous thirty-five years. But the movement was also a culmination of the First New South in the sense that it paved the way for the region's full readmittance to the Union. National reconciliation had gotten under way with the South's strong support for the Spanish-American War in 1898 and with the earlier participation of southerners in Grover Cleveland's two administrations. A more dramatic expression of national acceptance came with Woodrow Wilson's first presidential administration (1913–17). Wilson became the first southern-born president since Andrew Johnson (and the first elected one since 1848), as well as the last until Lyndon Johnson. His election in 1912 also renewed the ties within the Democratic party between the South and the West and returned the South to a position of power in the national government for the first time since the Civil War.

Southern progressives played a key role in the South's presidential primaries and at the Democratic national convention in securing support for the Virginia-born Woodrow Wilson, then the progressive governor of New Jersey. In a campaign that further revealed the cleavage between rural-driven Populism and urban-rooted Progressivism, former agrarian radicals such as Alabama's Tom Heflin, Mississippi's

James Vardaman, and Georgia's Tom Watson (who somehow determined that Wilson "kow-towed to the Roman hierarchy" and was "*ravenously fond of the Negro*,") supported the more conservative Alabama Representative Oscar Underwood, whereas urban progressives such as Georgia Governor and U.S. Senator Hoke Smith, Tennessee Senator Luke Lea, and North Carolina Supreme Court Judge Walter Clark supported Wilson.

After Wilson defeated William Howard Taft and Theodore Roosevelt in the presidential election, his southern supporters were rewarded with several cabinet positions. North Carolina's Josephus Daniels became secretary of the navy, Texas's Albert Sidney Burleson became postmaster general, and North Carolina native and former Texan David F. Houston became secretary of agriculture. Although they lived in New York, Attorney General James C. McReynolds was from Tennessee, and secretary of the Treasury William Gibbs McAdoo had been born in Georgia and raised in Tennessee. "Colonel" Edward M. House of Texas became Wilson's closest advisor.

Because Wilson carried with him a Democratic Congress, southern Democrats now turned the seniority that the Solid South had given them into key congressional leadership posts. Of the seventeen most important House committees, fifteen were chaired by southerners. Progressive chairmen of committees included Hoke Smith of the new Senate Committee on Education and Labor and fellow Georgian William C. Adamson of the House Interstate and Foreign Commerce Committee. But conservative southerners also wielded new power. Thomas Martin, the conservative Democratic boss of Virginia who had sought to block Wilson's nomination, became a somewhat reluctantly loyal Senate majority leader. Oscar Underwood, whom Wilson had defeated for the nomination, had some progressive credentials, but his stronger conservative preferences included opposition to women's suffrage. Evans Johnson, his biographer, called him a Bourbon (in the process demonstrating the problems with the traditional nomenclature), "a member of the old planter aristocracy who favored concessions to business and strict economy, and who extolled the glories of the Old South and envisioned a great industrial future for the New South." Having served as House majority leader before moving to the Senate in 1914, in 1920 he became the first man since Henry Clay to lead his party in both houses. As chairman of the House Ways and Means Committee, he was responsible for the Underwood-Simmons Tariff of 1913 (cosponsored by Senator Furnifold Simmons of North Carolina) that implemented the longstanding Democratic and bipartisan progressive principle of tariff reduction and provided for the first income tax following ratification of the Sixteenth Amendment.

Most other major legislative measures of Wilson's first term, arguably the most productive one since George Washington's, bore the names or imprint of southern committee chairmen, including the Glass-Owen Federal Reserve Act, the Clayton Anti-Trust Act, the Adamson Eight Hour [on Railroads] Act, and the Smith-Lever and Smith-Hughes bills that provided federal matching funds for agricultural and vocational education. Southern committee chairmen also played a crucial role in the mobilization effort during World War I, often managing to put aside their states' rights convictions in the interest of national policy making. On a less positive note, such chairmen, together with cabinet officials such as Secretary of the Navy Daniels and with the at least tacit support of the president, were responsible for the institutionalization of segregation in the federal government and armed forces.

Although the southern stamp on the Wilson administration was unmistakable, it is not always clear which southerners were most responsible. Arthur Link and George Tindall argue that southerners with agrarian roots were responsible for most of Wilson's "New Freedom" legislation. Indeed, to a great extent the dispute between Link and Woodward over the roots of southern Progressivism can be traced to Link's greater concern for the progressives' impact on the national level, whereas Woodward, whose *Origins* ends with the election of Wilson, focused on the local and state character of the movement. Yet, even though key leaders supported Wilson's legislation, especially that which moved in the direction of Theodore Roosevelt's more centralized "New Nationalism," southern delegations as a whole were less supportive, some agrarians were among the most reactionary and vociferous opponents, and Wilson himself as often led as followed Congress. Indeed Wilson enjoyed greater overall support for his program among western rather than southern agrarians. And, of course, key urban figures such as Birmingham's Oscar Underwood, Atlanta's Hoke Smith, Jacksonville's Duncan Fletcher, and Lynchburg's Carter Glass deserve at least equal billing with more rural-based figures, such as North Carolina's Furnifold Simmons or South Carolina's Asbury F. Lever.

But the triumphs of Wilson's first administration were cut short by America's entry into World War I in April of 1917. Entering the war was the high point of Progressivism. Having failed to democratize the eating clubs while he was president of Princeton, Woodrow Wilson had enjoyed greater success with New Jersey and the United States; now he sought to "Make the World Safe for Democracy." Most southern progressives supported this effort, but many of the old southern agrarians, such as Mississippi Senator James Vardaman and North Carolina Congressman Claude Kitchin, broke with Wilson and opposed American involvement in the war. But widespread southern support for the war and the region's popularity as the site for army and National Guard training camps ended any lingering doubts that the South was indeed finally back in the Union.

Wilson's Democratic party won the war, but did not fare as well in the politics of peace. The president tried to force the Treaty of Versailles down the collective throats of the Republican opposition and many American voters, and his party suffered an overwhelming defeat in the presidential election of 1920. The Democrats had already lost control of Congress in 1918. That also meant the loss of southern committee chairmanships and the end of the South's brief dominance over the national government, a position not again approached until the New Deal. At the same time that the political power of representatives of the First New South was being shattered, the "Great Migration" of blacks out of the South that began in 1914 highlighted the region's continued economic and social problems and undercut its claims to be the best place for blacks. As we shall see more clearly in the next chapter, southern Progressivism furthered rather than challenged the racial settlement of the 1890s and in that sense, too, was the culmination of the period that began with the end of the Civil War. Only by looking at Progressivism's impact on the cultural and social life of blacks and whites can we arrive at a complete assessment of the movement's place in the history of the First New South.

CHAPTER THREE

Society and Culture

Antebellum southern society was grounded in three elements: conservative evangelical religion, white racism, and an agrarian way of life that stressed mutual obligation between the white planter class and the self-sufficient white yeomanry. The Civil War and Reconstruction intensified white devotion to conservative religion and racism but, as we have seen, helped undermine the mutuality of interests linking planters and other whites.

The South's economic and political systems clearly influenced the nature of social and cultural life. Conversely, of course, the social structure and culture had helped determine the region's economics and politics. It is unrewarding to seek to determine which set of factors had the greater impact on the other, although some scholars try. For our purposes, it is the interaction of politics and economics with society and culture that is most important.

The fate of the three cornerstones of the Old South—white supremacy, conservative religion, and an agrarian way of life—

in large measure determined the structure of black life between the end of the Civil War, or, perhaps more important, the end of Reconstruction, and 1920. We will therefore begin with the blacks and then turn to the whites. Despite the rhetoric of intraracial solidarity, the lives of the great mass of southern whites were more like those of most blacks than anyone except an occasional "troublemaker" was willing to admit. Just above them on the white socioeconomic ladder was a smaller middle-class population, and at the top were the remnants of the old planter class and members of the new urban elite, who were the loudest proponents and defenders of a so-called New South.

Race over Class: Black Life

The economic and political realities for blacks largely determined their social and cultural lives during the end of the nineteenth and the beginning of the twentieth centuries. As we have seen, by the turn of the century most blacks worked as sharecroppers in the countryside or as servants and unskilled laborers in the cities. And whether by legal or other means, their brief period of political influence during Reconstruction had come to an end. Living largely in, or on the brink of, poverty, and with no recourse to the ballot box, the South's blacks attempted to make the best of a bad situation. Eventually growing numbers would come to believe that their only real prospects for change lay in the North.

The realities of New South race relations revealed the hollowness of Henry Grady's assurance that the "Negro Question" could be left with the South, "with the fullest confidence that the honor of the Republic will be maintained, the rights of humanity guarded, and the problem worked out in such exact justice as the finite mind can measure or finite agencies administer." For if sharecropping and disfranchisement dominated black economic and political life, segregation established the boundaries for black social and cultural life. Early generations of historians assumed that a rigid system of physical separation of the races had always characterized southern life. In *The Strange Career of Jim Crow* (1955, 1966, 1974), however, C. Vann Woodward argued that it was not until after 1890 that a rigid segregation code "lent the sanction of law to a racial ostracism that extended to churches and schools, to housing and jobs, to eating and drinking. Whether by law or by custom, that ostracism eventually extended to virtually all forms of public transportation, to sports and recreations, to hospitals, orphanages, prisons, and asylums, and ultimately to funeral homes, morgues, and cemeteries." The reference to custom was misleading, however, because for Woodward the existence of a law enforcing segregation has always been the key variable in evaluating the nature of race relations.

Most historians initially accepted the so-called Woodward Thesis concerning the late development of segregation in the South, and several provided further support for it. Some historians, however, discovered the earlier existence of segregation during the antebellum period in the South and even in the North. And Joel Williamson, in *After Slavery: The Negro in South Carolina during Reconstruction, 1861–1877* (1965), launched a frontal attack on the assertion that flexibility was the rule in southern race relations between the end of Reconstruction and the 1890s. Williamson found segregation so pervasive in the South's Radical stronghold that he argued for the existence of a "duo-chromatic order" by the end of Reconstruction. Other studies as well suggest that on the whole Woodward had exaggerated the importance of integration as a "forgotten alternative" in southern race relations prior to the 1890s.

Yet segregation and integration were not the only options available to white and black southerners. Indeed, prior to the Civil War and during its immediate aftermath, whites favored a policy of racial exclusion in most areas of southern public life. Blacks were excluded from schools, poorhouses, hospitals, institutions for the blind, deaf, and dumb, and a variety of public conveyances and places of public accommodation. Republican Reconstruction governments sought to change that policy. They guaranteed blacks access to the new public school systems, militia companies, social welfare institutions, street-cars, and theaters. In most instances, however, access was to be on a separate but equal basis. Because it replaced exclusion rather than integration, segregation, ironically, often marked an improvement rather than a setback in the status of blacks.

Although individual blacks occasionally used petitions, boycotts, or lawsuits to protest segregated treatment, most black leaders continued to be more concerned with removing the vestiges of exclusion and eliminating instances of unequal treatment. A black councilman in Montgomery, Alabama, for example, sought to have the black section of the city cemetery equally maintained, rather than try to have the cemetery de-segregated. A Norfolk, Virginia, black man, observing that the city was building a new opera house, suggested that "colored theatre-goers . . . petition the managers to give them a respect-able place to sit, apart from those of a lewd character." Throughout the South, other blacks demanded truly equal, albeit separate, accommodations in schools and welfare insti-tutions.

Black desires at times actually contributed to making seg-regation a more visibly ingrained fact of southern life. During the antebellum period, for example, many blacks had wor-shipped in segregated sections of white churches. At the end of the Civil War, however, blacks initiated a mass exodus from the white churches and formed their own Baptist and Meth-odist congregations, leaving behind a handful of generally el-derly blacks to worship in white Catholic, Presbyterian, Ep-iscopalian, and Congregational churches. But even those denominations had to adjust to black demands. About black Presbyterians, an Alabama preacher said in 1868, "we hardly know what to say, think or hope; they are disinclined to hear the word of God from us and are led astray by superstitious leaders." "Almost universally they prefer separate organiza-tions and preachers of their own color," said another minister the following year. By the late 1880s, the Presbyterians and most of the other holdouts had been forced to establish separate churches for their black congregants. Denied access to secular white organizations, blacks also initiated their own Masonic, Odd Fellow, and similar fraternal orders, as well as a variety of voluntary associations.

Black desires also were responsible for a more segregated educational system than most whites would have preferred. Although whites, whether northerners or southerners, Republicans or Democrats, were nearly unanimous in wanting segregated schools, most wanted to have whites teaching black students. As newly founded black colleges such as Fisk in Nashville, Howard in Washington, D.C., and Atlanta Baptist began to graduate their first classes of teachers, however, the black residents of communities throughout the South demanded that blacks replace white teachers in black schools. In 1882, for example, Richmond's black newspaper, the *Virginia Star*, led the fight to have the city's young blacks "instructed by those who have their interests at heart." Blacks argued that they were capable of teaching themselves and that black teachers would be role models and have better relations with the black community. Besides, no matter how good they were, black graduates were barred from teaching in white schools. Blacks also objected to the practice of staffing black public schools with whites who had scored lowest on teacher examinations. But even in schools staffed by able and sympathetic northern veterans of the schools established by the northern freedmen societies, blacks preferred black teachers.

Local school boards resisted hiring black teachers, especially in cities such as Charleston and New Orleans, where school systems grew slowly, if at all. By the turn of the century, however, most black schools were staffed entirely by black teachers and principals, although an occasional school could still be found with a mixed staff, an all-white staff, or, as in the case of Richmond's black high school, a black staff with a white principal. The boards were finally worn down by black petitions, the growing number of competent black graduates, the retirement of white teachers, and, perhaps most of all, by the fact that the boards could pay black teachers less than whites.

In other areas besides education, segregation, though initiated by whites, was often agreed upon by whites and blacks. The Reconstruction governments established separate black and white militia units, and some of the black companies remained in service, as in Georgia, until the early twentieth century. The same was true of local fire companies, such as the Grey Eagle Company in Montgomery, Alabama. Blacks reacted to their exclusion from a variety of welfare facilities by calling for equal access to services. After protracted negotiation with the army and the Freedmen's Bureau, the Richmond city council finally established separate quarters for blacks in the city's poorhouse in 1868. Tennessee's blacks gained segregated access to the state's lunatic asylum in 1868, the same year that North Carolina established the Negro Department at the Institution for the Deaf, Dumb and Blind.

Although most state and local welfare institutions had made segregated arrangements for blacks by the end of Reconstruction, some states lagged in providing any welfare services for blacks. When they finally did so, the new segregated quarters signified the end of exclusion rather than the end of integration. Georgia did not provide for the care of blind blacks until 1881 and the deaf and dumb until 1882; Alabama finally made provisions for all three categories of disadvantaged blacks in 1892; Virginia did not act until 1909. Virginia accepted support of the previously privately run Virginia Labor School of the Negro Reformatory eleven years after it had opened the Laurel Industrial School for white boys.

White and black desires also combined to produce a new pattern of housing segregation in southern cities. Prior to the Civil War, most urban slaves had lived in their masters' compounds. After the war, many blacks remained in alley dwellings behind the houses of prosperous whites, but most moved to the outskirts of town to the remnants of antebellum enclaves that had attracted some slaves and free Negroes or to freedmen's camps set up in the immediate postwar years by the victorious Yankees. Whites did not want blacks in their neighborhoods except as servants, and many blacks preferred to live among themselves in areas that contained their churches, schools, fraternal orders, places of amusement, and businesses. As early as 1881, an Atlanta reporter grasped, if only condescendingly, the extent to which residential segregation had become the foundation of the region's biracial society. "Far the largest proportion of Negroes are never really known to us," he wrote. "They are not employed in private homes nor in the business houses, but drift off to themselves, and are almost as far from the white people, so far as all practicable benefits of associations are concerned, as if the two races never met."

Whites demanded segregation in still other areas of life, including public conveyances, hotels, restaurants, and theaters, and blacks usually had no choice but to make the best of any limited flexibility open to them. Although the evidence is still unclear, it seems that integration was most common on city streetcars. Following an initial progression from exclusion to segregation, streetcars in Louisville, Richmond, New Orleans, and elsewhere evidently permitted a certain degree of integrated seating until the turn of the century. Integration existed less often on the region's railroads and was rarely, if ever, allowed on steamboats. With the exception of places frequented by the lower classes of both races, hotels, bars, and restaurants had either a black or a white clientele. Integration seems to have persisted in parks for a longer period—in the case of Raleigh's Pullem Park, well into the 1920s—but segregation was more common, and as early as 1890, the *Atlanta Constitution* could assure its readers that the city's new zoo contained separate seven-foot-wide aisles for blacks and whites, one on each side of the row of eight cages that occupied the center of the building. "There is no communication between them, and two large double doors at each side of the building serve as entrance and exit to the aisles." It is not known whether the animals were told which way to face.

Segregation, then, was pervasive in most areas of southern life during the immediate postwar years. Much of it was the legacy of the Reconstruction governments, which sought to end exclusion and assure that separate treatment would be equal treatment. The new Conservative governments accepted the shift from exclusion to segregation, but quickly abandoned all but the pretense of equal treatment. Everywhere the needs of poor and disadvantaged whites were met first; only then were the needs of blacks considered, provided, of course, that funds were still available. When Fulton County, Georgia, belatedly decided to erect new poorhouse facilities in 1889, $8,000 was spent for a one-story brick building for whites and $1,500 for six double wooden cottages for blacks on the other side of the woods. The quarters for blacks at the Tennessee School for the Blind were, in the view of an administrator, "ill adapted for a school—they were originally residences and are situated on a busy thoroughfare."

The separate but relatively equal school systems of Reconstruction bore the brunt of discriminatory attention. By the 1880s, appropriations were as much as ten times greater for white than for black education. Although educational opportunities were particularly lacking in the countryside, urban blacks confronted severe discrimination as well. Black teachers, regardless of their qualifications, were paid up to 40 percent less than whites; black schools were likely to be constructed of wood, whereas white schools were made of brick; many communities refused to establish black high schools; black school terms generally were much shorter; and serious overcrowding was widespread because of a combination of inadequate facilities and a growing black population that was eager to learn. In 1912, student-teacher ratios in Nashville, one of the South's more "progressive" systems, were 33:1 for whites and 71:1 for blacks.

Beginning in the late 1880s and accompanying the disfranchisement legislation, which weakened the ability of blacks to resist, the region's race relations entered a new phase that included alterations in the system of segregation. Several reasons have been offered for this shift, including worsening eco-

nomic conditions, increased political turmoil, and the withdrawal of northern support for black rights.

No single factor, however, was enough to account for the
changed nature of segregation. Some of the early segregation
had been *de jure*, that is, sanctioned by law. Whether by state
constitutions, state laws, or local ordinances, schools, cemeteries, militia companies, and welfare institutions were required to practice segregation. Most other instances of segregation, however, were sanctioned by custom, that is, were *de
facto*. Attempts to end both forms of segregation through the
passage of federal civil rights legislation proved unsuccessful.
The Civil Rights Act of 1875, which could be interpreted as
guaranteeing separate but equal access rather than integration,
had been stripped of the clauses covering schools and cemeteries before becoming law and was nevertheless already a dead
letter before the Supreme Court declared it unconstitutional
in 1883.

The Supreme Court's action, Congress's refusal to protect
southern blacks, the apathy or outright hostility of northern
voters, and other evidence that the North was ready to let the
South deal with its "Negro Problem" helped usher in a new
period in which customary practices were given the force of
law. Once the North made it clear that it would not interfere
with the South's new "peculiar institutions" and some blacks
challenged the *de facto* practices that had emerged in the immediate postwar years, white southerners institutionalized segregation and extended it to new areas of southern life.

Beginning in 1881 with Tennessee's separate coach law,
which mandated black access to separate first-class accommodations for a first-class fare, southern states passed new
legislation requiring separate accommodations for blacks in
theaters, parks, and public conveyances. There were even to
be "Jim Crow" (that is, separate) water fountains, bathrooms,
phone booths, and courtroom bibles. Prominently displayed
"Colored" and "White" signs and the laws that compelled
them served, according to one historian, as "public symbols
and constant reminders" of the southern black's inferior status.

In *Plessy* v. *Ferguson* (1896), a case that grew out of a Louisiana statute requiring segregation on that state's railroads, the U.S. Supreme Court held that such separation was constitutional as long as both races received equal treatment. That rarely occurred, but only in *Buchanan* v. *Warley* (1917), a decision that struck down government-enforced residential segregation in several southern cities, was any form of segregation successfully challenged in court. Even without the force of law, however, a combination of white discrimination and, to a lesser extent, black choice produced widespread *de facto* segregation in housing.

Although an occasional facility remained integrated into the twentieth century (usually ones where the lower classes of both races intermingled), and vestiges of exclusion persisted, the policy of separate and *unequal* treatment of the races had become firmly entrenched in the South by the turn of the century.

A deteriorating economic situation, disfranchisement, and institutionalized segregation were bad enough, but the new period of race relations also brought an escalation in anti-black political rhetoric and an epidemic of lynchings. The actual figures are unknown, but between 1882, for which we have the first relatively reliable statistics, and 1903 a reported 1,985 blacks (including 40 women) were lynched. After reaching a high of over 200 in the depression year of 1892, the numbers steadily declined, dropping to fewer than 100 a year between 1904 and 1920. An occasional white might be lynched, but between 1882 and 1930, 500 of Mississippi's 545 victims were black, as were 474 of Georgia's 508. Although the press and white politicians such as James Vardaman claimed that lynching was necessary to punish black rapists, fewer than one-third of the black victims were actually accused of rape, let alone guilty of it.

Lynching, which often was accompanied by grotesque mutilation and burning of the victim's body, was in fact most often employed as a social-control device to keep blacks "in their place" following real or imagined examples of black social, political, or economic "uppityness." It also provided a form of mass recreation for largely isolated, frustrated, and entertainment-starved white rural populations. In one instance, according to George Tindall, "mobs outraged by the killing of a white planter stormed across two South Georgia counties for a week, hanged three innocent men, strung up the pregnant widow of one by the ankles, doused her clothing with gasoline, and after it burned away, cut out her unborn child and trampled it underfoot, then riddled her with bullets. A man who finally confessed the original murder was shot, his body unsexed and dragged through the streets of Valdosta." Urban white populations preferred unprovoked and indiscriminate mass attacks on individual blacks and black neighborhoods, as in Wilmington, North Carolina (1899), New Orleans (1900), and Atlanta (1906). The situation was so bad in South Florida in 1898 that a Bahamian immigrant appealed to England's Queen Victoria for protection against lynching and injustice in Miami: "Some of our number have been lynched and others have had mock trials and [been] hanged or imprisoned unjustly—and we live in fear of mob violence from the southern white element."

Confronted by the increase in racial hostility, blacks had to choose among various strategies for survival that dated from the antebellum period. One possibility was to leave America. Emigrationist sentiment among blacks was already evident in the African colonization efforts of the black sea captain Paul Cuffee at the beginning of the nineteenth century and the Massachusetts-based, but Virginia-born, Dr. Martin Delany during the 1850s. The idea of blacks "returning" to Africa (most had never been there) had also been endorsed by the all-white American Colonization Society, whose membership had included James Madison and Henry Clay. Colonization agitation died down during the Civil War and Reconstruction, but flared up again in the late 1870s and continued through the 1890s. Delany, who had recruited black troops for the Union war effort and had been active in South Carolina politics, cosponsored a group of immigrants to Liberia. The leading proponent of colonization, however, was Henry M. Turner of Georgia, a bishop of the African Methodist Episcopal Church who urged his people to "Respect Black." Yet few blacks emigrated to Liberia; even Turner did not. Perhaps about as many went to Canada, which already contained enclaves of runaway slaves, antebellum free Negroes, and their descendants. The basic impact of the nascent "Back to Africa" movement was to strengthen interest in Africa among some black intellectuals and to add to a sense of ethnic pride and black nationalism. Black politician and journalist George Washington Williams of Ohio, for example, produced the *History of the Negro Race in America from 1619 to 1880* (1882), the first scholarly treatment of the subject. Not until Marcus Garvey's movement in the 1920s would emigration to Africa capture the imagination of the black masses, and even then it would be strongest among those in large northern cities.

A variant of black nationalism was internal colonization—the attempt to establish exclusively black communities within the United States. Benjamin "Pap" Singleton, a Nashville realtor, was the most visible black advocate for the "Exodus of 1879," the most important and largely spontaneous movement that drew thousands of black migrants to Kansas and led to the founding of such all-black towns as Nicomedus. Around the turn of the century, other blacks flocked to the towns of Langston (1891), Clearview (1903), and Boley (1908) in the new Oklahoma Territory. At least fifty black towns existed in the South in 1910. A black reporter proudly pointed in 1912 to the most famous one, Mount Bayou, Mississippi, "a town owned and operated by our people," a place where "a black mayor with his black aldermen sit in the council chambers making laws," where "a black marshall carries the billy, a black postmaster passes out the mail, a black ticket agent sells the tickets and the white man's waiting room is in the rear." Some of these towns enjoyed initial success, but none ever had more than 5,000 people and all were in decline by the second decade of the twentieth century. Their autonomy was limited by reliance on all-white county governments for a variety of public services. They were also going against the grain of twentieth-century life, in which small towns of all kinds were being overwhelmed. Most were little more than ghost towns by the 1920s and 1930s.

A third alternative for blacks was to remain in the South and try to change the system. An estimated 60,000 blacks were active in the Knights of Labor and many more joined the Populist ranks. Still others pressed for constitutional rights under the Thirteenth, Fourteenth, and Fifteenth amendments and the various civil rights acts. In conventions throughout the South, blacks demanded equal education, political rights, and equal justice. Most of them hoped that the Republican party would bring them relief. This protest orientation was epitomized by the Washington-based Frederick Douglass. A former slave who had escaped from Maryland in 1838, Douglass had been the country's leading black abolitionist. He emerged from the war as the most powerful black leader and retained that position until his death in 1895. In his view, "The Republican Party is the ship and all else the sea." A committed integrationist in both public and private matters (racists were appalled that his second wife was white), Douglass was personally rewarded with patronage positions, but his calls for fairer treatment of other blacks fell largely on deaf ears.

A new generation of blacks at both ends of the socioeconomic scale also engaged in various forms of protest against racial discrimination within the South. Blacks in some southern cities challenged the informal segregation on trains and streetcars. In Atlanta, groups of lower-class blacks, resentful of their treatment by the all-white police force, interceded physically on the streets to free black prisoners or prevent arrests. A young Memphis schoolteacher and newspaper editor, Ida Wells (later Wells-Barnett), unsuccessfully sued Tennessee because she had been forced to sit in a smoking car that had been designated for blacks, and began a lifelong crusade against lynching. After losing her teaching job and seeing her newspaper office destroyed, Wells was forced to flee for her life. She settled in Chicago, where she continued her campaign against racial injustice. Everywhere, members of the first generation of college-educated blacks asked why their educations, proper manners, and good behavior counted for so little. As the young editor of Nashville's *Fisk Herald* put it in 1889, "We are not the Negro from whom the chains of slavery fell a quarter of a century ago. . . . we are now qualified, and being the equal of whites, should be treated as such." The cumulative effect of such actions probably encouraged white southerners to codify many of their *de facto* forms of discrimination.

W. E. B. Du Bois became the nation's major black voice for challenging segregation, economic exploitation, disfranchisement, and lynching. Du Bois was born in Great Barrington, Massachusetts, graduated from Fisk in 1888, and in 1895 became the first black to receive a Ph.D. (in history) from Harvard. For several years, he taught at Atlanta University, where he edited a landmark series of volumes on the status of blacks in the South (1897–1914). He then moved to the North to become editor of *The Crisis*, the journal of the National Association for the Advancement of Colored People (NAACP), the new interracial protest organization he had helped found in 1910. Speaking for what he called the "Talented Tenth" of educated, middle-class blacks, Du Bois, most memorably in his powerful evocation of black life, *The Souls of Black Folk* (1903), called for an end to segregation, the return of the ballot, and governmental guarantees for black civil rights.

Prior to 1920, Du Bois and the NAACP had little impact on black life in the South. There were few challenges to the new Jim Crow system, and NAACP chapters did not become active in the South until the end of World War I. But even in the nation at large, the integrationist and protest orientation of Du Bois and the NAACP had less influence than the accommodationist approach of the new generally acknowledged leader of black America, Booker T. Washington.

Booker T. Washington was born in Virginia, the son of a black slave and an unidentified white man. After emancipation, he worked briefly in West Virginia coal mines and salt furnaces before obtaining a rudimentary education that eventually led him to study at Hampton Institute from 1872 to 1875. Hampton was founded by Samuel Chapman Armstrong, a former Union general who preached the virtues of personal morality, hard work, and industrial education as the best means for blacks to prosper in freedom. Washington adopted Armstrong's personal code of behavior and educational philosophy and sought to implement them at Tuskegee Normal and Industrial Institute, the school he founded in Tuskegee, Alabama, in 1881.

From his base in Tuskegee, Washington urged the substitution of racial pride for "amalgamation." In a sense, Washington endorsed a form of cultural pluralism practiced by some of the period's immigrants. He believed that blacks should have their own churches, businesses, and fraternal organizations. Washington subscribed to the American belief that "thrift, economy, and push" would result in improvement. The key for black success, he argued, was self-help. In his view, Reconstruction was a failure because it gave blacks rights and privileges they had not earned. Blacks, he said in his autobiography, *Up From Slavery* (1901), had to start at the bottom and work their way up. Not surprisingly, he inveighed against socialism, labor unions, and political agitation. Thus, he appealed to blacks to find a place in southern society without threatening whites, telling blacks to "cast down your bucket where you are."

Southern whites naturally welcomed such advice, which could be interpreted as black support for what has been called the New South Creed, and they warmly embraced and widely publicized a speech Washington gave at the Atlanta Cotton States and International Exposition in 1895. Taking place soon after Douglass's death, that appearance made Washington the natural successor to the old abolitionist's unofficial position as the nation's most important black leader. Dubbed by Du Bois the "Atlanta Compromise," Washington's speech announced that blacks should accept the status quo and seek progress through self-help and economic striving, and that "In all things that are purely social, we can be as separate as the fingers, yet one as the hand in all things essential to mutual progress." White northerners also were attracted to his message, and philanthropists and Republican politicians usually consulted Washington before making any decisions that would affect southern blacks. White southerners were comfortable with Washington's northern ties, except when his acceptance of President Theodore Roosevelt's invitation to have dinner at the White House in 1901 provoked a regionwide furor.

Thus Booker T. Washington's public approach to problems facing black America contrasted sharply with that of Du Bois, and each man attracted allies who shared his point of view. In large part the differences between Washington and Du Bois stemmed from their differences in background. Du Bois was northern-born of a free, "aristocratic" heritage and had a liberal arts education. Washington was a southern-born, lower-class slave who used industrial education as a path to power and influence. Washington was seeking primarily to help one segment of the black community (the southern masses); Du Bois focused on the needs of another (the "Talented Tenth" in both the South and North). Although he accommodated to segregation and inequality, Washington never endorsed either as a permanent solution to racial strife. Rather, he had as his final goal equality and integration, but he believed that the mass of blacks were not yet ready for them. Du Bois said his class *was* ready, although he too believed in racial pride and solidarity.

There was also a private side to Washington that was concealed until his personal papers were opened to the public in the 1950s. This hidden Washington was very different from the public image that the "Wizard of Tuskegee" projected. In addition to demonstrating that Washington was a ruthless manipulator who used the bestowal or denial of northern patronage and philanthropy to reward or punish black newspapers, colleges, and individual leaders, his correspondence reveals his behind-the-scenes efforts to challenge the southern racial system. He used his considerable power to veto the appointment of white Republican and Democratic federal officeholders whom he deemed unsympathetic to racial progress and secretly funded a series of court cases aimed at ending segregation and peonage in the South.

But in the end, it was the public Washington who had the most impact. One could argue that Washington was simply doing the best he could under the circumstances, but there were at least three serious problems with his program to help blacks. First, he uncritically accepted the dominant laissez-faire philosophy of American business by insisting that everyone's future was in his own hands, whereas in reality the nation had been transformed by large-scale industrial capitalism. His National Negro Business League (1900) was thus more successful as a cheerleader than as an agent for grass-roots economic development. Second, Washington advocated industrial education for blacks to produce blacksmiths and other artisans at the very time that these jobs were being phased out by the changing economy. Third, and most important, Washington counseled blacks to remain in the rural South, the least dynamic sector of the nation's economy and the place most hostile to blacks in economic, political, and social terms. It is likely that most blacks would have done so without Washington's advice, but he no doubt influenced many. And his words and actions legitimized southern white behavior at the same time that they funneled northern funds into southern black institutions, such as Tuskegee, that sought to keep blacks in the South.

As late as 1900, then, more than 90 percent of the nation's blacks remained in the South, about 80 percent of them living in the countryside. Rural and urban blacks led quite different lives, but both groups coped with their hostile environments by turning to the three primary institutions of southern black life—family, church, and mutual benefit society.

The black family was the core of black life. It was once commonly believed that slavery, with its nonrecognition of slave marriages, forced separations, and limitations on the authority of black males, had irreparably inhibited the creation of strong black families. More recent research, however, has demonstrated that black slaves were able to forge strong family ties that outlasted slavery. In the immediate postwar years, white and black newspapers were filled with evidence of former slaves seeking to be reunited with loved ones. One notice in a Nashville black newspaper in 1866, for example, was placed by a Samuel Dove, whose family had been broken up by sale in Richmond, and who wrote from the North "to know of the whereabouts of his mother, Areno, his sisters Maria, Neziah, and Peggy, and his brother Edmond, who were owned by Geo. Dove, of Rockingham county, Shenandoah Valley, Va." According to a Freedmen's Bureau agent in South Carolina, the former slaves "had a passion not so much for wandering, as for getting together . . . every mother's son among them seemed to be in search of his mother; every mother in search of her children."

Given the high mortality among blacks, the frequent separations as males looked for work, and the fact that a higher proportion of blacks than whites were in prison, it is not surprising that more black than white families were headed by females. Yet in most places more than three-fourths of black households with children had two parents. Whether one or two parents were present, black households frequently consisted of three or even four generations. And, especially in rural areas, nuclear and extended families were linked by strong kinship networks that kept alive elements of black culture and brought both economic and psychological support.

Families were particularly important as economic units, unlike in slavery, when the black family had virtually no economic function. In cities, black women commonly worked as domestics, laundresses, and unskilled workers in order to supplement the family income or support themselves and their children. Wives of middle-class urban blacks either worked as schoolteachers or in other white-collar positions, or remained at home. But the family was especially important in the countryside.

Ned Cobb, an Alabama sharecropper immortalized in Theodore Rosengarten's *All God's Dangers* (1974), began plowing when he was nine years old and worked alongside his mother on his family's small plot of land. He later was hired out by his father to plow and haul logs under a "white man's administration." As an adult, he was able to join the ranks of cash renters (white chicanery prevented him from becoming a landowner), thanks not only to his own hard work and his skills as farmer, blacksmith, hauler of logs, and maker of ax handles and baskets, but also to the help of his sons. He did not allow his educated wife to work in the fields or do washing for white folks, but in addition to doing the housework, she handled the accounts and kept the local storekeepers and planters honest. As Ned put it, "A man can't prosper here by himself." He continued to support his father (whom he hated), and when Ned in turn grew old, he was able to buy a small house with the help of his stepdaughter, who was a supervisor in a Boston hospital.

Family and kinship groups also provided a foundation for much of the region's religious life among blacks. This was especially true in the small churches of the countryside, but also was evident in the cities. The churches reflected the emerging class differences among blacks. The overwhelming majority of blacks were Baptists and Methodists, but there was a significant sorting out along class lines within these denominations following the formation of black churches during the immediate postemancipation years, particularly in the cities. Members of the black elite, which included teachers, ministers, small businessmen, lawyers and doctors, and self-employed craftsman, worshipped in Baptist and Methodist churches that were separate from those of the working and lower classes. Other members of the elite were drawn to the Congregational, Episcopalian, and Presbyterian denominations.

In general, the elite preferred educated preachers, learned sermons, and decorous services. The black masses, however, wanted their churches to provide an emotional experience that would help ease the burden of their difficult lives. W. H. Crogman, a black professor at Clark University, told of an old-fashioned preacher who decried the fact that Atlanta's twenty-five black public school teachers no longer attended his church, preferring instead "that fashionable church on the next street." The clergyman felt that it was a sign that the younger generation was less devout, but Crogman disagreed.

With their enlarged intellectual life, they [young blacks] are naturally craving for a higher order of pulpit instruction. Their fathers were satisfied to be made happy. The children, of necessity less emotional and excitable, desire to have their reason appealed to as well. They expect to be instructed and helped and strengthened. The pulpit that cannot supply this demand will not hold the rising generation.

As critical whites were fond of pointing out when they wished to belittle what one called "the hysteric emotionalism of revival preaching," there were many pulpits that chose to ignore the "rising generation." But even a member of the middle class, Montgomery's Bertha McClain, acknowledged that one of her reasons for attending Old Ship African Methodist Episcopal (AME) Zion church was "to hear the people mourn and shout."

The churches were more than houses of worship. They also functioned as social centers, the last refuge of self-government, and surrogates for unresponsive local governments. "They had many and varied programs for the young and old alike," remembered Bertha McClain. City churches were better than those in the country, she maintained, because "they could touch people more often than just once or twice per month which was customary in rural churches." As the *Atlanta Constitution* noted, "the colored man not only takes his spiritual information but also his special information from the pulpit." Many of the first postbellum black schools had been born in churches at a time when blacks were still excluded from the public schools. Congregations were responsible for organizing orphanages and hospitals and providing a variety of relief services. Although usually thought of as encouraging otherworldliness and accommodation to oppression, many churches and preachers drew on the prophetic dimension of black religion and were active in protests against racial injustice. Some churches even served an economic function within the black community.

The most important institutional impact of the black church, however, involved its relationship to the third basic element of the black community—the fraternal order and mutual benefit society. Beginning with the Free African Society of Philadelphia, founded in 1787, such voluntary associations of blacks were often either the progenitors or the offspring of black churches. After the Civil War, a bewildering array of national societies, including the black Masons, Odd Fellows, Elks, and Grand United Order of True Reformers, which often were composed of members of the same church, and other more local and directly church-related benefit societies provided outlets for social interaction and status seeking and performed needed charitable work. Most important, by providing low-cost burial insurance and a guaranteed group of mourners, the societies assured their members of the kind of respect in death that the larger society had denied them in life. "Insurance" was so important to blacks in rural Mississippi, for example, that sociologist Hortense Powdermaker found it to be as much a cultural staple as "church going, hunting and fishing." Nor was the benefit society an all-male world. Maggie Lena Walker, who became one of the wealthiest black women in the country and was a member of the board of directors of the NAACP, used her Richmond-based Independent Order of St. Luke to develop a broad range of institutions, including a savings bank, a newspaper, and a department store. As W. E. B. Du Bois observed in 1906, the beneficial societies were "next to the church ... the most popular organizations among Negroes."

Such societies also served as spawning grounds for such enterprises as North Carolina Mutual (1898) and Atlanta Life (1905), which sold insurance to blacks, whom white companies ignored. Like the societies, North Carolina Mutual was an expression of an ideology of self-help and racial solidarity. By 1924 it had established in Durham, "the Capital of the Black

Middle Class," a commercial bank, a savings and loan institution, a fire insurance company, a cotton mill, and the National Negro Finance Corporation, which functioned as a national financial clearinghouse and chamber of commerce.

The efforts of black churches and societies helped temper some of the neglect of black needs by white-controlled government agencies. This support was especially evident in the early postwar years, but it also was present during the Progressive Era. Although white progressives focused their efforts on controlling blacks and helping whites, many blacks, especially those in the cities, embraced much of the progressive agenda and sought to bring economic progress, political rights, and "social uplift" to other blacks. Leading this effort was the small but growing black elite, which was middle class in character but functioned as an upper class within the black community.

This identifiable black elite, or black bourgeoisie, as it is sometimes derisively called, had emerged in southern cities by the 1880s. Whether in fraternal organizations, political rallies, business ventures, or social gatherings, the same names continually reappeared. Nashville lawyer and businessman J. C. Napier was active in both St. Paul's AME and the First Colored Baptist, a state and city officeholder, a member of the state Republican Executive Committee, president of the Negro branch of the YMCA, and a member of several temperance and fraternal societies. N. P. Vandervall, a grocer, was a longtime member of Richmond's prestigious First African Baptist, in which he filled every position but pastor; he also belonged to the Mechanics Society and the Union Friendship Society, served as treasurer of a local Odd Fellows lodge, sat on the city council for six years, and was a trustee of the Negro orphanage, the Odd Fellows Hall, and the Union Burial Ground. Robert Steele, Atlanta's leading barber catering to whites, was an elder at Bethel AME Church, a trustee of the Carrie Steele Orphan Home (run by his mother), and a member of both the Masonic Lodge and the Afro-American Historical Society.

Middle-class blacks, whether as individuals or as members of civic and service organizations, drew on a strong tradition of self-help and racial pride and were especially concerned about the deplorable living conditions of poor blacks and the lack of services in black neighborhoods. Black women's clubs, whose members were barred from the all-white General Federation of Women's Clubs, were particularly active in the effort to increase public spending or provide privately funded support. Nashville's Phillis Wheatley Club, for example, supported a "day care home" for working mothers, and the Virginia Federation of Colored Women's Clubs sponsored the Virginia Industrial School for Colored Girls. The most successful women's club was Atlanta's Neighborhood Union, led by Lugenia Burns Hope, the wife of Atlanta Baptist (later Atlanta University) president John Hope. The union, begun in 1908 in an effort to establish a playground for black children, followed the example of Chicago's Hull House by launching cleanup campaigns, establishing a health center, and disseminating health information through home visits and instructional literature.

Other groups of blacks petitioned city governments to improve streets, housing, and sanitation, to build parks, and to enforce fire codes in black areas. Sometimes they were able to get new parks, often the first for blacks, by claiming that access to parks would reduce black crime. Similar arguments, based on appeals to white fears rather than a sense of justice, were also effective in securing correctional facilities for black juveniles. Blacks in more than twenty-five southern cities, including Atlanta, New Orleans, and Nashville, further demonstrated that they took the ideal of social justice more seriously than did white progressives by staging (unsuccessful) boycotts of streetcar lines after the imposition of legally enforced segregation.

But like progressives in general, black reformers were most concerned with education. In 1913 the Atlanta Neighborhood Union established a social improvement committee to "better conditions of the Negro in the public schools of Atlanta." After a six-month fact-finding investigation in which every black school was inspected, members of the committee lobbied the mayor, school board, city council, white religious leaders, and influential white women. With support from the northern-based Russell Sage Foundation and the NAACP, Atlanta blacks were able to use their small but pivotal vote to determine the outcome of local school bond referenda and gain an additional school and higher salaries for black teachers. They also helped defeat the effort in Georgia to divide the school fund between the races in proportion to the taxes each paid. In 1924, they finally secured the opening of Booker T. Washington High School, the city's first black high school. Similar protests produced the first Negro branches of city public libraries, ending decades of exclusion in such cities as Atlanta, New Orleans, and Birmingham.

Throughout the South blacks solicited funds from primarily northern-financed sources, such as the Slater Fund, the Jeanes Foundation, and the General Education Board, and raised money in their own communities for the expansion of their private schools and colleges. In 1917 the Georgia legislature finally established a normal school for black teachers and increased appropriations for the Savannah Industrial School. Protests over white control of black colleges also began to bear fruit. John Hope was appointed Atlanta Baptist's first black president and other black presidents followed elsewhere.

The black middle class also engaged in social uplift activities. Black churches were active in the numerous prohibition efforts that swept the South. They also were in the forefront of campaigns calling for crackdowns on prostitution, gambling, and other forms of vice in black neighborhoods, sections of the city to which white politicians, most notably in Memphis and New Orleans, had sought to confine various forms of illicit behavior. Such efforts were tinged by a self-righteous moralism that both reflected and exacerbated intrarace class divisions. They also further undermined features of a sometimes exaggerated, but no less real, antebellum communal lifestyle that already had been weakened by the breakup of the slave quarters, abolition of collective work patterns, and growing socio-economic differentiation. One Nashville black supported the "cleansing" of the city's notorious Black Bottom district because "the white people make no distinction between the different classes of negroes whereas we make several distinct grades."

In the end, efforts at self-help and racial solidarity and the feeble support of a few well-intentioned whites failed to convince a new generation of blacks that the South was indeed the best place for them. The outbreak of World War I gave them the opportunity to leave. There always had been a trickle of migration to the North, most notably in the first decade of the twentieth century as some of the "Talented Tenth" moved to northern cities. But between 1914 and 1920 an estimated 600,000 blacks went North. These migrants were quite different from their predecessors. Earlier twentieth-century migrants had been part of a gradual two-step migration that carried them from the rural areas to border cities of the upper South before they continued on to the urban North. But now participants in the so-called Great Migration tended to move in an explosive burst directly North from the rural areas of the Deep South, using the Illinois Central Railroad in the Midwest or coastal railroads and steamboat lines in the Mid-Atlantic states. These new migrants not only were less familiar with urban life, but also were poorer and less skilled and educated than their predecessors.

The black exodus of the war years testified to the emptiness of New South promises. Both "push" and "pull" factors drew blacks from southern farms to northern cities. Blacks were "pushed" out of the South by the increase in racial violence and political and social discrimination, and especially by the economic crisis associated with wide-scale flooding and the spread of the boll weevil—the boll weevil in particular proved to Ned Cobb that "all God's dangers ain't a white man." At the same time, blacks were "pulled" northward by prospects of fairer political and social treatment, and especially by the demand for labor in meat-packing, mining, steel, chemical, and other industries in the wake of the wartime cutoff of foreign immigration and the enlistment of white workers in the armed forces. The Great Migration was largely a spontaneous movement. Unlike previous black responses to the inadequacies of southern life, it did not have any national or even regional spokesmen. It was, however, encouraged by northern black newspapers such as the *Chicago Defender,* which asked, "Do you wonder at the thousands leaving the land where every foot of ground marks a tragedy, leaving the graves of their fathers and all that is dear, to seek their fortunes in the North?" For many blacks, the North would give less succor than they had hoped for. In 1917, whites in East St. Louis, Illinois, for example, produced the century's bloodiest race riot. However, there would be some, like the migrant to Akron, Ohio, who could write home, "I am making good."

As much as anything else, the exodus, which was accompanied by an even larger desertion by white southerners for many of the same economic reasons, announced the failure of the First New South.

Class over Race: White Life

For blacks in southern society, race counted far more than individual socioeconomic characteristics. Whether blacks were college-educated urban professionals or illiterate sharecroppers, they were equally likely to suffer from disfranchisement, segregation, and the threat of lynching. Whites, too, were defined by their race, although *their* color guaranteed rather than cost them access to certain rights and opportunities.

The various segments of the white population shared more than their race and a belief in white supremacy. As we have seen, southern whites shared a common belief in the ideals loosely associated with the Democratic party. And, like their black counterparts, they placed a high value on family and kinship ties. Although the nuclear family predominated, extended-family living arrangements were common and family honor was as prized as personal honor. Family dynasties frequently controlled local politics, particularly in the country-side, and businesses often depended on family financing. In theory, paternal authority was unchallenged and wives were expected to take care of the home and the children, whatever other responsibilities they might have to assume. Such atti-tudes also were common in the North, but southerners seemed to hold onto them more fiercely, as was revealed by their op-position to women's suffrage. Even today, regular family visits and special reunions, to say nothing of the tending of graves, seem far more common among southerners. And nowhere out-side of Mormon Utah was genealogy as entrenched. Although Charleston, South Carolina, carried family affiliation to ex-tremes, a local proverb nicely captured one of the region's basic traits: "Inquiring of a young stranger, it is asked in Boston, 'How much does he know?'; in New York, 'How much is he worth?'; in Charleston, 'Who was his grandfather?' "

Southern whites were ethnically the most homogeneous group of whites in the country. The region's small number of immigrants often has led historians (incorrectly) to ignore their impact on southern life. The Irish played a significant role in southern urban politics and as laborers, particularly in Mem-phis, Richmond, and New Orleans. Jewish merchants, usually of German descent, figured prominently in business affairs and politics; there was a "Jewish seat" on the Atlanta board of education, and during Reconstruction both the Radical mayor of Montgomery and his Conservative successor were Jewish. At the end of the century, New Orleans received a large number of Italian immigrants, and Cubans helped build Tampa's cigar industry.

But foreign immigration actually had declined in impor-tance in the South since the antebellum period. More than 25 percent of the urban population outside the South was foreign-born in 1880, but this was a true of only 10 percent of urban southerners. By 1910 that figure had dropped to 4.7 percent. Only the small Texas cities of Galveston (17 percent foreign-born), San Antonio (18 percent), and El Paso (37 percent) far exceeded the regional average because of their sizable Mexican populations. Although there were significant numbers of second-generation Irish- and German-Americans, most white southerners were of English and Scots-Irish stock—and defiantly proud of it. In the view of an Episcopal bishop, "The South above any other section represents Anglo-Saxon, native-born America"; to another clergyman, "The preservation of the American government is in the hands of the South, because Southern blood is purely American."

Such religious sanction was important, for, as also was true for blacks, religion occupied a special place in the lives of white southerners. Not only did the South lead the nation in the percentage of church members, but its religious practices also set it apart from the rest of the country. At a time when northern religion was becoming more heterogeneous, southern religion was becoming more homogeneous. Although small Jewish congregations flourished in the towns and cities, and Roman Catholicism was a powerful force in some Texas, upper South, and coastal communities and throughout Louisiana (where it attracted a majority of church members), a special kind of nondenominational Protestantism was practically the publicly sanctioned religion. Ever since the antebellum division of Methodists, Baptists, and Presbyterians into southern and northern wings, southern Protestantism had been set apart organizationally. It also differed doctrinally and in style of worship. There were many forms of Christianity, but evangelicalism was more important in the South than it was in the North.

In most states, at least 80 percent of white church members (close to 90 percent east of the Mississippi) were, like their black counterparts, Baptists and Methodists. There also were numerous adherents to Holiness, Pentecostal, Disciples of Christ, and other evangelical sects. The South was, as the writer Flannery O'Connor put it, "Christ-haunted." As historian Samuel Hill has noted, there were four basic characteristics of southern Protestantism: "(1) the Bible is the sole reference point of belief and practice; (2) direct and dynamic access to the Lord is open to all; (3) morality is defined in individualistic and personal terms; and (4) worship is informal." "On such concepts as heaven and hell, God and Satan, depravity and redemption, there was little dispute," writes historian Kenneth K. Bailey. "Few southerners doubted the literal authenticity of the Scriptures or the ever-presence of God in man's affairs." Most noteworthy was the emphasis on baptism, which, unique in western culture, was seen as more important than communion. This individualistic evangelical approach to religion focused on personal salvation. Thus it failed to encourage the kind of social ethic, present to a greater degree among otherwise similarly inclined black Protestants, that might have challenged the social, political, and economic status quo. Indeed, southern white Protestantism was one of the bulwarks of the existing social and political order. Although Populism and other protest movements at times resembled religious crusades, the Social Gospel movement, which transformed northern religion in the late nineteenth and early twentieth centuries by stressing an individual's responsibility to correct society's ills, largely bypassed the South.

A number of other shared values and activities set southerners apart as a group from whites in other sections of the country. Southern whites highly valued their "honor" and were not adverse to resorting to violence to defend it. Even more readily than in the rest of a violent nation, they found other reasons for violence as well. As Edward Ayers has noted in *Vengeance and Justice: Crime and Punishment in the 19th Century South* (1984), a mix of a sense of honor, sexual fears, and "republicanism" (the belief that corruption and the market economy were undermining the status of yeomen) prepared the way for a particularly disturbing outbreak of violence at the end of the century. Crystallized by the economic downturn that began at the end of the 1880s, these elements manifested themselves in the Black Belt in lynching and barn burning and in the upcountry in "whitecapping" (vigilante action), feuds, employer-labor violence, and moonshine battles.

There was certainly no shortage of weapons. In 1881 the appraised value of guns, pistols, and dirks in Alabama, for example, was greater than that of tools and farming implements. Not surprisingly, southern states far outdistanced the rest of the country in homicides. South Carolina reported nearly three times as many homicides as the six New England states in 1890. Similar statistics for other states led C. Vann Woodward to conclude that "The South seems to have been one of the most violent communities of comparable size in all Christendom."

Even when southerners used the legal system to punish acts of violence, they demonstrated their fascination with violence. Public hangings were especially popular community events. Some ten thousand to twelve thousand people showed up at the natural amphitheater chosen as the site for murderer Knox Martin's execution outside Nashville in 1879. One Nashville teacher was besieged with notes from parents of her students. "Please excuse Joseph—he wants to see the man hung—by request of his mother," said one. "If you will let the children go to see Knox Martin hung today, I will not ask you any more," proclaimed another. "Please let Thomas go to the hanging. I hope it will do him good," pleaded a third.

The ethnic homogeneity of the white South, its strong identification with a peculiar brand of Protestantism, and its penchant for violence help account for the popularity of the Ku Klux Klan. The original KKK of the Reconstruction Era was formed in Pulaski, Tennessee, in 1866 by six young former Confederates who sought college-fraternity-like activities to alleviate their boredom. Membership grew, and when Klan members tired of playing pranks on one another, they turned to the more vicious pleasures of attacking blacks and the "outsiders" who supported them. As a result of Republican-initiated federal and state suppression efforts and the fact that it had achieved its political goals of limiting local Republican influence, this Klan had died out in most states by the early 1870s.

The second Klan was founded by Alabama preacher, salesman, and history teacher William J. Simmons near Atlanta in 1915 at a time when southern blacks had been "put in their place." Simmons envisioned a fraternal order from which he could profit through the sale of memberships, robes, and insurance. Galvanized in its recruiting efforts by members of the new advertising industry after World War I, the new Klan was less obsessed than its predecessor had been with blacks. Although it did not ignore blacks, particularly those in the North, it also publicized the alleged threats posed by Jews, immigrants, and Catholics to "Americanism," and particularly to southern womanhood. Whatever their differences, both Klans elicited active or passive support from all classes of white southerners, and the brilliantly marketed message of the second Klan was enticing enough to attract a large nationwide membership.

Yet although their skin color assured all whites of a status above blacks, marked differentiation within the hierarchically organized white segment of society made it clear that not only race counted in the First New South.

The great mass of whites, about 80 percent, fell into two classes. Although the two groups were very different, they were linked by the facts that they were white in a world that discriminated against blacks, and that they occupied the middle position in society between the black population and the white elite.

The first group consisted of lower-class whites (more than half of the white population), known to the rest of society as "poor whites" or, more pejoratively, as "rednecks" and "white trash." Even blacks looked down on them. "I had a little dog/ His name was Dash./I'd rather be a nigger/Than po'h white trash./I'd rather be a nigger an' plow ol' Beck,/Dan a white hill-billy wid a long red neck," went a popular black ditty. Such whites were sharecroppers and wage laborers in the plantation districts, unskilled and semiskilled operatives in the mill villages, mining camps, and cities, and subsistence farmers in the mountains. Their lives were remarkably similar to those of most blacks. They generally could not vote, had little or no schooling, and sought relief in revivalistic religion (that might, however, include snake handling and speaking in tongues), and gambling, hunting, fighting, and drinking. One Georgia planter complained that field work suffered because "my farm hands white and black are making fish traps . . . fish is the paramount idea with them." Poor whites rarely traveled far from home, and when they did it was likely to be by foot, mule, or in no better than second-class train cars. If they could afford a theater ticket, it would be for the balcony.

Their vulnerable economic position forced wives and young children into the labor market and helped disrupt family lives. In the Georgia and Carolina cotton mills in 1880, almost half of the workers were women and almost a quarter were children. Thanks to a number of factors—more men leaving farming and becoming mill workers, new equipment and practices that placed greater emphasis on strength and skill, and the beginnings of child labor reform—the respective figures dropped to 29 percent and 18 percent by 1909, but even these participation rates for women and children far exceeded those for other classes of white southerners or, for that matter, northerners. Pay was low—perhaps no more than $2.50 a week—and seventy-hour weeks were common. "By 1900 the cotton-mill worker was a pretty distinct physical type in the South," wrote W. J. Cash. "A dead-white skin, a sunken chest, and stooping shoulders were the earmarks of the breed. Chinless faces, microcephalic foreheads, rabbit teeth, goggling dead-fish eyes, rickety limbs, and stunted bodies abounded—over and beyond the limit of their prevalence in the country. The women were characteristically stringy-haired and limp of breast at twenty, and shrunken hags at thirty or forty."

Not only mill workers, but also poor whites in general were victims of a wide array of diseases. Inadequate diets—salt pork, cornmeal, and syrup or molasses were the staples—and poor working and living conditions produced a high incidence of pellagra (caused by vitamin deficiency), malaria (for which blacks had a natural immunity), hookworm, black lung (from mines), brown lung (from cotton mills and thus absent among the excluded blacks), and tuberculosis. Hookworm was an especially serious problem. Dubbed by one sarcastic journalist the "germ of laziness," the blood-sucking hookworm burrowed into the soles of bare feet and produced anemia, lethargy, pale skin, and other easily identifiable symptoms. As one researcher discovered, it was "primarily a 'poor man's' malady, and in frequency it far exceeds even the most extreme limit which theoretical deductions seemed to justify."

Poor whites became objects of concern and scorn for the white middle and upper classes. The sharp increase in the number of cotton mills and workers between 1895 and 1905 led, for example, to discovery of the "mill problem" in South Carolina. Editorials and public surveys pointed to increased "lawlessness" and the "anarchy" of a sickly floating population comprising "unfortunate yeomanry," "poor white trash," and "mountaineers." Motivated by a combination of humanitarianism and the desire to assert social control, reformers sought to end child labor, initiate compulsory education, and institute public health measures that included the registration of births and mandatory medical inspections and smallpox vaccinations. Beginning in 1909, the Rockefeller Sanitary Commission for the Eradication of Hookworm Disease represented the most systematic public health effort during the period. But, as with pellagra and malaria, the war against hookworm was not won until after 1920.

Already concerned about attempts to introduce black textile workers, efforts at disfranchisement, and other suspected breaches of white solidarity, mill parents resented the intrusion of the state into health matters and family relations, especially when it threatened their authority over children upon whose income they depended. Playing upon such fears, Governor Cole Blease, in vetoing a law in 1912 that mandated medical inspections for all South Carolina schoolchildren, declared, "If I had a daughter I would kill any doctor . . . whom I would be forced to let examine her against her will and mine." Mill parents' opposition to health legislation and other reforms, including child labor laws, both reflected class antagonism and further exacerbated it.

The second group in the great mass of whites, the middle and "respectable" working classes, was higher on the socio-economic scale than the lower-class whites. Consisting of between a quarter and a third of the white population, this was a heterogenous group that included the prosperous tenant farmers and small landowners of the countryside and the clerks, bookkeepers, salesmen, small businessmen, and skilled workers and mill foremen of the towns. They were part of the less than 50 percent of the population that was qualified to vote. Relatively large and secure incomes might enable them to purchase a house and employ a servant. The women ordinarily were able to stay out of the labor market and the children could finish at least eighth grade. Like the poor whites, they were overwhelmingly Baptist or Methodist, but they were more likely to be active church members and to belong to less emotionally oriented churches. They had more leisure time than the lower-class whites and they joined a variety of associations that ranged from unions and fraternal lodges to fire companies, militia units, and athletic teams. They entertained in their homes but also frequented "respectable" bars and restaurants, sat in the better sections of the theater, and the most successful among them traveled in first-class train cars. The combination of leisure time and greater discretionary income made them the most likely spectators at horse races and other sporting events, including baseball, the new national pastime. They had frequent contact with the elite and might even belong to some of the same organizations, and could be counted on to support such "reforms" as prohibition and disfranchisement. Particularly in the countryside, they were likely to be related to the elite by marriage.

The remaining 10 to 15 percent of the white population consisted of the entrepreneurs, industrialists, and professionals of the cities—what historians have called the "commercial-civic elite" or "new business class"—and the planter class and their county-seat allies. The planters and the "new men" of the cities might disagree over specific issues and were often found in different wings of the Democratic party, but they produced the Conservative leadership that overthrew Reconstruction, battled the Populists, disfranchised blacks and poor whites, and largely shaped Progressivism's agenda.

They also were united by a lifestyle that set them apart from other whites. Their wealth, of course, gave them options unavailable to the rest of society. Wives supervised the servants and children at home and engaged in frequent visiting. The socially conscious among them did good works in the community, whether as individuals or as members of the growing number of women's clubs that in 1910 coalesced to form the General Federation of Women's Clubs. In less need of religious excitement than their poorer counterparts, the wealthy joined the more prestigious and restrained Baptist or Methodist congregations, or were Episcopalians, Presbyterians, and, in the lower South, Catholics. Barred from major leadership roles within congregations, the women were the prime movers behind such organizations as the Methodists' Board of Home Missions, the Baptists' Women's Missionary Union, and the Women's Christian Temperance Union.

Members of the elite entertained lavishly at home, attended gala social events, took frequent vacations, and sent their children to private schools and colleges, sometimes in the North, not merely to educate them but also to strengthen and perpetuate class identity. In what one historian has termed "architectural exhibitionism," the urban elite constructed elaborate homes in their own separate neighborhoods. These neighborhoods were located near the downtown areas of such older cities as Charleston and New Orleans, but in newer cities, such as Nashville, Atlanta, and Birmingham, they could be found increasingly in parklike suburban enclaves. The elite traveled in first-class accommodations on trains and steamships, stayed in the best hotels, ate in the best restaurants, and sat in the best sections of the theater. Active in the community, the men were the officers of the militia units and fraternal lodges and the founders of social clubs, such as Atlanta's Capital City Club, and boards of trade and chambers of commerce. Men and women supported an array of literary clubs, country clubs, symphony orchestras, and museum societies that began to appear for the first time in the 1880s. The men owned and often edited the leading newspapers and, even when not public officials themselves, had easy access to the centers of political power that magnified their economic power.

Thus, although they shared many of the same values, the members of each of the three major classes in white society expressed their common characteristics in different ways. White attitudes were most complex when it came to two issues at the heart of the First New South—the "Race Question" and the "Lost Cause."

As we have seen, black attitudes and decisions played a role in the creation of the new system of race relations that emerged to replace slavery. Yet the actions of whites were far more important. Commitment to white supremacy had been a constant among southern whites since the colonial period, but its expression varied according to changing national and regional circumstances. Too often white attitudes are seen as monolithic. In fact, suggested solutions to the "Race Question" or "Negro Problem" revealed a mixture of consensus and conflict among whites that often reflected class tensions in white society.

Although frequently lumped together under the rubrics "Jim Crow" or "racial oppression," the region's examples of racial discrimination had significantly different origins and sources of support. As we have seen, disfranchisement was largely the work of rural and urban elites who sought to reassure the white masses of the centrality of race solidarity at the same time as they were "purifying" the electorate by eliminating significant numbers of poorer whites who might challenge Conservative hegemony. Lynching and other forms of violence against blacks, on the other hand, although occasionally endorsed, encouraged, rationalized, or even participated in by the upper and upper-middle classes, primarily involved whites farther down the socioeconomic ladder. The segregation of the races, however, seems to have enjoyed the support of all whites, though often for quite different reasons.

Whites of all classes defended segregation as the only way to prevent "social equality." What they meant by the term was not merely integration, but eventual intermarriage or "amalgamation." Henry Grady, who assured the North that his region was best qualified to deal fairly with the Negro, argued that the South "must carry these races in peace, for discord means ruin. She must carry them separately, for assimilation means debasement." This fear was expressed most explicitly in the passage of antimiscegenation legislation, which ironically, if indirectly, acknowledged the forbidden thought that white women might indeed be interested in black men. It also was evident in efforts to prevent racial intermingling in schools, welfare institutions, public accommodations, or any other area of southern life. Such "intermingling" would necessarily lead to "social equality," that is, intermarriage. "The whole people of this state are not ready to accept the perfect social and political equality of the blacks with them," wrote the *Nashville Union and American* in opposing passage of the Fourteenth Amendment in 1866.

They are not prepared to admit the Negro . . . to indiscriminate mingling in the social circle, at church, in the ball room, in the theatre, in the concert hall, in railroad cars, in the parlor, and at hotels and watering places. They have not yet satisfied themselves of the superiority of the theory of miscegenation and the improving results of amalgamation; and are not, therefore, ready to open the doors of marriage between the races, either by legal enactment or in the more solemn form of constitutional provision.

Without any evidence for either assumption, Hilary Herbert, an Alabama congressman and secretary of the navy under President Cleveland, believed that blacks wanted the promise allegedly made to them by Radicals of "absolute and complete social equality, equal rights not only in public conveyances, hotels and theatres, but also in the relations of marriage."

Sexual anxieties and perceived challenges to the "manhood" of individual whites contributed to such fears of social equality, resulting in the stereotype of what historian Joel Williamson has called "the black beast rapist" that was used to justify lynching. Ignoring the statistical evidence that rape was the cause of less than a third of all lynchings, even a respectable Conservative gentleman such as Mississippi Senator John Sharp Williams could rant that "Race is greater than law now and then, and protection of women transcends all law, human and divine." On the other end of the social scale, the less-cultured, plebeian Cole Blease was more direct: "Whenever the Constitution comes between me and the virtue of the white women of South Carolina, then I say 'to hell with the Constitution!' "

Opposition to social equality could emerge in the most unlikely places. In the 1880s, for example, five blacks served as clerks under a Democratic postmaster in Atlanta, but, as the *Atlanta Constitution* was quick to point out, each of them was segregated from white co-workers. Upon the return of the Republicans in 1889, the appointment of a black man as clerk in the registered letter department caused a furor. A white man and his daughter immediately resigned from the department on the grounds that the woman should not be brought into such close contact with a Negro. The new Republican postmaster pointed out that the black's desk was separated from those of the two whites by a brick wall and that he had been given that position deliberately to keep him away from the public. Despite these measures, both the black clerk and his political sponsor were burned in effigy, and two of the signers of the postmaster's bond withdrew their names. No doubt fearing a similar reaction during the following year, the Republican postmaster in Raleigh refused to put a black man at the general delivery window because of the close contact with white women.

For the great mass of whites, such discrimination was a source of increased self-esteem and a sign of both their links with the elite and their superiority over blacks. For members of the elite, of course, such measures were less important in terms of their actual contact with blacks. Many sent their children to private schools, pursued expensive entertainments, purchased first-class travel accommodations, and in other

ways were able to avoid contact with blacks except on the
hierarchical level of employer-employee or businessman-cus-
tomer. Segregation laws, then, were not directly for their benefit. They favored them in order to appease the white masses,
but also because such practices enhanced the elite's prospects
for maintaining power and social control. Segregation kept the
rest of society divided, and, by preventing either collusion or
conflict, met the elite's long-term interests.

There also was an economic dimension to segregation.
After all, more was at stake than social status. It is now fashionable to see the South's racial system as an American form
of apartheid. Although there are obvious similarities, the South
in fact had nothing comparable to the wide-ranging South African laws enforcing segregated living arrangements and labor
practices. The Supreme Court, as we have seen, struck down
urban residential segregation ordinances, and nothing came of
North Carolina editor Clarence Poe's proposal in the second
decade of the twentieth century to extend segregation to rural
land ownership. Segregated work patterns did exist, but they
were not required by law. The cotton mills, of course, provided
the most notable example of exclusionary labor policy in the
South, but a 1915 law in South Carolina seems to have been
the only one that formally segregated employment. Still, job
discrimination was widespread, although it is not always clear
whether that was the responsibility primarily of white workers
or of their employers. When local industrialists hired black
workers for some Charleston cotton mills at the turn of the
century, white workers threatened race warfare. Opposition by
white workers and the reluctance of blacks to work for lower
wages than they could receive in the fields doomed these particular efforts. But, as when blacks were brought in earlier to
replace white strikers at the Charleston Shoe Factory, white
employers were not averse to ignoring worker demands when
it was in their interest to do so. And even in those industries
that employed blacks, owners sought to use the threat of black
advancement to limit white demands for better wages and
working conditions.

Nevertheless, organized labor sometimes sought to incorporate blacks. In the late 1880s, the Knights of Labor, most notably in Richmond, admitted blacks, though usually in segregated assemblies. New Orleans, with probably the strongest labor movement in the South, witnessed united action by black and white union members that resulted in increased wages, shorter work days, and improved conditions for most workers. Collapse of the city's general strike in 1892, the first in the nation, and the depression of the 1890s brought an end to what has been called "labor's golden era in New Orleans" and also largely ended racial cooperation. By the mid-1890s, white union and nonunion labor in New Orleans, as elsewhere in the urban South, was committed to blocking black access to skilled positions. The replacement of the Knights by the racist American Federation of Labor spelled the doom of prospects for a revived biracial alliance. Interracial labor forces on relatively equal footing could only be found in southern coal mines.

An occasional white liberal, such as New Orleans author George Washington Cable, might challenge the system of segregation, but even he did so without attacking the cherished goal of race purity, arguing instead that integration in certain sectors of southern life need not extend to private relations. At the opposite extreme, some southerners continued to favor total exclusion from services ranging from education to health care. As one North Carolina editor put it, "Nothing is so surely ruining Negroes of the South as the accursed free schools." A few who predicted that the race could not survive in freedom and was on the verge of extinction even welcomed emigration efforts, though most did not. Southern authors, such as Thomas Dixon, Jr., whose *The Leopard's Spots: A Romance of the White Man's Burden—1865-1900* (1902) and *The Clansman: An Historical Romance of the Ku Klux Klan* (1905) were later adapted for the landmark pro-Klan film *The Birth of a Nation,* pictured the black male as subhuman and incapable of improvement, "a possible beast" who "roams at night and sleeps in the day, whose speech knows no word of love, whose passions, once aroused, are as the fury of the tiger."

More often, however, whites disagreed about how blacks should be treated within a segregated society. Some whites sincerely believed that segregation per se was not enough; separate treatment, they said, should also be equal treatment. This had been the view of the white Republican leadership during Reconstruction and of enlightened white Populists. Both groups favored the policy because of mixed motives of political expedience and a sense of fair play that varied in emphasis from person to person. But by the end of the century, when Republican influence was gone and such former Populists as Tom Watson were among the worst race baiters, this philosophy was most likely to be found within the Conservative elite. With blacks largely disfranchised, political expediency was no longer a factor. Members of the elite were moved instead by a combination of humanitarianism and concern for the greater benefits to southern society that would accrue from a moral, educated, highly disciplined and "loyal" black population. Although they often shared the broader white community's belief in Negro inferiority and concerns about possible "contamination," they nevertheless believed in the ameliorative effects of equal treatment.

Edgar Gardner Murphy, a Montgomery, Alabama, Episcopal minister, was typical of those elite whites who sought to make separate but equal more than empty rhetoric. One of the South's few advocates of the Social Gospel, Gardner, as a young minister in Laredo, Texas, had led a protest against the burning of a black man accused of rape and murder. After briefly moving to the North, he was called to Montgomery's St. John's Episcopal Church in 1898. A tireless worker on behalf of child labor reform and public education, he left the ministry in 1903 to serve as executive secretary of the Southern Education Board. Alarmed by racial fanatics who progressed "from the contention that no negro shall learn, that no negro shall labor, and (by implication) that no negro shall live," in

1900 he organized the Southern Society for the Promotion of the Study of Race Conditions and Problems in the South.

Accurately described as a white paternalist, Murphy acknowledged that segregation had "made of our eating and drinking, our buying and selling, our labor and housing, our rents, our railroads, our orphanages and prisons, our recreations, our very institutions of religion, a problem of race as well as a problem of maintenance." Yet because "ours is a world of inexorable divisions," integration was not an alternative; the only practical and humanitarian alternative was separate but equal treatment. As his biographer concluded, despite his many "advanced ideas . . . Murphy still held that the Negro could be granted his civil, political, and industrial rights without social integration and race amalgamation."

Similarly inclined whites thought that the region's race relations could be improved through meetings of concerned leaders from both races, studies of racial problems in white and black universities, and systematic educational campaigns. A white woman who attended a meeting of the National Association of Colored Women in 1920 clearly needed such exposure. "I saw women of education, culture and refinement," she observed afterwards. "I had lived in the South all my life, but didn't know such as these lived in the land." Organizations such as the Southern Sociological Congress (1912) and the Commission on Interracial Cooperation (1919) sought, as one founder put it, "good will, cooperation, and practical helpfulness." The focus was to be on immediate problems of "better homes, a fuller conception of religion, and a more efficient system of education." Uneasy with the assertiveness of the "New Negro," such southern "liberals" were like most whites, who, as journalist Ray Stannard Baker put it in 1908, "want the New South and the Old Negro." It would be decades before they would move haltingly beyond separate but equal solutions to embrace desegregation as their primary goal.

In the meantime, the pleas of moderates for racial equity within a segregated system were largely ignored. Such pleas did not begin to gather support until the Great Migration, a series of other economic and social changes, and renewed agitation for a truly new South in the 1920s again tipped the balance against racial extremists.

White supremacy supplied a needed element of continuity in the midst of rapid social, political, and economic change. The same was also true of attachment to the "Lost Cause," an idealization of the Old South and the Confederate generation that likewise revealed the strengths and limits of white solidarity and had fundamental implications for the "newness" of the First New South.

The fascination with the Lost Cause had its roots in an antebellum cultural nationalism that drew on a mixture of southern agrarianism, evangelical religion, and "master race" democracy. White southerners had entered and fought the Civil War believing that God was on their side. Northerners, of course, believed that they too had God's blessing, but because they won, this belief presumably had been confirmed. Southerners had to choose between admitting that they had been wrong to secede and finding some other reason for their defeat. Given the tremendous loss of life and property and the even greater emotional investment, to admit error would have been too much of a burden. Instead, Richmond editor Edward A. Pollard, in *The Lost Cause* (1866), called for a "war of ideas" to preserve southern identity.

The problem was how to hold onto the past while still embracing the future. Support for the Lost Cause can be seen as part of what C. Vann Woodward termed the region's larger "Divided Mind," which reflected the tension between change and continuity. But as with the idea of the New South itself, it seems more accurate to see that division as existing both between different groups of southerners and within the minds of individual southerners. Some southerners were unreconstructed Rebels—they sought to use the Lost Cause to keep alive hatred of the Yankees and were consumed with rehashing battles and mourning the dead. (The most unreconstructed, aside from the occasional suicide, established what turned out usually to be temporary Confederate colonies in Mexico, Brazil, and Venezuela.) A larger number of southerners sought to put the past behind them but were not averse to using it when it might further their interests. But perhaps the greatest number were genuinely torn between the security of the past and the uncertainty of the future.

For whites, particularly those of the old planter class and the Protestant clergy, the South's defeat did not negate the value or virtue of the Lost Cause. The South had lost the war, not because the Cause was unjust, but because of the North's superior numbers and the mistakes of certain generals. As far as the Cause itself, it was not slavery, they asserted, but states' rights and an identity and a value system that conformed more closely than those of the North to the ideals of the Founding Fathers. Even more vaguely, it was often claimed in sermons and on monuments that southerners had fought "in simple obedience to duty," or because of "a small voice in their bosoms, the voice of God, which was the voice of duty." But the reason for secession was always less important than the conduct and consequences of the war. The memory of the war and its heroes therefore had to be kept alive. The virtuous society and individuals who had fought the war were to be models for the postwar generation. The creation myth of the southern nation could not avoid the fact of temporal defeat, but spiritual victory was still possible. As the Reverend Moses Drury Hoge of Richmond's Second Presbyterian Church told the almost 50,000 people who had come to Richmond in 1875 to dedicate the first monument in the South to Stonewall Jackson, "Defeat is the discipline which trains the truly heroic soul to further and better endeavors." Confederate sacrifices had not been in vain.

It is not surprising, therefore, that the initial response to the memory of the war during the late 1860s and the 1870s was solemn and religiously oriented. Beginning in Georgia, local groups of women tended the graves of the Confederate dead, memorials were built in cemeteries, and the embittered members of such organizations as the Association of the Army of Northern Virginia (1870) and the Southern Historical Society (1873) kept alive memory of the Lost Cause. Special days for fasting, thanksgiving, and prayer were common. Such colleges as Stonewall Jackson Institute, Washington and Lee, and the University of the South (Sewanee) became monuments to the Lost Cause, filling their faculties with Confederate heroes and their campuses with memorials. Clergymen figured prominently in all these activities and reminded the survivors that the Lost Cause had been "baptized in blood."

But this early effort at "revitalization" or attempted restoration soon was transformed into a celebration of the past that could be used to help white southerners of all classes adjust to a new South. This transformation is ably charted in Gaines Foster's *Ghosts of the Confederacy: Defeat, the Lost Cause, and the Emergence of the New South 1865 to 1913 (1987)*. Although some Lost Cause champions, particularly among the clergy, railed against the "*money mania*" of the New South, the Lost Cause soon became a tool in the hands of both the sincere and the insincere to link the Lost Cause and the New South and in the process to encourage white solidarity. Democratic politicians became especially good at recalling the Confederate uniform and the alleged horrors of Republican-sponsored Reconstruction in their effort to stay in power, and a Confederate pedigree remained an important part of the job description for the highest political offices even into the twentieth century. But whites of all classes and ranks welcomed being wrapped in the common cloth of Confederate gray. And all found comfort in the depiction of allegedly loyal slaves who defended family members, built fortifications, and kept the plantations going. Such views not only justified the institution of slavery, but also provided a welcome contrast to postwar blacks, who were considered by troubled whites to be "uppity," "ungrateful," "lazy," or, worse still, "retrogressing to an animal state." As Georgia's Rebecca Felton, who later became the first woman to serve in the U. S. Senate, put it, the black race "was more honest, more upright, and more virtuous in the South, at the time of the surrender at Appomattox, than they are today."

Accompanying the new response to the Lost Cause was a broadening of support for it. Memorials now were placed in the town squares, and they now were celebratory rather than funereal, usually featuring a defiant soldier, gun in hand, looking North. New, more inclusive organizations, such as Robert E. Lee Camp #1, Confederate Veterans (1883), although not neglecting such stock heroes as Robert E. Lee, Stonewall Jackson, and the previously maligned Jefferson Davis, made space in the pantheon for the private soldiers and the heroic women of the Confederacy. Such changes brought working- and middle-class whites to what had been primarily an elite movement. The emphasis on white solidarity came at a time in the 1880s and 1890s when the South encountered economic and political turmoil, a fact that no doubt helped account for it. Praise for women that emphasized their traditional roles of nursing the wounded, making clothing, or resisting Yankee rapists drew on the traditional idealization of southern women, what W. J. Cash called "downright gyneolotry." But it was especially comforting at a time when white women were entering the work force in larger numbers and campaigning for rights that included the vote.

Appeals to cross-class and cross-gender white solidarity also were accompanied by greater attention to the need for reconciliation with the North. The memory of the common suffering and heroism of enlisted men served to bring the North and South together, a development that was further stimulated by the joint effort in the Spanish-American War and World War I, which in turn lessened the need to sentimentalize the Lost Cause. By then southerners were again observing Thanksgiving Day and the national Memorial Day and enthusiastically celebrating the Fourth of July, holidays long disdained because of their association with the Union's victory in the Civil War. It helped that a southerner was in the White House, but even in 1913 the Presbyterian minister James H. McNeilly was careful to point out that southern good will should not be "interpreted as condoning the barbarities of burning and butchery with which the war was conducted against our people." Southerners were ready to forgive, but they were unwilling to forget.

By the time of the Spanish-American War, the Lost Cause had reached its organizational peak. The formation of local and state veterans' groups finally led in 1889 to the founding in New Orleans of the United Confederate Veterans. General John B. Gordon, a Confederate war hero and prominent New South businessman and politician who was described as "handsome, compelling, and magnificent on a horse," was an especially fitting choice for commander. As Gaines Foster observed, "Except for politics, he probably succeeded best at being a professional southerner." The UCV was soon followed by the United Daughters of the Confederacy (1895) and the Sons of Confederate Veterans (1896). The UDC played a central role in UCV functions and was more active in general than its male counterpart, demonstrating a zealous guardianship of partisan history that was capped in 1912 by the dissemination of the "U.D.C Catechism for Children." Beginning in 1891, veterans assembled annually for a reunion that might attract close to 100,000 participants and spectators. Each Confederate veteran's death was the occasion for a procession, sermons, and other celebrations of the Lost Cause, all done according to the "Confederate Veteran's Burial Ritual." The clergy themselves organized a Chaplain's Association before the Atlanta reunion in 1898. After initially being unable to agree on a day, by 1916 ten states had designated June 3, Jefferson Davis's birth date, as Confederate Memorial Day.

What had begun as a solemn worship of the past had become a celebration of the links between North and South, Old South and New South, the past and the future. Yet even here the divisions among white southerners were evident. About 30 percent of Lee Camp's membership came from the working class, but this was true of less than 10 percent of the more elite-oriented Association of the Army of Northern Virginia. The UCV itself was dominated by the middle classes, but reduced dues for the poor attracted many workers and farmers. Parades with leaders on horseback and followers marching on foot must have been a reassuring symbol of social solidarity and deference. The common soldier was honored, but "in his place." The reunion became an ideal world, freed not only from the reality of wartime strife but from the economically and politically competitive, divisive South of the 1880s and 1890s. "When we feel that we have made poor crops, and mortgages and debts have pressed upon us, when we feel utterly discouraged and cast down—go ahead and read our record," one wealthy speaker told the veterans at the 1894 reunion, at the height of Populist insurgency. "You will rejoice that there is a country where honor is first, not wealth; where patriotic endeavor and duty are everything, riches only a secondary consideration."

At the same time, however, the reunions provided ample evidence of the class divisions that threatened white solidarity. By the turn of the century, as cities came to compete for reunion sites at least as much to make money from the veterans as to honor them, various forms of commercialization seeped into the celebrations. Elaborate floats appeared, including one memorable one for the National Casket Company—complete with a Confederate flag–draped coffin, a daughter and uniformed son of the Confederacy, and a sign reading "Your Sons and Daughters will forever guard the memory of your brave deeds."

But more than commercialization threatened the illusion that the reunion was the occasion for a united society to honor the symbols of the Lost Cause. Particularly among the SCV and UDC, membership was increasingly drawn from the middle and upper classes, and the Sons especially lost interest in promoting the Lost Cause as other than an excuse for a good party. Lavish balls and galas threatened to overshadow the simpler parties of the veterans. At the 1906 reunion in New Orleans, for example, one newspaperman found in the fashionable St. Charles Hotel, "beautiful women, stately, well-clad wearers of the gray and the 'fair women and brave men' of the old Confederacy gathered—with music and laughter and gaiety. Down in the Hotel Royal, where the ghosts of the past

seemed lurking even in the glare of gas and electricity—bi-
vouacked 3000 old soldiers ... men who came from the
ranks." They wore the "plainest" clothes, ate the "simplest"
food, and slept on cots. One veteran complained that at the
1910 reunion in Memphis, the leaders were "banqueted,
wined, dined, and quartered in the very best hotels," but the
common soldier had to "shift for himself, stand around on
the street, or sit on the curbstone."

By 1920 Richmond, Virginia, had become as much the
capital of the Lost Cause as it had been capital of the Confederacy. According to one catalogue of its Confederate nec-
rophilia,

the city boasted a sixteen-acre Hollywood Cemetery, holding the
graves of 16,000 Confederate soldiers, including 3,000 from the Get-
tysburg battlefield; the Hollywood Cemetery Monument, a massive,
ninety-foot-high Egyptian-like pyramid of James River granite; the
Soldiers' and Sailors' Monument in Libby Hill Park, a seventy-two-
foot-high shaft, topped by an eighteen-foot-high bronze Confederate;
the Confederate Memorial Institute, known as the South's Battle Ab-
bey; the White House of the Confederacy, which had been made into
the United Daughters of the Confederacy Museum; and a carefully
maintained Monument Boulevard [Avenue], with statues of J. E. B.
Stuart, Stonewall Jackson, Robert E. Lee, and an elaborate Jefferson
Davis monument, dedicated in 1907 before 200,000 people, the largest crowd ever to assemble to honor the Confederates.

But no town of any size in the South was without similar
expressions of devotion to the Lost Cause. Indeed, by 1914
there were over a thousand monuments to Confederate heroes
in the South. There were living monuments to the Cause as
well. It was not until 1910 that William Hodges Mann became
the last Confederate veteran to be elected governor of Virginia;
in that same year Confederate veterans still filled almost half
of the South's seats in the U. S. Senate. Never in the history
of the world had the losing side of a civil war been permitted
such a public and honored institutionalization of its defeat.

Yet by at least the late teens, interest in the Lost Cause
had declined to the point where it had become a hollow shell

of its initial self. The Civil War generation was largely gone, New South boosterism had triumphed, and two new wars had brought an outpouring of American patriotism. It was fitting that the 1917 Confederate Veterans' reunion occurred in Washington, DC, the first time a reunion was held outside the boundaries of the Confederacy. Vindication had finally been achieved, and the Lost Cause would play a much smaller role during the Second New South efforts of the 1920s. Indeed, as personified by the Nashville Agrarians, a Vanderbilt University–centered group of historians and English professors who revered the Old South, it would be used mostly to challenge the dominant New South ideology. Some white southerners to this day proudly display the Confederate flag and sing "Dixie" in celebration of the war's triumphant nationalism and martial glory. But in doing so they trivialize the tragic dimension of the war. That was true also of late-nineteenth-century southerners, who, as Gaines Foster notes, "gained little wisdom and developed no special perspective from contemplating defeat."

For many, then, the Lost Cause had become an end in itself rather than the means to an end, an aberrant form of the nation's more prophetic "civil religion" that grew out of a more forward-looking, optimistic sense of mission. In a similar fashion, the idea of a new South became more important than its reality, at the same time that it, too, became an end in itself rather than a means to a greater end. If there was a larger goal, it was for the South to be more like the North while somehow retaining its "southernness," but if that were the case, why? Was it to make up for a humiliating defeat and the end of southern independence? Or was it to win the war the next time? Despite some exceptions, particularly among progressives, New South advocates did not envision a new South as the means to improve the lives of the mass of southern whites, and it certainly was not for the benefit of blacks. By 1920, with reintegration into the nation complete, no one suggested a second War for Southern Independence. That was just as well, for, given the relative lack of southern economic, social, and political progress, the prospects for southern success were even slimmer than they had been sixty years earlier.

A Real New South?

By the 1980s it seemed as if a genuine new South had finally appeared. Some observers focused on the contrast between the decaying Frost Belt and the seemingly vibrant Sun Belt, in which the South was the junior partner of the West. Others noted the new realities in agriculture. Not only had mechanization finally come to cotton and tobacco, but two western states, California and Arizona, were now the leading producers of cotton. The number-one crop in the South's newly diversified farming sector was, of all things, soybeans. Cotton was no longer king in the South, and the South was not even king of cotton. New automobile plants in Tennessee and the appearance of high technology firms throughout the South testified to the region's increasing industrialization. Per capita income in the South, which had been roughly half of the nation's average as late as the 1930s, had reached 85 percent of parity. With Dallas, Houston, and San Antonio among the nation's ten most populous cities, and with Atlanta having the busiest airport and most convention business, an impressive urban South had finally emerged. And a new generation of young southern governors from both parties was carrying on a more inclusive and wide-ranging educational crusade than had occurred during the Progressive Era.

But it was in the realm of race relations that change was most evident. Elements of continuity remained, but the forces of change had finally begun to triumph. The South was still distinctive, but this time because conditions for blacks seemed better, not worse, than elsewhere. This is not just boosterism. To a certain extent the South looked so good only because of its own tragic past and the more severe problems elsewhere in the country. Yet by a variety of standards there were finally some grounds for the claims of Henry Grady and Booker T. Washington that blacks were better off in the South. Though in no sense truly "integrated," southern schools and neighborhoods were less segregated than those elsewhere, and southern blacks, especially women, had significantly narrowed the racial income gap since the early 1970s, whereas it had remained the same or even grown in most of the rest of the country, particularly in the economically depressed Midwest. In the process, southern blacks had overtaken their midwestern counterparts and had almost reached income parity with northeastern and western blacks. Thanks to the Voting Rights Act of 1965 and increased black turnout, the South had more than 60 percent of the nation's black officeholders, including Virginia's Douglas Wilder, the nation's first elected black governor. In the wake of Wilder's victory in 1989, politicians such as North Carolina's Harvey Gantt and Georgia's Andrew Young could launch more than symbolic efforts to become the South's first black U.S. senators since Reconstruction. Whether because the South looked so good, or the North looked so bad, for the first time since the Civil War the South experienced a net increase in black migration during the 1970s. The process continued during the 1980s, so that by 1990 the region's percentage of the nation's black population had increased from about 52 percent to 56 percent.

Much of what has happened in recent years would have amazed and delighted Henry Grady's generation, though one doubts that the kinds of advances for blacks were the sort of "moderate race relations" that whites had in mind. As long as the South continues to rank at the bottom of most income, educational, and social service indices, it will be unable to rest on its laurels. But, though there can never be complete breaks with the past, the region, if not yet ready for the title of "the Perfect South," can be at long last correctly called "the New South."

The reasons for this relative success cast light on why previous efforts, particularly that between 1865 and 1920, failed. First, there could be no real change until the southern economy was radically altered. This could only be achieved by ending the enslavement to cotton. Beginning with the post–World War I decline and continuing under the impact of Depression and New Deal policies, cotton's privileged position was eroded. The exodus of black workers, the spread of mechanization, the worldwide cotton competition, and what economist Gavin Wright calls the end of the South's separate labor market prepared the way for the transformation of the southern economy that would have been impossible before 1920.

But more than economics was involved. Thanks to black migration to the North, northern blacks became a crucial voting bloc, initially important to both the Republican and Democratic parties. Aligning themselves largely with the Democrats after the mid-1930s, blacks were able to move the national government to provide the kind of support for efforts at racial justice in the South that had been unthinkable one hundred years ago. What has been called the New or Second Reconstruction of the 1950s and 1960s would have been unlikely, however, without the support of southern and northern white liberals driven to action by both pragmatic and idealistic motives. These liberals, together with a few supportive conservatives, were partly influenced by foreign policy concerns that also had been absent a hundred years earlier. To ignore demands for racial justice in the South would have lost the

United States key points in the cold war struggle for the allegiance of third world nations. Conditions in the world at large, support from white liberals, and the new importance of the black vote provided an environment in which the grass-roots efforts of southern blacks could be nourished and finally triumph.

As Henry Grady and other First New South boosters had realized, real progress in the South depended upon racial progress. His generation's definition of racial progress, however, was quite different from ours, so it is not surprising that a "real" New South was so long in coming. When judged according to the goals of New South spokesmen and the spectacular developments in the North, the First New South was characterized to a greater degree by continuity than by change. Even some of the undeniable changes that occurred between 1865 and 1920 reinforced traditional aspects of southern society. The end of economic self-sufficiency, for example, contributed to the continuation of the region's economic backwardness, and the new system of race relations anchored by segregation, sharecropping, disfranchisement, and lynching simply marked another stage in the region's commitment to white supremacy. During the Depression, President Franklin Delano Roosevelt would identify the South as "the Nation's No. 1 one economic problem," and the region's economic, political, and social problems would long continue as a source for national concern. The essential failure to alter southern society in fundamental ways also became graphically evident in the North after 1920, as lower-class southern migrants, both white and black, contributed disproportionately to the high rates of illiteracy, infant mortality, homicide, unemployment, and family instability in northern cities.

The point is not that the First New South was not new, but that it was not new enough.

BIBLIOGRAPHICAL ESSAY

The history of the South between 1865 and 1920 has become one of American history's most exciting and productive fields. Historians and other scholars have been drawn to the period in part out of a desire to put into historical perspective the remarkable changes that began to transform the South in the 1960s. Fascination with the era of the First New South, however, is also the byproduct of an earlier interest in the antebellum South, and especially the institution of slavery, as scholars carry debates about the nature of antebellum southern life into the postbellum period. How well had slavery prepared blacks for freedom? What did the planters' reactions to postwar economic developments reveal about their antebellum attitudes? What happened to the antebellum yeomanry in the postwar years? And, most basically, to what extent was the Civil War a watershed in southern history?

There is no historiographical survey that covers the entire period between 1865 and 1920. For the best introduction to recent trends in the literature, therefore, readers should first consult several of the essays in *Interpreting Southern History: Historiographical Essays in Honor of Sanford W. Higginbotham* (1987), edited by John Boles and Evelyn Nolen. See especially La Wanda Cox's "From Emancipation to Segregation: National Policy and Southern Blacks"; Harold D. Woodman's "Economic Reconstruction and the Rise of the New

South, 1865–1900"; Dan Carter's "From Segregation to Integration"; and Richard L. Watson's "From Populism through the New Deal: Southern Political History." For equally thorough though more traditionally arranged assessments of the relevant literature written prior to the mid-1960s, see the essays by Vernon L. Wharton, Paul M. Gaston, George B. Tindall, Allen J. Going, Horace H. Cunningham, and Dewey W. Grantham, Jr., in *Writing Southern History: Essays in Historiography in Honor of Fletcher M. Green* (1965), edited by Arthur S. Link and Rembert W. Patrick.

The arguments among scholars are especially noteworthy because they echo the debates between northerners and southerners or among southerners themselves at the time. Postwar southerners were, after all, the first to claim that a new South had appeared, a view that was embraced by the first generations of (primarily southern-born) historians of the South. The best introduction to the New South advocates is Paul Gaston's *The New South Creed: A Study in Southern Mythmaking* (1970). Among the highly laudatory initial assessments of the New South are A[mory]. D[wight]. Mayo's "Is There a New South?" *Social Economist* (1893); Philip A. Bruce's *The Rise of the New South* (1905); Holland Thompson's *The New South: A Chronicle of Social and Industrial Evolution* (1921); and Broadus Mitchell and George S. Mitchell's *The Industrial Revolution in the South* (1930). For the purest statement of New South aims, see Henry W. Grady's *The New South and Other Addresses* (1904). For more on Grady, see Raymond B. Nixon's *Henry W. Grady: Spokesman of the New South* (1943); and Harold E. Davis's study of the relationship between Grady and his adopted city, *Henry Grady's New South: Atlanta, A Brave and Beautiful City* (1990).

The New South that emerged from such accounts allegedly had reconciled with the North and adopted northern values while still retaining its essential "southernness." The South had become more urban and industrialized, its agriculture more diversified, and its race relations more moderate. It had been necessary to disfranchise and segregate blacks in order to promote racial harmony and enable the whites, under the leadership of a united Democratic party, to promote progress for both races. Although urban businessmen and manufacturers enjoyed unprecedented prominence in this New South, members of the antebellum planter class continued to exercise considerable economic and political power.

Although there were piecemeal attacks on this picture of a thriving, united South, it remained the dominant view until the publication of C. Vann Woodward's *The Origins of the New South, 1877–1913* (1951). Perhaps no other book has so dominated a single field in American history and done so for so long. As should be evident in the preceding chapters, practically everything written about the period from 1877 to 1913 since *Origins*' appearance has been either explicitly or implicitly a response to it. Finding more evidence of discontinuity than continuity in postbellum southern history, Woodward argued that the Civil War had destroyed the antebellum planter class. In its place arose a class of "new men" from urban and middle-class backgrounds. Overcoming opponents from within a society that was more deeply divided than had been previously acknowledged, the "Redeemers" (whom Woodward called in an earlier work "New Departure Democrats") determined the political and economic life of the postbellum South. They committed the South to a dependence on cotton and the pursuit of industrial growth. Their ruinous promotional activities failed to close the gap in industrialization and urbanization that set the region apart from the rest of the nation, and left the South an economic colony of the Northeast. As leaders of the Democratic party, the Redeemers ran corrupt governments that were unresponsive to the needs of most of the population, suppressed the more enlightened Populist and other independent movements, disfranchised black voters, and prepared the way for Progressivism "for whites only."

Two excellent assessments of the literature in the field by former Woodward students reveal the extent to which *Origins* determined our understanding of the period even twenty years after its publication. See Charles Dew's "Critical Essay on Recent Works," in *Origins of the New South* (2nd ed., 1971); and Sheldon Hackney's "*Origins of the New South* in Retrospect," *Journal of Southern History* (1972). Although Hackney understated the extent to which some of Woodward's findings had been undermined and ignored the controversy surrounding Woodward's interpretation of race relations, he correctly concluded that "the remarkable thing is that there has been so little fundamental challenge to the outlines of the story established by Woodward." Thus, "the pyramid still stands." This was the case, Hackney believed, because "Woodward's sensibility is both Beardian and Faulknerian," that is, combines an appreciation of economic conflict with a tragic vision.

Since the mid-1970s, *Origins* has come under increasing attack from a new generation of scholars, though it has not lacked for defenders, many of whom were students of Woodward. Woodward himself graciously noted in the preface to the 1971 paperback edition that the time for revision was long overdue. For more recent assessments of the book, see J. Morgan Kousser and James M. McPherson's "Introduction: C. Vann Woodward: An Assessment of His Work and Influence," in *Region, Race, and Reconstruction: Essays in Honor of C. Vann Woodward* (1982), edited by J. Morgan Kousser and James M. McPherson; John Herbert Roper's *C. Vann Woodward, Southerner* (1987); and Woodward's response to his critics in *Looking Back: The Perils of Writing History* (1986).

The most heavily debated aspect of the First New South involves the impact of the Civil War on the nature of southern agriculture. For the argument that wartime devastation per se had minimal impact, see Peter Temin's "The Post-Bellum Recovery of the South and the Cost of the Civil War," *Journal of Economic History* (1976). The end of southern agricultural self-sufficiency is noted and the prevalence of cotton explained in Gavin Wright's *The Political Economy of the Cotton South: Households, Markets and Wealth in the Nineteenth Century* (1978). Useful surveys of southern agriculture are Gilbert Fite's *Cotton Fields No More: Southern Agriculture, 1865–1980*

(1984), an encyclopedic account that takes a detached stance; and Pete Daniel's *Breaking the Land: The Transformation of Cotton, Tobacco, and Rice Cultures since 1880* (1985), a more impassioned study that stresses the negative effects of mechanization on rice, tobacco, and cotton farmers and does not see those changes as inevitable. The findings of both authors are summarized in Daniel's "The Crossroads of Change: Cotton, Tobacco, and Rice Cultures in the Twentieth Century South," *Journal of Southern History* (1984); and Fite's "Southern Agriculture Since the Civil War: An Overview," *Agricultural History* (1979). Accounts of specific crops include Peter Coclanis's *The Shadow of a Dream: Economic Life and Death in the South Carolina Low Country, 1670–1920* (1989); Henry C. Dethloff's *A History of the American Rice Industry, 1685–1985* (1988); Nannie May Tilley's *The Bright-Tobacco Industry, 1860–1929* (1948); and J. Carlyle Sitterson's *Sugar Country: The Cane Sugar Industry in the South, 1753–1950* (1953).

Thanks to the extensive interest of economists, the origins of sharecropping have received especially close attention from scholars. Much of the often-heated debate is between Marxists, who emphasize class-determined power relationships, and neoclassical economists, who stress the role of market-based individual choice, but neither side is monolithic. Harold Woodman's "Sequel to Slavery: The New History Views the Postbellum South," *Journal of Southern History* (1977) is the best introduction to the issues.

In the Woodwardian tradition, and based on the study of parts of five Deep South states they call "The Cotton South," the economists Roger L. Ransom and Richard Sutch argue in *One Kind of Freedom: The Economic Consequences of Emancipation* (1977) that a new merchant class took control of the countryside from a weakened planter class and forced blacks to raise cotton or other staple crops. Two Marxist interpretations, Jonathan M. Wiener's *Social Origins of the New South, Alabama: 1860–1885* (1978), based on five Black Belt Alabama counties, and Jay Mandle's *The Roots of Black Poverty: The Southern Plantation After the Civil War* (1978), a more general account, however, argue that the Civil War did not "destroy" the antebellum planter class. Instead, planters retained their dominance and were most responsible for the creation of the sharecropping system. A balance of sorts is reached in Lacy Ford's "Rednecks and Merchants: Economic Development and Social Tensions in the South Carolina Upcountry, 1865–1900," *Journal of American History* (1984), which quite sensibly argues that the merchants and planters divided power in the South as a whole and even in local areas where one or the other might be dominant. Although more whites than blacks were ensnared by sharecropping, the percentage of black farmers who were croppers was much higher, and these authors see racism as the prime obstacle to black advancement. Peonage or debt servitude is examined in Pete Daniel's *The Shadow of Slavery: Peonage in the South, 1901–1969* (1972); and in William Cohen's "Negro Involuntary Servitude in the South, 1865–1940: A Preliminary Analysis," *Journal of Southern History* (1976). See also Harold Woodman's "Post–Civil War Southern Agriculture and the Law," *Agricultural History* (1979).

Conspiratorial explanations for the emergence of sharecropping have been challenged from a variety of perspectives. See Ronald F. Davis's *Good and Faithful Labor: From Slavery to Sharecropping in the Natchez District, 1860–1890* (1982) for the extreme claim that the blacks forced white landowners to accept sharecropping instead of the gang-wage-laborer system that whites preferred. A diverse group of free-market economists, however, argues that sharecropping was a compromise between the desires of landowners and blacks. As such, it was a rational response to market conditions that included a scarcity of capital and a high worldwide demand for cotton. Robert Higgs's *Competition and Coercion: Blacks in the American Economy, 1865–1914* (1977) emphasizes the availability of options for blacks and examples of economic progress; Stephen J. DeCanio's *Agriculture in the Postbellum South: The Economics of Production and Supply* (1974) argues that cotton was so popular because it was the region's most profitable crop;

and Ralph Shlomowitz's " 'Bound' or 'Free'? Black Labor in Cotton and Sugarcane Farming, 1865–1880," *Journal of Southern History* (1984) stresses black initiative, especially the rejection of an intermediate stage of squad day labor on individual plots of land, and reminds us that wage labor rather than sharecropping predominated in sugar areas. See also Joseph D. Reid's "Sharecropping as an Understandable Market Response," *Journal of Economic History* (1973).

The extent of planter power also has implications for the nature of southern industrialization. Jonathan Wiener's *Social Origins of the New South*, the classic statement of planter dominance, argues that the planters took the South down a "Prussian Road" to industrialization. Like the Junkers, the large landowning class in late-nineteenth-century Prussia, the postwar southern planter class allegedly was a precapitalist or even anticapitalist elite that sought to mold the South's industrialization so that it would not threaten the interests of labor-intensive single-crop agriculture. Wiener expanded his argument to include the rest of the South in "Class Structure and Economic Development in the American South, 1865–1955," *American Historical Review* (1979). In *Planters and the Making of a "New South": Class, Politics, and Development in North Carolina, 1865–1900* (1979), Marxist sociologist Dwight Billings agreed with Wiener about the persistence of planter power, but argued that conditions in North Carolina produced a different outcome. North Carolina had less demand for black plantation labor than did Alabama, and in an effort to control the state's surplus white labor force, the planter class turned to cotton textile manufacturing to produce a "revolution from above." Two older claims for planter control over the cotton textile industry are Broadus Mitchell's praise-filled *The Rise of Cotton Mills in the South* (1921); and the more critical assessment in *The Mind of the South* (1941) by W. J. Cash, the tormented southern white liberal journalist.

Several other local studies have demonstrated the remarkable staying power of the antebellum planter elite. Among those that found that a majority of planters survived the Civil

War with their holdings largely intact are Kenneth S. Greenberg's "The Civil War and the Redistribution of Land: Adams County, Mississippi, 1860–1870," *Agricultural History* (1978); Randolph B. Campbell's *A Southern Community in Crisis: Harrison County, Texas, 1850–1880* (1983); Steven V. Ash's *Middle Tennessee Society Transformed, 1860–1870: War and Peace in the Upper South* (1988); and J. William Harris's "The Transformation of a Social Order: Augusta's Hinterlands, 1850–1880," unpublished paper, 1980. A. Jane Townes's "The Effect of Emancipation on Large Land Holdings: Nelson and Goochland Counties, Virginia," *Journal of Southern History* (1979) also finds high rates of planter persistence, but concludes that large planters as a group held fewer of their counties' acres than before the war.

Yet the persistence of the same people does not necessarily mean that class attitudes and values also survived the war. And if they did not, then can one justifiably talk about the survival of the "class?" In *The Reshaping of Plantation Society: The Natchez District, 1860–1880* (1983), Michael Wayne chronicles the process by which the paternalistic, precapitalistic antebellum planter class was forced by market realities to diversify its economic interests and rethink its relationship to the former slaves. Wayne's findings support Harold Woodman's assertion in "Sequel to Slavery" that the postwar South was "an evolving bourgeois society." See also Woodman's "How New Was the New South?" *Agriculture History* (1984), and his forthcoming *The Revolutionary Transformation of the Agricultural South, 1860–1930*; as well as Robert L. Branfon's *Cotton Kingdom of the New South: A History of the Yazoo Mississippi Delta from Reconstruction to the Twentieth Century* (1967). In *Patronage and Poverty in the Tobacco South: Louisa County, Virginia, 1860–1900* (1982), Crandall Shifflett depicts a capitalistic postwar planter class that was interested in diversification, but sees this as a continuation of antebellum behavior. The Louisa planters' relations with blacks and poor whites were governed by a system of "patronage capitalism" that left the planters in control of the means of production and produced an employer-employee relationship that was somewhere between free and bound labor. For a study of a special group of capitalistic planters who had difficulty applying their "free labor" rhetoric, see Lawrence Powell's *New Masters: Northern Planters during the Civil War and Reconstruction* (1980).

The relationship of planters to southern industrialization is also open to dispute. Even Billings's *Planters in the Making of a "New South"* acknowledges that the North Carolina tobacco industry was in the hands of "new men." For a good discussion of the most important of the tobacco magnates, see Robert F. Durden's *The Dukes of Durham, 1865–1929* (1975). David Carlton's superb *Mill and Town in South Carolina, 1880–1920* (1982) demonstrates that "new men" were responsible for that state's textile industry. James C. Cobb's "Beyond Planters and Industrialists: A New Perspective on the New South," *Journal of Southern History* (1988) finds a mutuality of interests to be more important than any conflict between the two groups.

Yet too much credit has been given to postwar southerners, whether "persisting planters" or "new men," in shaping the course of southern industry. William N. Parker's "The South in the National Economy, 1865–1970," *Southern Economic Journal* (1980) and Gavin Wright's *Old South, New South: Revolutions in the Southern Economy Since the Civil War* (1986) convincingly argue that the Old South's decision to build on the region's rich natural resources, pool of unskilled labor, and limited capital restricted options in the New South. Wright's useful historiographical essay, "The Strange Career of the New Southern Economic History," *Reviews in American History* (1982) anticipates many of the arguments in his book, stressing the structural legacy of slavery and the isolation of low-wage southern labor markets from higher-wage national labor markets. Less deterministic, but equally nonconspiratorial when it comes to postwar leaders, David Carlton's "The Revolution from Above: The National Market and the Beginnings of Industrialization in North Carolina," *Journal of Amer-*

ican History (1990) argues that the North's domination of the new postwar national market determined southern production and consumption patterns. And Steven Hahn, in "Class and State in Postemancipation Societies: Southern Planters in Comparative Perspective," *American Historical Review* (1990), reminds us that the planter class had not only lost power within the South, but had also become the weakest among the industrialized world's planter classes. As such, it had been unable to shape either Reconstruction policy or the South's economic future. Hahn also notes that Wiener underestimated the bourgeois character of German industrialization. For a Mississippi planter's perspective, see William A. Percy's *Lanterns on the Levee: Recollections of a Planter's Son* (1941).

A useful summary of the debate over southern industrialization and an introduction to what actually took place is James C. Cobb's *Industrialization and Southern Society, 1877–1984* (1984). Whoever or whatever was responsible for the South's industrialization, its effects on specific industries aside from tobacco and textiles can be followed in Thomas D. Clark's *The Greening of the South: The Recovery of Land and Forest* (1984); Paul Wallace Gates's "Federal Land Policy in the South, 1866–1888," *Journal of Southern History* (1940), which shows how northern businessmen took advantage of the Homestead Act to amass huge quantities of the South's best timber land; John S. Spratt's *The Road to Spindletop: Economic Change in Texas, 1875–1901* (1955); and Justin Fuller's "From Iron to Steel: Alabama's Industrial Evolution," *Alabama Review* (1964), and "Boom Towns and Blast Furnaces: Town Promotion in Alabama, 1885–1893," *Alabama Review* (1976). For summaries of the ways in which industrialization transformed Appalachia and how other Americans interpreted that process, see Ronald Eller's *Miners, Millhands and Mountaineers: Industrialization of the Appalachian South, 1880–1930* (1982); and Henry D. Shapiro's *Appalachia on Our Mind: The Southern Mountains and Mountaineers in the American Consciousness, 1870–1920* (1978).

The effects of industrialization on the white labor force in the cotton textile mills are explored sympathetically in Jacquelyn Dowd Hall et al.'s *Like A Family: The Making of A Southern Cotton Mill World* (1987) and I. W. Newby's *Plain Folk in the New South: Social Change and Cultural Persistence, 1880–1915* (1989). Dolores Janewski's *Sisterhood Denied: Race, Gender, and Class in a New South Community* (1985) delineates the intersection of class, race, and gender among tobacco and textile workers in Durham.

John Stover's *The Railroads of the South, 1865–1900* (1955) documents the expansion of the region's rail network and the dominance of northern interests. Mark W. Summers's *Railroads, Reconstruction, and the Gospel of Prosperity: Aid Under the Radical Republicans, 1865–1877* (1984) reveals the corrupt machinations of both southern Conservatives and Republicans. Harold D. Woodman's *King Cotton and his Retainers: Financing and Marketing the Cotton Crop of the South, 1800–1925* (1968) demonstrates the railroad's impact on cotton and the old factorage system.

The railroads also shaped the region's urban expansion. Beginning in the mid-1970s, urban historians broke away from their fixation on the Northeast and Midwest and began to study the South. The classic statement of unremitting continuity in southern urbanization is David R. Goldfield's sprightly *Cotton Fields and Skyscrapers: Southern City and Region, 1607–1980* (1982). Lawrence H. Larsen emphasized the degree of change that occurred between 1865 and 1900 in *The Rise of the Urban South* (1985), but then settled for a position closer to Goldfield's in *The Urban South: A History* (1990). A more balanced account that nevertheless also comes down on the side of continuity is Howard N. Rabinowitz's "Continuity and Change: Southern Urban Development, 1860–1900," in *The City in Southern History: The Growth of Urban Civilization in the South* (1977), edited by Blaine A. Brownell and David R. Goldfield. See also, in the same volume, Blaine A. Brownell's "The Urban South Comes of Age, 1900–1940." The strongest case for change in late-nineteenth-century southern urbanization is

Don H. Doyle's *New Men, New Cities, New South: Atlanta, Nashville, Charleston, Mobile, 1860–1910* (1990).

Among the best studies of individual cities are James M. Russell's *Atlanta 1847–1890: City Building in the Old South and the New* (1988); Joy J. Jackson's *New Orleans in the Gilded Age: Politics and Urban Progress, 1880–1896* (1969); Durward Long's "The Making of Modern Tampa: A City of the New South, 1865–1911," *Florida Historical Quarterly* (1971); Michael B. Chesson's *Richmond After the War 1865–1890* (1981); and Don H. Doyle's *Nashville in the New South, 1880–1930* (1985). Useful older studies include Thomas Wertenbaker's *Norfolk: Historic Southern Port* (1931); and William D. Miller's *Memphis during the Progressive Era, 1900–1917* (1957).

Scholars have devoted increasing attention to various aspects of urban life. For studies of urban blacks, see Howard N. Rabinowitz's *Race Relations in the Urban South, 1865–1890* (1978); John Blassingame's *Black New Orleans, 1860–1880* (1973); Robert Engs's *Freedom's First Generation: Black Hampton, Virginia, 1861–1890* (1979); George C. Wright's *Life Behind a Veil: Blacks in Louisville, Kentucky, 1865–1930* (1985); and Mamie Garvin Fields and Karen Fields's *Lemon Swamp and Other Places: A Carolina Memoir* (1983). For assessments of the impact of new public utilities, see Kenneth Lipartito's *The Bell System and Regional Business: The Telephone in the South, 1877–1920* (1989); and Harold Platt's *City Building in the New South: The Growth of Public Services in Houston, Texas, 1830–1915* (1983). For examinations of urban politics, see William Miller's *Mr. Crump of Memphis* (1964); Carl V. Harris's *Political Power in Birmingham 1871–1921* (1977); Eugene J. Watts's *The Social Bases of City Politics: Atlanta, 1865–1903,* (1978); and Samuel M. Kipp III's "Old Notables and Newcomers: The Economic and Political Elite of Greensboro, North Carolina, 1880–1920," *Journal of Southern History* (1977). For an analysis of the inadequacy of public health efforts, see John H. Ellis's "Business and Public Health in the Urban South during the Nineteenth Century: New Orleans, Memphis, and Atlanta," *Bulletin of the History of Med-*

icine (1970). Dale A. Somers's *The Rise of Sports in New Orleans, 1850–1900* (1972) is a thorough account of a neglected subject. For coverage of another neglected topic, see Howard L. Preston's *Automobile Age Atlanta: The Making of a Southern Metropolis, 1900–1935* (1979).

The immediate postwar economic changes occurred within the political framework of Reconstruction. The work in this field is so extensive that an entire essay could be devoted to it. Michael Perman has done exactly that at the end of *Emancipation and Reconstruction, 1862–1879* (1987). Many of the historiographical essays I have cited are also useful introductions to the Reconstruction literature, and I mention works that deal with specific aspects of Reconstruction throughout this bibliographical essay. William Archibald Dunning's *Reconstruction, Political and Economic, 1865–1877* (1907) and a series of less restrained state studies by Dunning's students established the traditional academic version of Reconstruction as a terrible mistake promoted by vindictive northern Republicans and implemented by mercenary carpetbaggers, traitorous scalawags, and illiterate freedmen. Claude Bowers's widely read *The Tragic Era: The Revolution After Lincoln* (1929) brought these ideas to a larger popular audience that had already been less systematically exposed to some of them in numerous historical novels, school textbooks, and D. W. Griffith's landmark film, *Birth of a Nation* (1915).

Early revisionist accounts that documented the limitations of the "Dunning School" and the achievements against great odds of the Reconstruction governments were W. E. B. Du Bois's pathbreaking Marxist account, *Black Reconstruction in America: An Essay Toward a History of the Part Which Black Folk Played in the Attempt to Reconstruct Democracy in America, 1860–1880* (1935); John Hope Franklin's *Reconstruction After the Civil War* (1961), which drew attention to what white southerners were actually doing during "Reconstruction Confederate Style" between 1865 and 1867; and Kenneth Stampp's *The Era of Reconstruction, 1865–1877* (1965). The standard account now is Eric Foner's *Reconstruction:*

America's Unfinished Revolution, 1863–1877 (1988), an impassioned but scholarly defense of Reconstruction that effectively combines extensive primary research with a thorough
knowledge of the secondary literature. It is especially good at
describing the experiences of blacks during the period.

C. Vann Woodward's *Reunion and Reaction: The Compromise of 1877 and the End of Reconstruction* (1951) presents
the case for the centrality of political patronage and economic
subsidies in settling the disputed 1876 Tilden-Hayes presidential election. Woodward's interpretation (repeated in abbre-
viated form in *Origins*) is challenged effectively by Alan Peskin's "Was There a Compromise of 1877," *Journal of
American History* (1973); Keith Ian Polakoff's *The Politics of
Inertia: The Election of 1876 and the End of Reconstruction*
(1973); and Michael Les Benedict's "Southern Democrats in
the Crisis of 1876–1877: A Reconsideration of *Reunion and
Reaction*," *Journal of Southern History* (1980). But Woodward
scores some points in his reply to Peskin in "Yes, There Was
a Compromise of 1877," *Journal of American History* (1973),
and in his response to his critics in general in *Thinking Back*.
Vincent P. DeSantis thoughtfully summarizes the debate, and
takes the traditional view of the importance of Hayes's promise
of "Home Rule" for the South in ending the filibuster that had
prevented counting of the electoral ballots, in "Rutherford B.
Hayes and the Removal of the Troops and the End of Reconstruction," in Kousser and McPherson's *Region, Race, and
Reconstruction*. Carl V. Harris's "Right Fork or Left Fork?
The Sectional-Party Alignments of Southern Democrats in
Congress, 1873–1897," *Journal of Southern History* (1976) further undermines Woodward's position by demonstrating that
both before and after the Compromise of 1877 southern Democrats aligned themselves on key issues more often with west-
ern Democrats than with northern business interests. See also
Terry L. Seip's *The South Returns to Congress: Men, Economic
Measures, and Intersectional Relationships, 1868–1879* (1983).

Useful accounts of the broader role of the Republican
party in the failure of Reconstruction and its aftermath are

William Gillette's *Retreat from Reconstruction 1869–1879* (1979) and Vincent DeSantis's *Republicans Face the Southern Question: The New Departure Years, 1877–1897* (1959). Many of the essays in *Southern Black Leaders of the Reconstruction Era* (1982), edited by Howard N. Rabinowitz, demonstrate how the end of Reconstruction affected the careers of black politicians and the lives of their black constituents.

Accounts of southern politics after Reconstruction are dominated by the debates over the value of Woodward's Redeemer model. The term "Redeemer" was an inspired choice—much better than the rather clumsy "New Departure Democrats"—but, like "Bourbon," it carries too much ideological baggage. And because it contains so many elements, its essence is difficult to pin down. Some accounts of the post-Reconstruction regimes focus on the importance of former Whigs, others on the role of agrarian types, and still others on the continuity/discontinuity debate. In other words, scholars can choose up sides over any or all of the following: who the leaders were, what they did, why they did it, and what it meant in terms of southern history. Complicating matters still further are the unsettled debates over the actual nature of antebellum society.

In a number of books and articles, Thomas B. Alexander has lent support to Woodward's view of the Redeemers by documenting the power of former Whigs within the postwar Democratic party. See, for example, Alexander's "Persistent Whiggery in the Confederate South, 1860–1877," *Journal of Southern History* (1961). But it is not entirely clear what former party affiliation meant in terms of economic background or postwar attitudes. Woodward's conclusion about the destruction of the antebellum planter class depended heavily on Roger Shugg's *Origins of Class Struggle in Louisiana: A Social History of White Farmers and Laborers during Slavery and After, 1840–1875* (1939). Among the few works that strongly support Woodward's view of a more forward-looking group of political leaders composed of "new men" are Jack P. Maddex's *The Virginia Conservatives 1867–1879: A Study in*

Reconstruction Politics (1970); and Judson Clements Ward, Jr.'s "The New Departure Democrats of Georgia: An Interpretation," *Georgia Historical Quarterly* (1957), which, though somewhat more positive about the Conservative regimes, largely confirms Woodward's assessment for the state on which the Redeemer model was largely based.

William Cooper's *The Conservative Regime: South Carolina, 1877–1890* (1968) was the first book to directly challenge Woodward's model. Using the terms Bourbon and Conservative interchangeably, Cooper argued convincingly that the men who overthrew Reconstruction in South Carolina were all former Democrats, were primarily from planter backgrounds, and, though not ignoring industry, were more concerned about improving the state's agricultural situation. The most direct attack on Woodward is James Tice Moore's "Redeemers Reconsidered: Change and Continuity in the Democratic South, 1870–1900," *Journal of Southern History* (1978), which unintentionally reveals the difficulty of engaging the "Woodward Synthesis" on its many different levels, but effectively argues that the South's postwar leadership enjoyed the support of and responded to the region's agrarian elements. Charles L. Flynn Jr.'s "Procrustean Bedfellows and Populists: An Alternative Hypothesis," in *Race, Class, & Politics in Southern History: Essays in Honor of Robert F. Durden* (1989), edited by Jeffrey J. Crow, Paul D. Escott, and Charles L. Flynn, Jr., agrees, and argues that studies of New South leaders overemphasize their interest in industrial growth and neglect their appeals for agricultural diversification. Studies that argue for the centrality of agrarianism in postwar leadership and/or the limitations of traditional approaches to "Bourbonism" are Willie D. Halsell's "The Bourbon Period in Mississippi Politics, 1875–1890," *Journal of Southern History* (1945); Dewey W. Grantham, Jr.'s "The Southern Bourbons Revisited," *South Atlantic Quarterly* (1961); and Michael Perman's *The Road to Redemption: Southern Politics, 1869–1879* (1984). John Mering's "Persistent Whiggery in the Confederate South: A Reconsideration," *South Atlantic Quarterly* (1970) reveals that several of the politicians whom Woodward lists as "Redeemers" did not, in fact, fit the profile. See also William B. Hesseltine's *Confederate Leaders in the New South* (1950), which examined the postbellum careers of 656 ex-Confederate leaders and found that only 71 failed to recover their previous position and prestige. There clearly was a high degree of continuity between Confederate and New South leaders, but without knowing more about the sample's antebellum backgrounds, this study cannot be used to address the basic question of continuity between the antebellum and postbellum periods.

Overviews of state politics tend to find plenty of "new men" but generally testify to a greater degree of continuity or heterogeneity in Conservative leadership than the Redeemer model would allow. They are likely, however, to emphasize the abuses of the Conservative regimes. See Allen W. Moger's *Virginia: Bourbonism to Byrd, 1870–1925* (1968); William Ivy Hair's *Bourbonism and Agrarian Protest: Louisiana Politics, 1877–1900* (1969); Roger L. Hart's *Redeemers, Bourbons, and Populists: Tennessee, 1870–1896* (1975); Allen J. Going's *Bourbon Democracy in Alabama, 1874–1890* (1951); William W. Rogers's *The One-Gallused Rebellion: Agrarianism in Alabama, 1865–1896* (1970); Edward C. Williamson's *Florida Politics in the Gilded Age, 1877–1893* (1976); and Paul D. Escott's *Many Excellent People: Power and Privilege in North Carolina, 1850–1900* (1985). For the Readjusters, the South's most important pre-Populist insurgency movement, see James T. Moore's *Two Paths to the New South: The Virginia Debt Controversy* (1974). See also Gordon B. McKinney's *Southern Mountain Republicans, 1865–1900* (1978).

After years of neglect because of the influence of John Hicks's *The Populist Revolt: A History of the Farmers' Alliance and the People's Party* (1931), which emphasized the importance of midwestern Populism, southern populism has become a hot topic. Although Alex M. Arnett's *The Populist Movement in Georgia: A View of the "Agrarian Crusade" in Light of Solid South Politics* (1922) began the reexamination of southern populism, C. Vann Woodward was most responsible for the new and more favorable assessment of the movement. First in his marvelous sympathetic biography *Tom Watson: Agrarian Rebel* (1938), and then in *Origins*, Woodward established that southern populism was more radical and more persistent in the face of greater opposition than the more celebrated midwestern wing. And in "The Populist Heritage and the Intellectual," *American Scholar* (1959–60), Woodward convincingly took on Richard Hofstadter, Oscar Handlin, Edward Shils, and other critics who argued that the Populists were irrational, anti-Semitic, and generally small-minded opponents of a new economy that they did not understand.

Lawrence Goodwyn's *Democratic Promise: The Populist Moment in America* (1976) and its abridged version, *The Populist Moment: A Short History of the Agrarian Revolt in America* (1978), built on Woodward's foundation to argue that Populism was the nation's "last democratic mass movement." Although Goodwyn exaggerates the extent of Populism's "alternate vision" for America, its dependence on the "cooperative idea," and its roots in a "movement culture," his work remains a challenging and powerfully written account that, together with Robert McMath's *Populist Vanguard: A History of the Southern Farmers' Alliance* (1975), has firmly established the key place of the Farmers' Alliance in the movement. McMath's *Populist Vanguard*; Bruce Palmer's *"Men Over Money": The Southern Populist Critique of American Capitalism* (1980); Theodore Saloutos's *Farmer Movements in the South, 1865–1933* (1960); and Stanley Parsons et al.'s "The Role of Cooperatives in the Development of the Movement Culture of Populism," *Journal of American History* (1983), although favorable accounts of Populism, provide a needed corrective to Goodwyn's excesses. For the alleged role of restrictive fence laws in launching the movement, see Steven Hahn's *The Roots of Southern Populism: Yeoman Farmers and the Transformation of the Georgia Upcountry, 1850–1890* (1983); and Charles L. Flynn Jr.'s *White Land, Black Labor: Caste and Class in Late Nineteenth-Century Georgia* (1983).

For reasons that are not entirely clear, but no doubt prompted by the tendency to romanticize the Populists (and related to the academic penchant for revisionism), scholars are now reevaluating the Populists and looking at them more critically. The initial attacks came in the area of attitudes towards blacks, as represented by Gerald Gaither's *Blacks and the Populist Revolt: Ballots and Bigotry in the "New South"* (1977); Charles Crowe's strident "Tom Watson, Populists, and Blacks Reconsidered," *Journal of Negro History* (1970); and Herbert Shapiro's more balanced "The Populists and the Negro: A Reconsideration," in *The Making of Black America: Essays in Negro Life & History* (1969), edited by August Meier and Elliott Rudwick. Gregg Cantrell and D. Scott Barton's "Texas Populists and the Failure of Biracial Politics," *Journal of Southern History* (1989) further documents the importance of "racial stigma" among white Populists in that key state.

Even more critical of Populist racial attitudes, which are seen as part of the broader values and attitudes that Georgia Populists shared with Conservatives, is Barton C. Shaw's *The Wool Hat Boys: Georgia's Populist Party* (1984). Drawing on Robert Durden's depiction of the Populists as "angry agrarian capitalists" in *The Climax of Populism: The Election of 1896* (1965), Eric Anderson's "The Populists and Capitalist America: The Case of Edgecombe County, North Carolina," in Crow et al.'s *Race, Class, & Politics in Southern History*, also found common values and even sources of support among Democrats and Populists. See also Flynn's "Procrustean Bedfellows," cited above. Shawn E. Kantor and J. Morgan Kousser's "Common Sense or Commonwealth? The Fence Law and Institutional Change in the Postbellum South," *California Institute of Technology Social Science Working Paper* (1989) found more angry agrarian capitalists, and argues that the fence laws provoked the strongest opposition from small landholders, whose profits from cotton were threatened.

Southern progressives have fared much better lately. Peter Filene's "An Obituary for 'The Progressive Movement,' " *American Quarterly* (1970), which questioned the utility of the concept of Progressivism, has not struck a responsive cord in the study of southern Progressivism. For a thoughtful examination of the trends in the approach to national Progressivism, see Daniel T. Rodgers's "In Search of Progressivism," *Reviews in American History* (1982).

Historians generally have continued to view Progressivism's southern branch in the tradition either of Woodward's *Origins* or of Arthur Link's landmark article, "The Progressive Movement in the South, 1870–1914," *North Carolina Historical Review* (1946). Woodward stressed the urban roots of southern Progressivism and, while allowing for its considerable achievements, emphasized what it left undone and its less noble aspects, which he summed up in the phrase "Progressivism for Whites Only." Link, however, emphasized the movement's rural roots and downplayed its support for prohibition, disfranchisement, and segregation. In part the contrasting emphases of these two giants of the historical profession grew out of their personal readings of southern history. But Link, who became the biographer of Woodrow Wilson, was more concerned than Woodward with the national manifestation of southern Progressivism. Yet part of the difference between the two historians also can be traced to the men with whom they studied at the University of North Carolina. Woodward worked with Howard K. Beale and Rupert B. Vance, two scholars noted for their criticisms of southern society. Link's mentor, however, was Fletcher Green, who was famous for finding evidence of democracy and progress in what others pictured as a uniformly conservative and benighted South. Like other Green students, Link stressed the progress that the South made, whereas Woodward, although conscious of the effects of change, was more impressed by the failure of the South to accomplish more.

Two magisterial works by former students of Fletcher Green sought a balance between Woodward and Link, but in the end largely embraced Link's more positive assessment of the movement. George Tindall's *The Emergence of the New South, 1913–1945* (1967) is, like *Origins* (a companion volume in the invaluable "A History of the South" series), jam-packed with facts but beautifully written; Dewey W. Grantham's *Southern Progressivism: The Reconciliation of Progress and Tradition* (1983) is a comprehensive account that leaves the reader wondering whether tradition or progress got the edge. Grantham summarizes his main themes and thoughtfully assesses the literature in "Review Essay: The Contours of Southern Progressivism," *American Historical Review* (1981). Studies of Progressivism in individual states include Raymond Pulley's *Old Virginia Restored: An Interpretation of the Progressive Impulse, 1870–1930* (1968); Sheldon Hackney's *From Populism to Progressivism in Alabama* (1969), which stresses the differences between an allegedly parochial and reactionary Populism and a more forward-looking, positive, Progressivism; and two studies that find greater continuity between the two movements—Jeffrey Crow's " 'Populism to Progressivism' in North Carolina: Governor Daniel Russell and His War on the Southern Railway Company," *The Historian* (1975); and Robert Worth Miller's "Building a Progressive Coalition in Texas: The Populist-Reform Democrat Rapprochement, 1900–1907," *Journal of Southern History* (1986).

Scholars who are critical of Progressivism tend to emphasize its inherent racism. J. Morgan Kousser's *The Shaping of Southern Politics: Suffrage Restriction and the Establishment of the One-Party South, 1880–1910* (1974) sees disfranchisement as preparing the way for Progressivism in some states while being the tool of the progressives in others. Richard L. Watson, Jr.'s "Furnifold M. Simmons and the Politics of White Supremacy," in Crow et al.'s *Race, Class & Politics in Southern History*, challenges Kousser's assertion that a major aim of North Carolina's disfranchisers was to disfranchise poor whites. Jack T. Kirby's *Darkness at the Dawning: Race and Reform in the Progressive South* (1972) and Bruce Clayton's *The Savage Ideal: Intolerance and Intellectual Leadership in the South, 1890–1914* (1972) emphasize the ways in which Progressivism embraced and expanded the racial settlement of the 1890s. Two state studies that criticize white progressives while documenting the reform efforts of black progressives are John Dittmer's *Black Georgia in the Progressive Era, 1900–1920* (1977) and Lester C. Lamon's *Black Tennesseans, 1900–1930* (1977). Three studies that review the discriminatory aspects of progressive educational policy are Louis Harlan's *Separate and Unequal: Public School Campaigns and Racism in the Southern Seaboard States, 1901–1915* (1958); Carl V. Harris's "Stability and Change in Discrimination Against Black Public Schools: Birmingham, Alabama, 1871–1931," *Journal of Southern History* (1985); and James Anderson's *The Education of Blacks in the South, 1860–1935* (1988), a challenging revisionist account that exaggerates the role of southern blacks, especially ex-slaves, in shaping southern educational policy.

A growing number of books have detailed the efforts of southern white progressives to reform specific areas of southern life. For a study of one of the leading progressive governors, see William Larsen's *Montague of Virginia: The Making of a Southern Progressive* (1965). In many cases the objects of reform resisted the efforts of the reformers. See, for example, William A. Link's *A Hard Country and a Lonely Place: Schooling, Society, and Reform in Rural Virginia, 1870–1920* (1986), and "Privies, Progressivism, and Public Schools: Health Reform and Education in the Rural South, 1909–1920," *Journal of Southern History* (1988); John Ettling's *The Germ of Laziness: Rockefeller Philanthropy and Public Health in the New South* (1981); Elizabeth Etheridge's *The Butterfly Caste: A Social History of Pellagra in the South* (1972); William Graebner's *Coal-Mining Safety in the Progressive Period: The Political Economy of Reform* (1976); Joseph Cannon Bailey's *Seaman A. Knapp: Schoolmaster of American Agriculture* (1971); Roy V. Scott's *The Reluctant Farmer: The Rise of Agricultural Extension to 1914* (1970); Bradley R. Rice's *Progressive Cities: The Commission Government Movement in America, 1901–1920* (1977); David Carlton's previously cited *Mill and Town in South Carolina* for efforts at child labor reform in the textile industry; and Wayne Flynt's *Cracker Messiah: Governor Sidney J. Catts of Florida* (1977) and Paul E.

Isaac's *Prohibition and Politics: Turbulent Decades in Tennessee, 1885–1920* (1965) for the link between Progressivism and prohibition.

Southern progressives played a key role in Woodrow Wilson's two presidential campaigns. Arthur S. Link, in a series of articles in southern journals in 1945 and 1946 and in *Wilson: The Road to the White House* (1947), emphasized their indispensable contribution to Wilson's nomination and election in 1912. Dewey Grantham, Jr.'s *Hoke Smith and the Politics of the New South* (1958) and J. Wayne Flynt's *Duncan Upshaw Fletcher: Dixie's Reluctant Progressive* (1971) are good biographies of two leading southern progressives. William Holmes's *The White Chief: James Kimble Vardaman* (1970) is a thoughtful if at times too generous assessment of a leading demagogue who often backed progressive legislation. Evans C. Johnson's *Oscar W. Underwood: A Political Biography* (1980) is a solid study of the most powerful southern congressional leader. For biographies of two of the South's more colorful leaders, see Francis Butler Simkins's *Pitchfork Ben Tillman, South Carolinian* (1944) and Raymond Arsenault's *The Wild Ass of the Ozarks: Jeff Davis and the Social Bases of Southern Politics* (1984). For a study of Congress's most prominent "gentleman politician," see George Coleman Osborn's *John Sharp Williams: Planter-Statesman of the Deep South* (1943). Robert Dean Pope's "Of the Man at the Center: Biographies of Southern Politicians from the Age of Segregation," in Kousser and McPherson's *Region, Race, and Reconstruction*, is an intelligent assessment of the South's political leaders and the literature about them. For a less subtle approach, see Allan A. Michie and Frank Ryhlick's *Dixie Demagogues* (1939).

Arthur Link's "The South and the 'New Freedom': An Interpretation," *American Scholar* (1951) makes a strong case for the importance of rural southerners in pushing Wilson's New Freedom legislation, and Anne Firor Scott's "A Progressive Wind from the South, 1906–1913," *Journal of Southern History* (1963) stresses the southern agrarian contribution to congressional Progressivism prior to Wilson's election. But

Richard M. Abrams's "Woodrow Wilson and the Southern Congressmen, 1913–1916," *Journal of Southern History* (1956) provides a useful corrective to such an emphasis on southern agrarians in the development of Wilson's program. See also Dewey W. Grantham's "Southern Congressional Leaders and the New Freedom, 1913–1917," *Journal of Southern History* (1947); and Seward W. Livermore's *Politics is Adjourned: Woodrow Wilson and the War Congress, 1916–1918* (1966). For the South during World War I, see Tindall's *Emergence of the New South*; and David M. Kennedy's *Over Here: The First World War and American Society* (1980).

Since the mid-1970s, historians have become increasingly interested in the everyday lives of ordinary people. Social and cultural history, broadly defined, has sought to go beyond or at least be incorporated into more traditional economic and political history. This emphasis in southern history has manifested itself most clearly in the study of black life and race relations.

C. Vann Woodward's *The Strange Career of Jim Crow* (1955, 1957, 1966, 1974) initiated an ongoing debate over the origins of segregation after the Civil War. Noting the relatively late appearance of laws enforcing segregation in public conveyances and public accommodations, Woodward argued that segregation did not become the rule in the South until after 1890. Joel Williamson's *After Slavery: The Negro in South Carolina During Reconstruction, 1861–1877* (1965), however, found extensive segregation both by custom (*de facto*) and by law (*de jure)* in South Carolina even during Reconstruction. Since the battle was joined, historians have jumped in on both sides of the debate. Some support Woodward, others report findings for the immediate postwar period similar to those of Williamson, and still others have documented widespread segregation in the antebellum North and South. Howard N. Rabinowitz's *Race Relations in the Urban South*, cited above, however, noted that even though segregation appeared earlier than Woodward had claimed, the more interesting point was that it replaced exclusion rather than integration and thus marked an improvement rather than a setback in the lives of southern blacks. For that reason it was generally supported by blacks and their white allies, especially because separate treatment was to be equal treatment. John Cell's *The Highest Stage of White Supremacy: The Origins of Segregation in South Africa and the American South* (1982) supports this assessment and provides a useful comparative framework for the study of southern race relations. But see also Jeffrey J. Crow's "An Apartheid for the South: Clarence Poe's Crusade for Rural Segregation," in Crow et al.'s *Race, Class, & Politics in Southern Society.* Charles A. Lofgren's *The Plessy Case: A Legal-Historical Interpretation* (1987) notes that the Supreme Court's support for separate but equal treatment reflected both existing case law and the reality of a segregated society. For a convenient summary of the debate over the "Woodward Thesis," see Howard N. Rabinowitz's "More than the Woodward Thesis: Assessing *The Strange Career of Jim Crow*," *Journal of American History* (1988). See also Woodward's response to his critics in "*Strange Career* Critics: Long May They Persevere," *Journal of American History* (1988), and in *Thinking Back.*

A number of other works reveal the range of white attitudes towards blacks. Joel Williamson's *The Crucible of Race: Black-White Relations in the American South Since Emancipation* (1984) is a moving though often repetitious tour de force that divides white southerners into three groups—Liberal, Conservative, and Radical—in an effort to explain the triumph of white racism at the end of the nineteenth century. Unfortunately, Williamson pushes his psychoanalytical interpretation too far. Less ambitious but more compelling is George M. Fredrickson's *The Black Image in the White Mind: The Debate on Afro-American Character and Destiny, 1817–1914* (1971), which originated the term "herrenvolk democracy" to describe white support for discrimination against blacks. For studies of "white liberals," see Hugh C. Bailey's *Edgar Gardner Murphy: Gentle Progressive* (1968) and *Liberalism in the New South: Southern Social Reformers and the Progressive Movement* (1969); Arlin Turner's *George W. Cable: A Biography*

(1956); and Morton Sosna's *In Search of the Silent South: Southern Liberals and the Race Issue* (1977). For the argument that southern race relations have finally achieved the pace-setting position within the nation that First New South spokesmen once unjustly claimed, see Howard N. Rabinowitz's "The Weight of the Past vs. The Promise of the Future: Southern Race Relations in Historical Perspective," in *The Future South: An Historical Perspective for the Twenty-First Century* (1991), edited by Joe P. Dunn and Howard L. Preston.

In recent years scholars have sought to view black life as something more than simply the product of white oppression. Even though whites set the ground rules, blacks themselves helped create their own institutions within the larger segregated society. In the process, as subjects rather than simply as objects of history, they were able to maintain a degree of autonomy and a sense of self-respect that previously went unrecognized. For a pioneering interpretation, see Lawrence Levine's *Black Culture and Black Consciousness: Afro-American Folk Thought from Slavery to Freedom* (1977). For studies of the assertiveness of the former slaves immediately after emancipation as they sought to take control over their own lives, see Peter Kolchin's *First Freedom: The Responses of Alabama's Blacks to Emancipation and Reconstruction* (1972); and Leon F. Litwack's kaleidoscopic *Been in the Storm So Long: The Aftermath of Slavery* (1979). For examinations of the strong family ties among blacks, see Herbert Gutman's *The Black Family in Slavery & Freedom, 1750–1925* (1976) and Jacqueline Jones's *Labor of Love, Labor of Sorrow: Black Women, Work, and the Family from Slavery to the Present* (1985). Theodore Rosengarten's *All God's Danger's: The Life of Nate Shaw* (1974) is the remarkable "oral autobiography" of the Alabama sharecropper son of former slaves (his real name was Ned Cobb) who managed to move part of the way up the "agricultural ladder" and had a colorful tale to tell about his experiences and those of his contemporaries. At the other end of the black class structure, one of the region's most successful black businesses is ably charted in Walter B. Weare's

Black Business in the New South: A Social History of the North Carolina Mutual Life Insurance Company (1973). The classic and highly critical account of middle- and upper-middle-class blacks is black sociologist E. Franklin Frazier's *Black Bourgeoisie: The Rise of a New Middle Class in the United States* (1957). More appreciative studies are Loren Schweninger's *Black Property Owners in the South, 1790–1915* (1990) and Willard B. Gatewood's *Aristocrats of Color: The Black Elite, 1880–1920* (1990). See also Schweninger's "Prosperous Blacks in the South, 1790–1880," *American Historical Review* (1990).

For examinations of attempts by middle-class black women to improve the lives of southern blacks, see Gerda Lerner's "Early Community Work of Black Club Women," *Journal of Negro History* (1974); *The Afro-American Woman: Struggles and Images* (1987), edited by Sharon Harley and Rosalyn Terborg-Penn; Jacqueline Anne Rouse's *Lugenia Burns Hope: Black Southern Reformer* (1989); and Cynthia Neverdon-Morton's *Afro-American Women of the South and the Advancement of the Race, 1895–1925* (1989). See also William J. Breen's "Black Women and the Great War: Mobilization and Reform in the South," *Journal of Southern History* (1978). Clarence E. Walker's *A Rock in a Weary Land: The African Methodist Episcopal Church During the Civil War and Reconstruction* (1982) is one of the few full-length studies of black religious and fraternal life for this period, but there is a great deal of material on these and other aspects of black life in several of the books already cited, and in Vernon Wharton's *The Negro in Mississippi 1865–1890* (1947); George Tindall's *South Carolina Negroes, 1877–1900* (1952); and Lawrence D. Rice's *The Negro in Texas, 1874–1900* (1971).

There is now an impressive body of work on post-Reconstruction black leaders. The best introduction to the subject is August Meier's *Negro Thought in America 1880–1915: Racial Ideologies in the Age of Booker T. Washington* (1963). Louis Harlan's work on Booker T. Washington is indispensable. See for example, his (with others) thirteen-volume edition of *The Papers of Booker T. Washington* (1972–1984); his two-volume biography, *Booker T. Washington: The Making of a Black Leader, 1856–1901* (1972) and *Booker T. Washington: The Wizard of Tuskegee, 1901–1915* (1983); and "Booker T. Washington in Biographical Perspective," *American Historical Review* (1970). For a study of Washington's predecessor as the nation's acknowledged black leader see William S. McFeely's *Frederick Douglass* (1991); and for examinations of his chief rival, see Elliott Rudwick's *W. E. B. Du Bois: Propagandist of the Negro Protest* (1960); and Thomas C. Holt's "The Political Uses of Alienation: W. E. B. Du Bois on Politics, Race, and Culture, 1903–1940," *American Quarterly* (1990). See also Du Bois's impressive *Souls of Black Folks: Essays and Sketches* (1903) and Washington's ghost-written *Up From Slavery* (1901).

Other major southern black leaders have been overshadowed by the three giants of the period, but also see the essays on John Mercer Langston, Martin R. Delany, Alexander Crummell, Henry McNeal Turner, William Henry Steward, Isaiah T. Montgomery, and Mary Church Terrell in *Black Leaders of the Nineteenth Century* (1988), edited by Leon Litwack and August Meier; and Thomas C. Holt's "The Lonely Warrior: Ida B. Wells-Barnett and the Struggle for Black Leadership," in *Black Leaders of the Twentieth Century* (1982), edited by John Hope Franklin and August Meier.

For a study of the earliest mass migration of blacks out of the South, which began once it became clear that such leaders could do little to significantly improve conditions for blacks, see Nell Irvin Painter's *Exodusters: Black Migration to Kansas after Reconstruction* (1976), which strongly identifies with the black masses as opposed to the "representative colored men"; and Robert G. Athearn's less impassioned *In Search of Canaan: Black Migration to Kansas, 1879–80* (1978). Norman Crockett's *The Black Towns* (1979) is a fact-filled study of efforts to build black towns, primarily in the Midwest and Oklahoma, that fails to engage a number of critical conceptual issues. Kenneth Marvin Hamilton's *Black Towns and Profit: Promotion and Development in the Trans-Appalachian*

West, 1877–1915 (1991) appeared too late to be consulted here but may correct some of these oversights. For interest in Africa, see Edwin S. Redkey's *Black Exodus: Black Nationalist and Back-to-Africa Movements, 1890–1910* (1969). William Cohen's *At Freedom's Edge: Black Mobility and the Southern White Quest for Racial Control, 1861–1915* (1991) thoroughly analyzes the entire range of black migration efforts and white reactions to them prior to the so-called Great Migration.

General accounts of the Great Migration are less satisfying than the numerous studies of migration to specific northern cities. Unlike earlier studies, such as Gilbert Osofsky's *Harlem: The Making of A Ghetto* (2nd ed., 1971) and Allan H. Spear's *Black Chicago: The Making of a Negro Ghetto, 1890–1920* (1967), which emphasized ghetto formation, Peter Gottlieb's *Making Their Own Way: Southern Blacks' Migration to Pittsburgh, 1916–30* (1987) and James T. Grossman's *Land of Hope: Chicago, Black Southerners, and the Great Migration* (1989) begin the story in the South and follow the migrants North. Both works are excellent, but Gottlieb minimizes the discontinuities inherent in the movement, whereas Grossman provides a more balanced account. Elliott M. Rudwick's *Race Riot at East St. Louis July 2, 1917* (1964) is a model study of the nation's bloodiest race riot that was the white response to the migration in one city.

Scholars have paid less attention to the everyday lives of southern whites. For example, despite all the attention given to black migration, by 1920 there were two-and-a-half times as many southern whites as blacks living outside their states of birth, yet we know very little about them. The books by Charles Flynn, Steven Hahn, Gilbert Fite, and Pete Daniel cited above, begin to get at the impact of economic change on the lives of the rural yeomanry. The books by I. W. Newby, Jacquelyn Dowd Hall et al., and Dolores Janewski explore the lives of the first generation of southern industrial workers. For a useful overview, see J. Wayne Flynt's *Dixie's Forgotten People: The South's Poor Whites* (1979); also see Pete Daniel's

Standing at the Crossroads: Southern Life in the Twentieth Century (1986).

Examples of social mobility studies, whose popularity peaked in the early 1970s, are Paul Worthman's "Working Class Mobility in Birmingham, Alabama, 1880–1914," in *Anonymous Americans: Explorations in Nineteenth-Century Social History*, edited by Tamara K. Hareven (1971); Alwyn Barr's "Occupational and Geographical Mobility in San Antonio, 1870–1900," *Social Science Quarterly* (1970); and Richard J. Hopkins's "Occupational and Geographic Mobility in Atlanta, 1870–1896," *Journal of Southern History* (1968).

For examinations of the limited successes and more numerous failures to unionize southern workers, see Leon Fink's *Workingmen's Democracy: The Knights of Labor and American Politics* (1983); David Alan Corbin's *Life, Work and Rebellion in the Coal Fields: The Southern West Virginia Miners, 1880–1922* (1981); Melton A. McLaurin's *Paternalism and Protest: Southern Cotton Mill Workers and Organized Labor, 1875–1905* (1971); Eric Arnesen's *Waterfront Workers of New Orleans: Race, Class, and Politics, 1863–1923* (1990); and Jacquelyn Dowd Hall, Robert Korstad, and James Leloudis's "Cotton Mill People: Work, Community, and Protest in the Textile South, 1880–1940," *American Historical Review* (1986).

There is an extensive literature about southern white Protestantism. See, for example, Rufus B. Spain's *At Ease in Zion: A Social History of Southern Baptists, 1865–1900* (1967); Jean E. Friedman's *The Enclosed Garden: Women and Community in the Evangelical South, 1860–1900* (1985); Kenneth K. Bailey's *Southern White Protestantism in the Twentieth Century* (1964); Samuel S. Hill's *The South and The North in American Religion* (1980); *Religion and the Solid South* (1972), edited by Samuel S. Hill; *Religion in the South* (1985), edited by Charles Reagan Wilson; and H. Shelton Smith's *In His Image, But . . . Racism in Southern Religion, 1780–1910* (1972).

For the centrality of violence among southern whites, see George C. Rable's *But There Was No Peace: The Role of Vi-*

olence in the Politics of Reconstruction (1984); Edward L. Ayers's *Vengeance and Justice: Crime and Punishment in the 19th Century American South* (1984); Albert C. Smith's " 'Southern Violence' Reconsidered: Arson as Protest in Black Belt Georgia, 1865–1910," *Journal of Southern History* (1985); William F. Holmes's "Whitecapping: Agrarian Violence in Mississippi, 1902–1906," *Journal of Southern History* (1969); Walter F. White's *Rope and Faggot: A Biography of Judge Lynch* (1929); Altina L. Waller's *Feud: Hatfields, McCoys, and Social Change in Appalachia, 1860–1900* (1988); Allen W. Trelease's *White Terror: The Ku Klux Klan Conspiracy and Southern Reconstruction* (1971); David M. Chalmers's *Hooded Americanism: The History of the Ku Klux Klan* (1965); and Robert P. Ingalls's *Urban Vigilantes in the New South: Tampa, 1882–1936* (1988).

Anne Firor Scott and Jacquelyn Dowd Hall's superb "Women in the South," in Boles and Nolen's *Interpreting Southern History,* ably summarizes the literature in this burgeoning field and is itself an important contribution to that literature. Among the most useful studies of white women, in addition to those by Hall, Newby, and Janewski, are Anne Firor Scott's "The 'New Woman' in the New South," *South Atlantic Quarterly,* (1962) and *The Southern Lady: From Pedestal to Politics, 1830–1930* (1970); Jacquelyn Dowd Hall's *Revolt Against Chivalry: Jessie Daniel Ames and the Women's Campaign Against Lynching* (1979), which goes well beyond the antilynching campaign; A. Elizabeth Taylor's series of articles on state suffrage campaigns and *The Woman Suffrage Movement in Tennessee* (1957); Julie Roy Jeffrey's "Women in the Southern Farmers' Alliance: A Reconsideration of the Role and Status of Women in the Late Nineteenth Century South," *Feminist Studies* (1972); John Patrick McDowell's *The Social Gospel in the South: The Woman's Home Mission Movement in the Methodist Episcopal Church, South, 1886–1939* (1982); and James L. Leloudis II's "School Reform in the New South: The Woman's Association for the Betterment of Public School Houses in North Carolina, 1902–1919," *Journal of American History* (1983).

Little has been done on immigrants to the South, and most of what exists is about Jews. See, for example, Steven Hertzberg's *Strangers Within the Gate City: The Jews of Atlanta, 1845–1915* (1978); Myron Berman's *Richmond Jewry, 1769–1976* (1979); Mark Elovitz's *A Century of Jewish Life in Dixie: The Birmingham Experience* (1974); and Howard N. Rabinowitz's "Nativism, Bigotry and Anti-Semitism in the South," *American Jewish History* (1988). The best study of Mexican immigrants is Mario T. Garcia's *Desert Immigrants: The Mexicans of El Paso, 1880–1920* (1981). See Robert Ingalls's *Urban Vigilantes* and Gary Ross Mormino, and George E. Pozzetta's *The Immigrant World of Ybor City: Italians and Their Latin Neighbors in Tampa, 1885–1985* (1985) for studies of Cuban, Italian, and Spanish immigrants in the cigar industry. Pete Daniel's *Shadow of Slavery* examines the use of peonage against immigrants in rural-based industries. For a study of the German migration to Texas, see Terry G. Jordan's *German Seed in Texas Soil: Immigrant Farmers in Nineteenth-Century Texas* (1966). See also the mobility studies by Hopkins, Worthman, and Barr cited above. For studies of nonwhite immigrant groups, see Lucy M. Cohen's *Chinese in the Post Civil War South: A People Without a History* (1984); and Raymond A. Mohl's "Black Immigrants: Bahamians in Early Twentieth-Century Miami," *Florida Historical Quarterly* (1987).

Historians of the Lost Cause have made up for the neglect of the subject in Woodward's *Origins*. Rolin G. Osterweis's *The Myth of the Lost Cause, 1865–1900* (1973) exaggerates the role of racism in the movement; Charles Reagan Wilson's *Baptized in Blood: The Religion of the Lost Cause, 1865–1920* (1980) views the Lost Cause as a "southern civic religion" and stresses the key role of the clergy; and Gaines M. Foster's *Ghosts of the Confederacy: Defeat, The Lost Cause, and the Emergence of the New South, 1865 to 1913* (1987) imaginatively shows how the Lost Cause was used to ease the transition from Old to New South.

I have slighted the literary aspects of the First New South because of a lack of space and the gaps in my own knowledge.

Interested readers should consult C. Vann Woodward's excellent discussion of this and other intellectual matters in *Origins*, in which Woodward emphasizes the First New South's "Divided Mind." Other works that catch the transitional nature of the era's culture are Daniel J. Singal's *The War Within: From Victorian to Modernist Thought in the South, 1919–1945* (1982); Wayne Mixon's *Southern Writers and the New South Movement, 1865–1913* (1980); and Anne Goodwyn Jones's *Tomorrow Is Another Day: The Woman Writer in the South, 1859–1936*. See also *The History of Southern Literature* (1985), edited by Louis D. Rubin, Jr.

Finally, readers are encouraged to consult two impressive encyclopedias that treat all of the matters discussed in this book and many others, especially in the area of cultural history: *The Encyclopedia of Southern History* (1979), edited by David C. Roller and Robert W. Twyman, which consists primarily of relatively brief alphabetical entries about traditional subjects; and the incomparable *Encyclopedia of Southern Culture* (1989), edited by Charles Reagan Wilson and William Ferris, a topically arranged (and often idiosyncratic) compilation of longer essays about a stunning and innovative variety of subjects.

INDEX

The First New South, 1865–1920 was copyedited by Anita Samen and proofread by Andrew Davidson. Production editor was Lucy Herz. The index was compiled by Sandi Schroeder. The book was typeset at Impressions, a division of Edwards Brothers, and first printed and bound at Edwards Bros., Inc.

Book design by Roger Eggers.